Eco-Journeys
The World Guide
to Ecologically Aware
Travel and Adventure

STEPHEN FOEHR

D1051856

The Noble Press, Inc.

CHICAGO

Publisher's Note: The author and the publisher have attempted to provide current and accurate information, but they cannot be held responsible for any changes or discrepancies. We suggest that you contact the organizations listed here to verify the information.

Printed in the United States of America

Library of Congress Cataloging-in-Publication data:
Foehr, Stephen, 1943-
    Eco-journeys : the world guide to ecologically aware travel
  and adventure / Stephen Foehr.
       p. cm.
   Includes index.
   ISBN 1-879360-21-7 (pbk): $14.95
    1. Ecotourism   I. Title
  G155.A1F63   1992
  910'.2'02–dc20   92-50436
                                            CIP

Noble Press books are available in bulk at discount prices. Single copies are available prepaid direct from the publisher:

The Noble Press, Inc.
213 W. Institute Place, Suite 508
Chicago, Illinois, 60610
800/486-7737

To all who treat Mother Earth as a neighbor, a friend, and a lover.

To all who recognize the Earth as a sentient being, alive and responsive to our presence.

To all who respect the Earth and consciously act for her well-being.

To travelers of the heart and spirit who have fun.

Contents

Preface   **xiii**

Part I: Safe Thrills

AFRICA
Botswana   3
Kenya/Tanzania   5
Namibia   20
Rwanda/Zaire   21
Zambia   24
Zimbabwe   26

ANTARCTICA   29

ASIA
Borneo   36
India   43
Nepal   47
Papua New Guinea   55
Russia   60
Thailand   63

CENTRAL AMERICA
Belize   67
Costa Rica   69

NORTH AMERICA
Canada   72
Mexico   82

United States   89
West:
    Alaska   89
    Arizona   104
    Colorado   106
    Hawaii   107
    Montana   109
    New Mexico   111
    Utah   112
    Wyoming   119
Northeast:
    Maine   124
South:
    North Carolina/Tennessee   125

SOUTH AMERICA
Argentina/Chile   127
Brazil   129
Ecuador   133
Peru   139
Venezuela   142

Part II: Comfortable Wilderness

AFRICA
Botswana   149
Kenya/Tanzania   155
Namibia   162
Zambia   166
Zimbabwe   168

ASIA
India/Nepal   170

CENTRAL AMERICA
Belize   174
Costa Rica   177

NORTH AMERICA
United States   184
West:
    Alaska   184
    California   188
    Colorado   190
    Hawaii   191
    Oregon   194
    Washington   197
Midwest:
    Minnesota/Ontario   198
Northeast:
    Maine   200
    Vermont   201
South:
    Florida   202
    Georgia   204

SOUTH AMERICA
Argentina   206
Brazil   208
Ecuador   212
Peru   221
Venezuela   224

Part III: Family

AFRICA
Kenya/Tanzania   232

ASIA
Nepal   233

CENTRAL AMERICA
Costa Rica   237

NORTH AMERICA
Canada   239

United States   243
West:
    Alaska   243
    California   245
    Colorado   246
    Hawaii   247
    Montana   248
    Utah   249
    Washington   251
Midwest:
    Minnesota   251
Northeast:
    New York   252

SOUTH AMERICA
Ecuador   254

Part IV: Raw Adventure

Irian Jaya   259
Nepal   264
Pakistan   266

Part V: Not Ordinary Trips

AFRICA
Mali   271
Tanzania   274
Zimbabwe   277

ASIA
Nepal   278
Thailand   280

CENTRAL AMERICA
Belize   283
Costa Rica   284

NORTH AMERICA
Canada   285
Mexico   286
United States   289
West:
    Alaska   289
    Hawaii   291
    Montana   293
    Utah   294
    Washington   295
Midwest:
    Minnesota   297
South:
    Florida   299

SOUTH AMERICA
Chile   300
Ecuador   302
Peru   303

Part VI: Special Needs

CENTRAL AMERICA
Belize   308
Costa Rica   309
Panama   309

NORTH AMERICA
Canada   311
Mexico   315
United States   316
West:
    Hawaii   316
Midwest:
    Minnesota   316

East:
    Maine   318
South:
    Florida   320
    Georgia   323
River trips   323

Listing of Tour Operators   327

INDEX

    General Index   337
    Geographical Index   341

Preface

This book is about fun, excitement, and discovery.

Riding on an inner tube through limestone caves on the River of Caves in Belize is pure fun. The gentle river carries you into dim caverns and tunnels of dappled green light filtered through the jungle canopy. Monkeys, toucans, and macaws answer your laughter with exclamations points of hoots and squawks hurled from the treetops.

Tracking elephants, lions, and Cape buffalo on foot through African forest is delicious excitement. Anticipation and wonderment spiked with a dash of fear pump you up. You are alert, almost giddy, as you push through the thickets.

Visiting the people of the rain forests in South America, Borneo, Irian Jaya, or Papua New Guinea is a voyage of discovery. You journey into a world of beliefs and values so fundamental that your modern mind becomes befuddled. The real adventure is to open yourself to the "primitiveness" of living so attuned to the environment. Do you dare step beyond analyzing why people paint their bodies with earth's pigments and dance to nature spirits and actually join them?

This book is a reference guide to fun and exciting ecologically aware vacations. It describes tour destinations all over the world and is divided into sections according to comfort level.

Safe Thrills includes backpacking, sea kayaking, and trekking trips. These trips require physical effort but stop short of life-threatening risks—for the most part. You sweat, get dirty, and deal with the local people on close terms. You are not a tourist but a traveler.

Comfortable Wilderness covers trips that delve into the back-country yet do not deprive you of a bed. After a day of watching wild animals on the African plains or taking a canoe trip through a rain forest, you return to a comfortable safari camp or lodge. You have a wilderness experience with creature comforts: the best of both worlds.

Family trips are designed for children under ten years old accompanied by a parent(s). The trips cater to children without compromising the adult experience. Whether hiking the forest of New York State or trekking the Himalayas of Nepal, the physical demands do not overtax children, but the wilderness is authentic. The children meet children of the host country, play their games, and visit their schools. The local ecosystems are explained in ways children can easily understand.

Not Ordinary Trips are wilderness experiences that allow you to participate in research projects. For example, you study river dolphins in Peru, track wolves in Minnesota, or help establish a refuge for chimpanzees in Mali. The trips provide an in-depth look at the intricate workings of the natural world. They are a way for you to actively participate in helping an animal species or a piece of wilderness survive while having a fun vacation.

Special Needs includes journeys that consider the needs of people with physical disabilities. Physical limitations do not mean limited opportunities on these trips. Running white-water rapids in foreign lands, canoeing North American rivers, traveling through a tropical rain forest are a few of the choices offered. These trips do not provide a watered-down version of a wilderness experience, but rather make it possible for people with disabilities to experience the real thing. Most of the tours are suited for both able-bodied people and people with disabilities.

Raw Adventure includes trips take you to the edge and make you curl your toes over it—a trip to remote Irian Jaya or a trek through the mountains of Pakistan. The trips are strenuous, both physically and mentally. You must be self-reliant and mentally flexible to cope with the demands.

More than five hundred companies sell tours to environmentally sensitive areas worldwide. But selling a tour and being environmentally responsible are not the same thing. When choosing a tour operator, closely scrutinize the firm's operating principles. Simply practicing low-impact camping—haul out your trash, leave no trace of your presence—is not enough.

To determine a tour operator's commitment to ecologically aware travel, ask the company the following questions:

- How do they contribute to the local economies of the places they visit?
- Do they hire local guides and staff assistants?
- Do they buy local supplies as much as possible?
- Do they contribute to or otherwise support environmental organizations, especially those in the host country?
- Do they make a conscious effort to inform on the environmental and cultural issues of the places they visit?
- How do they show respect for the local culture, people, and wildlife?
- Do they provide information on products that should not be purchased, such as those made from sea turtle shells; reptile skin or leather; ivory from elephants, whales, walrus, or narwhals; bird feathers or skins; or fur?

This book does not include all firms that practice responsible eco-tourism; but the firms listed here have a record of responsible ecotourism and practice what they preach.

For example:

Ancient Forest Adventures will discount 5 percent off the price of your trip and donate that money to the conservation organization of your choice.

Nature Expeditions International donates to education and conservation organizations, most recently to the Oregon Natural

Resources Council to help preserve the ancient forest in the northwest region of the United States.

Turtle Tours will donate fifty dollars in your name to a cultural survival organization of your choice.

Journeys International and Wildland Adventures founded the non-profit Earth Preservation Fund. The fund's purpose is to identify and support village- and community-level projects that promote environmental or cultural preservation. For example, staff and client volunteers clean up trails while trekking in Peru. In Nepal, the tour participants distribute vegetable seeds and forestry seedlings and help in planting projects. They volunteer in repairing monasteries and helping schools.

Part of the companies' profits are donated to the Ladakh Ecological Development Group, Costa Rica's Monteverde Cloud Forest Reserve, the Endangered Wildlife Trust, the Chobe Wildlife Trust, and Wildlife Clubs of Kenya. Monies also help support a local Costa Rican organization working to develop community-based ecotourism on the Caribbean coast. In the Yucatan region of Mexico, the firms contribute to the Punta Laguna Project, a community-based conservation program to protect spider monkey habitat and develop eco-tourism for local Mayan residents near Coba. And in Belize, they support the Mayan community's efforts to organize a cooperatively owned guest house for eco-travelers.

Inca Floats contributes via the Smithsonian Institute to the Darwin Research Station in the Galapagos Islands. Nature Conservancy raised $150,000 for the research station by gathering contributions from people who had visited the station.

International Expeditions helped establish the nonprofit Amazon Center for Environmental Education and Research (ACEER) Foundation and the Peruvian Amazon Biosphere Reserve. The company raised $60,000 for the center, which serves both as a research base for scientists and a rain forest education center.

Mountain Travel/Sobek Expeditions works with the Rainforest Action Network on projects in Mexico and Brazil.

The cost of each adventure depends upon the size of the group (generally from eight to a maximum of sixteen), the time of year, the comfort level of accommodations, the accessibility of the region, and the mode of ground transportation. The mode(s) of transportation, the types of accommodations, the land cost (per person for the entire trip unless otherwise noted), the length of the trip, and the best seasons to visit are given for each tour described. After each description, the tour operators that go to that area are listed. The addresses and phone numbers of all tour operators mentioned in the book are included in an appendix in the back of the book. Please contact the tour operators for additional information.

The pros and cons of eco-tourism is a lively debate among the proponents and opponents.

Proponents of eco-tourism argue that travelers' dollars help conserve wildlife and wildlife habitat. Many developing countries cannot adequately fund wildlife preserves on their own and use the revenue eco-tourism generates to develop conservation projects. Park fees and other use-charges support ecological studies, implementation of management plans, and other conservation projects.

Eco-tourism also aids local economies. Game parks and service infrastructure (hotels, lodges, guide services, etc.) generate 30 percent of Kenya's national revenue, according to government figures. Each lion in Kenya's Amboseli National Park is worth $27,000 U.S. per year net in tourism revenues. The entire elephant herd is valued at $510,000. Wildlife viewing brings in an estimated $40 per hectare; farming the same land would yielded just eighty cents per hectare. (*Ecotourism: The Potential and Pitfalls*, by Elizabeth Boo, World Wildlife Fund, 1990)

A women's cooperative at Costa Rica's Monteverde reserve grosses about $50,000 per year selling homemade souvenirs to eco-tourists.

The survival of Rwanda's mountain gorillas is due in large part to tourists who pay up to $170 to watch the gorillas in the Parc National des Volcans. The revenue helps pay for the park's maintenance and staff.

Eco-tourism generates jobs for people, especially those in rural areas. Local people may be the best interpreters, managers, and guardians of protected areas because of their experience and familiarity with the environment. In Namibia, tribesmen were converted from poachers to game wardens once eco-tourism became a local economic factor.

Detractors argue that eco-tourism contributes to the degradation of wilderness and the weakening of native cultures. Twenty years ago almost no tourist lodges existed in Nepal's Annapurna region. Now, approximately fifty lodges cater to the tourist trade. The demand for wood to heat the lodges and prepare meals has lowered the forest line by several hundred feet. In the Nepalese village of Ghorepani, which sees an average of eighteen thousand trekkers in nine months, food and lodging cost have soared, creating inflationary prices for the local people. Yet, without the tourist trade, Nepal would be in dire economic straits.

Responsible tour operators carry their own cooking kerosene and avoid guest houses or tea houses that overstress local resources. And, they spur the government of Nepal to formulate policy that mitigates the impact of increased tourism.

Antarctica is often cited as a place that should be off limits to tourism because of potential long-lasting environmental damage. Often cited as a harbinger of potential disasters to come is the Argentinean tourist boat that ran aground in 1988, spilling most of its 250,000 gallons of fuel into Antarctic waters. However, according to an Environmental Defense Fund report, tourism is not the main culprit fouling Antarctica's environment. Despite the dramatic rise in the number of tourists to the area—from 2,500 in 1988 to 7,200 in 1989, most aboard cruise ships—most of pollution of the continent comes from the inhabitants of the fifty-seven scientific research stations.

Nature in its pristine state, or close to it, is the capital resource for those in the eco-tourism business. They have a vested interest in protecting that resource. But they are not the only ones who must conserve and protect the environment. You, the eco-tourist, have responsibilities.

Here are some suggestions offered by tour operators on how to be a responsible eco-tourist.

- Learn a little of the local language and the names of local staff.
- Acquaint yourself with local etiquette and respect the customs.
- Do not make a point of driving a hard bargain; have a generous heart and share the wealth.
- Join local conservation organizations of the countries you visit and make regular contributions.
- Donate to locale temples, schools, monasteries, and park visitor centers.
- Invite local people, students, and teachers to your camp and on day hikes. Learn from them and share your knowledge without seeming to preach or lecture.
- Bring negative environmental practices to the attention of government officials.
- Do not distribute nondegradeable, breakable gifts, or items in nondegradeable packaging.
- Respect privacy when taking photographs.

The sensibilities of being a good eco-tourist should extend to the animal world, since viewing wild animals is a large part of most the tours. Mahatma Gandhi observed that the greatness of a nation and its moral progress can be determined by the way in which its citizens treat animals. It is a measure of their consciousness that all living things are part of the same whole. What is hurtful to one diminishes all others.

Guidelines to follow when watching wild animals include:

- Moving cautiously and quietly to keep from disturbing wildlife and plants.

- Maintaining a respectful distance, perhaps twenty to thirty feet.
- Be aware when animals become uneasy with your presence and leave. If you get too close, the animals expend energy unnecessarily to run from you or to defend their territory. Birds must leave their young and eggs vulnerable to predators or the elements to ward off intruders with cameras. Crowds can disrupt breeding, hunting, and feeding patterns, and even cause animals to abandon their nests.
- Animals need private moments for mating, nesting, feeding, or tending to their young. Do not be an intrusive voyeur. Put yourself in the animal's place. Animals are not without sensitivity or intelligence, so be respectful.

Being a responsible eco-tourist is a state of mind that honors the unity of the earth's ecosystems, of which *Homo sapiens* are only one element.

If we continue to destroy the diversity in the natural world there will be "nothing left to instruct us about what life is, where sacredness lies with the landscape," Gandhi writes. "Conflict erupts, death follows. The spirits of humans and animals go, whole cultures and natural processes vanish. This is a warning. The endangerment of one wildland stands for global and human demise."

Eco-tourism is part of the environmental grassroots movement that has gained momentum in the past decade. The movement has found a nascent structure in the Green Party, which has run candidates for political office in the United States and Europe. In Germany, the Greens became a force in the national parliament. Environmentalism has become a staple in mainstream politics, international business, and community action groups, such as the Global Action Plan that organizes neighborhood Ecoteams.

Within the context of environmental politics your choice of vacation has ramifications beyond your own pleasure. By choosing a firsthand experience with wilderness and its denizens you participate in the environmental movement. You open your consciousness to the places, animals, peoples, plants, and psychologically make them part of your own backyard. You are more apt to defend the rights and to take action to protect the inherent integrity of life in your backyard.

So, go take a tour of your worldwide backyard. Enjoy yourself while contributing to the well-being of the Earth and all who live on her.

Acknowledgments

Diane O'Donnell's sharp eye and critical mind strengthened and honed the essential underpinnings of this book's prose. Miriam Morgan added polish and style to the words and their flow across the pages. If thanks were given in flowers, I would need to turn the world into a flower garden to express my gratitude to these two friends. But the biggest bouquet goes to my mother, Eileen Foehr, whose years of support allowed me to get into position to actually write the book.

PART I

Safe Thrills

The trips described in this section require physical effort and some roughing it: backpacking, camping, sea kayaking, high mountain trekking. Expect to exert yourself, especially when climbing Mount Kilimanjaro. These trips will allow you to become physically involved with the land. You will be able to invest a part of yourself in the places you visit, the wildlife, and the people. You are more than a spectator, you will forge bonds with the places you visit that will test and reward you.

These trips take you into the real African scrub tracking wild animals or sea kayaking among ice floes. The hill tribes of Northern Thailand as well as the jungle tribes of the Amazon will welcome you to their homes. You can trek the Arctic North Slope and raft down its rivers or walk on the ice shelves of the Antarctic. These are adventure trips into the wilderness that may also take you on an unexpected inner journey.

Africa

BOTSWANA

Transportation: motor vehicles/hiking
Accommodations: tents
Land cost: $1,400-$2,450
Duration: 10 to 23 days
Seasons: year-round

The Okavango, located in northern Botswana, is technically a delta; a triangular-shaped tract of alluvial land at the mouth of a river. But it feels like a swamp, all water and marsh and low islands with tall reeds and grasses hiding wildlife. On these trips to the delta you backpack your gear across islands, help pole the *mokoro* (dugout canoe) through the waterways, pitch your own tent, and cook simple meals over a campfire. You often sleep on the ground in two-person tents.

Experiencing Botswana in this way is like removing a layer of protective cellophane wrap between you and the natural world. As you ride the *mokoro* through reeds, you push dense vegetation aside to get through narrow passages. You may encounter a crocodile, a group of red lechwe, a breed of aquatic antelope, or perhaps the rare and beautiful sitatunga antelope. Fish eagles, plentiful in the delta, hunt overhead.

The water is clear and cool, very unswamp-like, with a gentle current, the result of a 200-foot drop in altitude, which occurs over a 150-mile expanse from the top of the delta to the bottom.

You sense the strangeness of this delta. Normally, a river delta runs into an ocean or sea. The Okavango Delta empties into the Kalahari Desert. The Okavango River starts in the Angolan highlands and heads for the Atlantic Ocean, but then it veers toward the desert as if on a suicide run.

The delta trips start in Maun, a dusty little town on the southeastern tip of the Okavango. The town's round houses with thatched roofs made of mud and wattle (reeds or branches woven together) are of the same style that existed before Europeans landed in Africa. The form and materials of the houses tell of a relationship between humans and nature in Africa that scholars rarely capture in their books. Natural forms in Africa are sensuous, curved, and flowing. Native peoples shape both their buildings and their outlook on life to the landscape.

On the eastern edge of the delta you camp in the Moremi Wildlife Reserve—1,100 square miles of permanent swamps, forests, floodplains, and islands—and search on foot for herds of buffalo, kudu (large antelope with spirally twisted horns), antelope, and other big animals. You track lions and elephant herds across the savanna, mopane (low-lying scrub land), and arid sandveld (sandy, lightly vegetated land). You actually hope to find big crocodiles in the swamps.

The 4,200-square-mile Chobe National Park is renowned for large elephant herds, especially in the Serondela region. The park's three other main regions—Kasane, the corridor around Ngwezumba and Nogatsaa, and the Linyanti Swamps—offer nearly every type of game-viewing in Africa.

Some tour operators take you from the delta into the Kalahari Desert, which surrounds the Okavango. You trek the Makgadikgadi and Kudikam salt pans (an indented area where water gathers leaving a deposit of salt when it evaporates) after herds of zebra and two types of desert antelope—springbok and gemsbok. The springbok, an antelope thirty inches high at the shoulder, springs in five-foot vertical leaps to escape predators—hence the name.

A raft trip down the Zambezi River to Victoria Falls concludes some tours. Otherwise you reach the falls by road, where all tours end.

For more details on the Okavango Delta, the Kalahari Desert, and Victoria Falls, see COMFORTABLE WILDERNESS: Africa/Botswana.

Tour operators:

Above the Clouds Trekking
Africa Adventure Company
Exodus Adventure
Explore Worldwide

Guerba Tours and Safaris
Journeys International
Safaricentre
Trek Africa

KENYA/TANZANIA

Transportation: motor vehicle/hiking
Accommodations: tents
Land cost: $1,000-$3,700
Duration: 7 to 23 days
Seasons: year-round

It's hot and dusty. You're banging along in a Land Rover over a rough dirt track somewhere in northern Kenya. You haven't seen another vehicle, dwelling, or person all day—besides the eight people in your party. You did spot a small group of elephants and tracked them on foot for an hour through the scrub of low, flat-topped acacia trees. Pushing into a thicket where the elephants disappeared you nervously asked the guide about lions lurking about. He shrugged. "Buffalo are meaner. Dangerous to go into the bush after buffalo," he replied. "Probably buffalo around here. Why don't you lead for a while."

It had been a good day, just as you imagined a nontourist-tourist trip into the African wilds would be. You are far removed from the recognizable reference points around which you normally orient your life.

Now you look forward to pitching camp. "Where are we?" you ask the driver/guide.

"Nearby."

"Nearby" on a camping tour of Kenya could be the Kakamega Forest, the Sibiloi National Park in North Horr close to the Ethiopian border, or the Shaba Game Reserve near Mount Kenya. "Nearby" in Tanzania could be Mount Kilimanjaro or the Tarangire and Lake Manyara national parks. Most of the camping tours head out to these remote places, although tours also go to the better known game parks: Serengeti, Masai Mara, Amboseli, and Samburu (see COMFORTABLE WILDERNESS: Africa/Kenya/Tanzania).

Looking for wild animals is encouraged on the daily hikes in the outback. In the evening you help set up the camp, eat around a campfire, and sleep in simple tents with or without cots. A portable shower is set up and a hole dug in the ground serves as a latrine. The one luxury is that meals are prepared by the guide/driver. Occasionally you stay in a lodge with modern conveniences.

In western Kenya at Lake Naivasha, 55 miles from Nairobi, you camp near Hell's Gate Gorge. Lammergeyers, 4-foot-long birds of prey with 10-foot wingspans, nest in the towering basaltic cliffs. The area around the freshwater lake is populated by some four hundred species of birds.

The best way to observe the bird life is from the water. You can rent a canoe and paddle out to Crescent Island, a bird and game sanctuary. On a walk around the island you see zebra, giraffe, several species of antelope, and a few camels. You also encounter lots of people, since the park is a popular recreation area for Nairobi residents.

Lake Nakuru, a short drive to the northwest, is an alkaline lake that attracts hundreds of thousands of lesser flamingos and water birds that migrate from Europe for the winter. Leopards, hippos, baboons, Rothschild's giraffe, and waterbucks live in the national park around the lake. The park is also a designated black rhino sanctuary.

The 78-square-mile park, covered mostly by the lake, is near the Kakamega Forest, the easternmost limit of the West African rain forest. You camp at the Kakamega Forest Station, where botanists study the flora and fauna unique to this part of Kenya. A network of trails, many hand-cut by the botanists, leads into the trees and to the Ikuywa and Lugasida rivers.

At Mount Elgon National Park you camp in a grassy meadow in the montane forest that covers most of the mountain. Mount Elgon, a huge, extinct volcano and the second highest peak in Kenya (14,178 feet), fully occupies the 65-square-mile park on the Ugandan border, 225 miles from Nairobi.

Trails up Mount Elgon's slopes pass through cedar and olive trees and then into a zone of bamboo before emerging into open moorlands of giant heather. Elephants, buffalo, waterbucks, and bushbucks all live in the forest.

You follow elephant tracks through the bush to the Kitum and Makingeny caves. Elephants often enter the caves at dusk to spend hours mining salts with their tusks. Over the years they have enlarged the caves so that now small herds fit inside, along with thousands of bats.

Saiwa Swamp, a short distance away, is Kenya's smallest national park. It was created specifically to protect the rare sitatunga antelope. At strategically located game-viewing platforms, you see blue flycatchers, double-toothed barbets, broad-billed rollers, and, with luck, a sitatunga. From the swamp you descend the Kongelai escarpment to dry country and the Suam River.

In eastern Kenya, tours follow the Tana River as it arcs north around the Aberdares Mountains before plunging down to the Indian Ocean. You camp not far from the river in the Kora National Reserve, the last home of George Adamson—famous for his work with lions and the author of *My Pride and Joy*. In the early morning, and again in the late afternoon, you walk through the rough land of scrub and bush looking for elephants, cheetahs, lesser kudu, giraffe, and impala. Prolific bird life thrives along the river.

Farther downstream you stop at the Arawale National Reserve for a boat trip or a hike to search for crocodiles, hippos, lions, buffalo, and elephants. The Pokomo tribe raises mango trees, bananas, cassava, rice, and maize on the land close to the river. You can buy produce from them, although they do not have trailside stands.

You camp in the relatively undisturbed riverine habitat of the Tana River Primate Reserve on the lower Tana. The Tana River red colobus monkey, the Tana River crested mangabey, and a subspecies of Syke's monkey are native to the reserve's lowland evergreen forests. Baboons, buffalo, gazelle, and lions add a tinge of excitement to forest walks.

Tours in northern Kenya stop at the Samburu and neighboring Shaba game reserves, 220 miles from Nairobi, before continuing to the frontier region around Lake Turkana near the Ethiopian border. You travel on dirt roads around the Aberdares Mountains, a long ridge, now well-weathered, formed by molten rock when volcanos shaped this region.

The Kikuyu and Dorobo people populate this area. Kenya's first president, Jomo Kenyatta, was a Kikuyu. Kenyatta documented the tribe's customs and practices in his book, *Facing Mount Kenya*, which he wrote as a sociologist before devoting his life to politics.

You drive across the slopes of Mount Kenya, a dormant volcano, and down into the town of Isiolo. Soon past the town you turn into the Samburu Game Reserve and set up camp along the Ewaso N'giro (also Uaso Nyiro) River at the Buffalo Springs Game Reserve within the larger 40-square-mile Samburu reserve.

A game drive in Samburu takes you through various habitats: scrub desert, riverine forest, and swampland, each favored by different animal populations. Elephants tend to stay close to the forest where they forage among the trees. The herds bathe daily in the river not far from your camp. Lions, Somali ostriches, oryx, and herds of gazelle roam the scrub that stretches south to Mount Kenya, where the mountain's snowcapped peak looks like a mirage shimmering in the heat waves.

You shift camp to the smaller Shaba reserve, 10 miles east of Samburu. Few people stay in the reserve of rocky hills and thornbush scrubland because more animals live in Samburu. But at a marsh in the park's center you can find the same animal species as in Samburu's swamps. Elephants and crocodiles muck up the Ewaso N'giro River on the reserve's northern border just as they do in Samburu. Instead of seeing Mount Kenya, though, you have a view of Mount Shaba, a 5,300-foot volcanic cone just south of the reserve.

A palm-fringed river meanders through Shaba's acacia-covered plains, black rock lava flows, and reed-filled marshes. A good hike along the river goes to the remote Penny's (Chandler's) Falls.

Continuing north into the wild semidesert country, you drive to the Kitich Game Reserve, a forested valley tucked between the peaks of the Mathews Range. An armed park ranger and a spear-carrying Samburu warrior guide you on hikes searching for elephants, rhino, Cape buffalo, and forest antelope. On a moderately strenuous climb to one of the wooded ridges enclosing the valley, you pass through the "mist forest" of giant podocarpus trees (a conifer of the yew family) and cycads, cone-bearing trees that look like palms. Cycads are among the oldest African plants, relics of the ancient "supercontinent" Gondwanaland.

Floodlights for nighttime viewing at the permanent tented camp reveal leopards, hyenas, and honey badgers going about their business.

Several tour options are offered in the Northern Frontier Territory. You can hike in the Mathews Range, in the Ndoto Mountains on the edge of the Chalbi Desert, or on Mount Nyiru. This rough, remote wilderness of lush vegetation offers cool relief from the surrounding semidesert plains. Local people guide you through scenery seldom visited by outsiders.

A three-day camel safari ("safari" is Swahili for "voyage") takes you to remote valleys and plateaus. Samburu guides lead the camels that serve as pack animals. You ride, or walk, through mopane forests where elephants, lions, buffalo, rhino, and leopards live. Unfortunately, poaching has reduced the animal population in recent years.

Next, the tours drive to South Horr Valley, in the heart of Samburuland, and camp beside a stream. The wooded valley, a catchment area for the streams tumbling down the encircling hills, is a haven from the lava desert that surrounds the base of Mount Kulal. Leaving the valley, you descend to Lake Turkana (or Lake Rudolf). On the way, you pass through Loiyangalani, an oasis trading center for the Samburu people.

The Samburu are often called the northern Masai, not because of tribal affiliation, but because of their attitude. They regard themselves as "the world's top people." Like the Masai, they are herdsmen who disdain menial work. They call themselves *il-oikop*, fierce ones. The Masai call them *il-sampurrum*, after the white butterflies that flutter around sheep and goat dung.

The Samburu are a tall, handsome people with a regal manner. A Samburu *morani* (young warrior) often paints his body with red ochre and wears his hair in cornrow braids, pulled forward from the nape of the neck to jut over his forehead, like a bill of a cap.

You camp near the shore of the 175-mile-long, 10- to 13-mile-wide Lake Turkana, also known as the Jade Sea for its deep green color. The lake may once have been connected to the Mediterranean Sea via the Nile River, because puffer fish, which are found in the Mediterranean, also live in the lake. Nile perch, the world's largest freshwater fish, some weighing four hundred pounds, also live in the lake, which is fed by the Omo River flowing out of the Ethiopian highlands.

The water is a tempting escape from the heat, but you must beware—Africa's largest concentration of crocodiles calls the lake home. They live a long time and grow to abnormally large sizes here because they are not hunted. The lake's bitter alkaline and saline water renders their skin unattractive and commercially useless.

At the El Molo village near the campsite, you can rent rafts, or shallow dugouts that tend to flip faster than the money market. The El Molo, the smallest tribe in Kenya with about five hundred members, also live as fishermen on islands in the lake. You can paddle to their island homes or to the Central Island and South Island national parks. An excursion boat ride from the Lake Turkana Lodge or the Oasis Lodge saves you a long, hot, tiring raft trip.

Both volcanic islands have crocodiles and little else. The 2-square-mile Central Island National Park is the most concentrated crocodile breeding ground in Africa.

Trekking tours in southern Kenya go to the Tsavo National Park on the Kenya-Tanzania border. The Mombasa-Nairobi highway splits the park. In Tsavo West, which has a larger wild animal population than Tsavo East, you camp on the banks of the Tsavo River, which runs along the edge of the Taru Desert. You hike along the palm-fringed banks looking for Nile crocodiles, hippos, elephants, Cape buffalo, and a wide variety of antelope. The park's black rhino sanctuary is a must stop.

An armed park ranger accompanies you on treks through the rugged bush. The hikes, usually five to six hours, start in the predawn coolness. By midday you return to camp to rest up for an evening exploration. Besides wild animals, you see fortifications left from battles between British and German forces during the first World War.

In Tsavo East you hike along the Galana River and camp on its white-sand beaches—safely away from the crocs and hippos that live in the river. Herds of Cape buffalo and elephants often come to the river. Herds of gazelle, elands, oryx, and giraffe are easily spotted on the surrounding plains.

Loita Hills, northeast from Tsavo near the Masai Mara National Reserve, is the country of the Laiser clan, from which the Masai's spiritual leaders (Laibon) come. On hikes through this remote area of rolling hills, dramatic escarpments, and open savannas, you visit with the most tradition-bound clans of the Masai. Spear-carrying warriors guide you to lions, buffalo, monkeys, baboons, giraffe, bushbucks, and other game.

In Tanzania, the hiking tours stay in the north, dropping no farther south than the Lake Manyara National Park near Arusha. You can see the snow-tipped peak of Mount Kilimanjaro from the lake on a clear day.

In the Arusha National Park, you hike the forested slopes of Mount Meru to its crater (8,500 feet high). Approximately 250,000 years ago, half of the 14,900-foot mountain was blown away by a violent volcanic explosion. The resulting crater is awe-inspiring. A perfectly formed 12,000-foot ash cone rises from the crater floor, surrounded on three sides by the vertical walls of the old volcano. African cedar and podocarpus cover the crater and its slopes. Black-and-white colobus monkeys, bushbucks, perhaps elephants, and a profusion of birds—touracos, parrots, and hornbills—live in the forest.

You next track game on foot through the forest that crowns the summit of Ol Doinyo Sambu Mountain, an extinct volcano east of Tarangire National Park in the Rift Valley. Expert trackers demonstrate the skills necessary to find Cape buffalo and greater kudu. Lions and leopards live in the area but are difficult to find. Animals in areas outside national parks are much more elusive than those accustomed to visitors. The guides build blinds and apply their bushcraft skills to attract the big cats.

Tarangire National Park, Tanzania's third largest, is best in August, September, October, December, and January. This is the dry season when large numbers of animals migrate from southern

Masailand and congregate around the Tarangire River. (November is a short rainy season; much of the wild game migrates out of the park and the roads become difficult to travel.) The park's nine distinct vegetation zones—ranging from grassland to woodland, deep gullies to rocky hilltops—provide habitats for a wide diversity of animals.

No trip to Tanzania is complete without a stop at Ngorongoro Crater (see COMFORTABLE WILDERNESS: Africa/Kenya/Tanzania). You pitch camp on the rim because camping is prohibited on the floor of the 12-mile-wide caldera of the extinct volcano. You descend through forest by jeep to explore the 100-square-mile natural amphitheater for buffalo, rhino, lions, antelope, zebra, elands, and elephants. The crater's soda lake, where the animals come to drink, also attracts crested cranes, flamingos, egrets, herons, and other birds.

A short drive south from the crater is Lake Manyara National Park, at the foot of the Rift Valley escarpment. This lush, small park (123 square miles) is known for its birds, particularly water varieties. Springs flowing from the escarpment nourish five distinct vegetation zones, each a favorite habitat for different animal species. Elephants, baboons, impala, giraffe, and tree-dwelling lions live in the palm jungles and forests of mahogany and fig trees. Hippos love the pools in the marshlands. Antelope, kudu, zebra, and elands graze on the open plains. For more information, see COMFORTABLE WILDERNESS: Africa/ Kenya/Tanzania.

Tour operators:

Above the Clouds Trekking
Africa Adventure Company
Exodus Adventure
Explore Worldwide
Guerba Tours and Safaris
Mountain Travel/Sobek
   Expeditions

Nature Expeditions
   International
Overseas Adventure Travel
Safaricentre
Special Interest Tours and
   Travel
Trek Africa

Tusker Trail and Safari
Wilderness Travel
World Expeditions

Woodswomen Adventure
Travel (women and
children only)

Mount Kenya/Aberdares Climb

Transportation: hiking

Accommodations: tents

Land cost: $3,000-$3,300

Duration: 10 to 12 days total for both climbs

Seasons: best times are early December to mid-March; mid-June to October

The five-day Aberdares Mountain trek starts at the Njabini Forest Station at the foot of the range, where two park rangers join you. They carry rifles as a precaution to ward off charges by wild animals. The dense vegetation in the bamboo forest zone (4,000- to 6,000-feet altitude) can conceal a Cape buffalo or an elephant until you nearly stumble into them.

On the hike you carry only a daypack. Porters tote the heavier gear and do most of the camp chores, including cooking. You set up your own tent and generally help out.

From the trailhead, you hike four hours up through the cedar and podocarpus forest where bushbucks, blue and colobus monkeys, tropical boubou, Hartlaub's touracos, and other birds live. The first campsite is on the edge of the bamboo forest zone.

On the second day, you clear the forest dripping with Spanish moss and come out into open moorlands. The rounded humps of Elephant and Kinangop peaks are across the moorlands. Technical skills are not required to climb the peaks; you just walk up and stroll along the 10,000-foot ridge to the summit. On some tours a vehicle meets you below the summit and takes you to the nearby campsite—a reward for conquering the mountain.

The third day is a pleasant walk across the moorlands through shallow valleys with stands of conifers. The mornings are bright and clear, but by afternoon towering clouds usually envelop the mountain.

The ascent of Satima, the highest point (13,120 feet) of the Aberdares, is the goal of the fourth day. You walk along game trails in the footsteps of buffalo and elands. Lions follow the same trails. The thought of sighting a lion is exciting, too, until you realize you have no place to run or hide. You keep the armed guide in sight.

The next day you hike down to the starting point for a hot shower and a day's rest in camp before driving to Mount Kenya, several hours to the west. The Masai call Mount Kenya "Kere Nyaga," named for *Nyago*, the Masai word for God.

Several routes lead to Point Lenana (16,355 feet), the goal for nontechnical climbers of Mount Kenya. Different tours may take different routes, but none require technical climbing skills. Some tours make a beeline for Point Lenana, getting up and down in four days; others take a circuitous route requiring up to six days. Tours do not attempt the two highest peaks, Batian (17,058 feet) and Nelion (17,023 feet), which do demand technical rock-climbing expertise. The descent takes one or two days.

Tour leaders take the hike at a reasonable, almost slow, pace. In a relatively short time you walk up to over two miles in altitude, which can cause pulmonary edema, a respiratory disorder brought on by insufficient oxygen at high altitudes.

Other potential dangers are buffalo and forest elephants. They forage in the thick vegetation but are rarely seen, having no more desire for a confrontation than you do.

The trip requires no climbing skills but is physically demanding. You will enjoy the hike better if you are in good condition. Although Mount Kenya straddles the equator, nights at 13,000 feet can be bitterly cold, so pack warm clothes and extra socks.

One popular summit route is the Naro Moru Track. The first hour of the hike—up a gentle slope through conifer, hardwood, and bamboo forests—softsells the climb. You carry only a daypack, the trail is in reasonable shape, porters lug the heavy stuff, and the temperature is pleasant. It is on the second day you find out you are in for a challenging climb: you hit a vertical bog.

Tours try to reach the Met Station, just below the treeline, by the first night. Some tour leaders prefer to push on for another hour to Old Mosses Camp, just above the treeline at 10,500 feet.

The second day's objective is Mackinders Valley Huts or Shipton's Camp, a short but steep climb above Mackinders Valley. The 3,000-foot climb to the huts takes six to seven hours. On the way, you encounter the vertical bog—spongy, oozy ground, and a series of muddy hills. After the bog, you ford the Naro Moru River and hike across moorlands dotted with giant groundsel, wildflowers and lobelia—some 30 feet tall—to Teleki Valley, the starting point for a direct assault on Point Lenana. If it is sunny you will get your first clear look at Mount Kenya's top peaks from the valley.

If you leave Teleki Valley by 4 A.M., you can reach Point Lenana's summit and return to your campsite by nightfall. A longer route takes you over the Simba Col to Kami Hut (14,564 feet) on the north side of the peaks. You pass Emerald Lake and other lakes on the trek through the high valleys.

You top Point Lenana after a four- to five-hour hike up the north ridge. A magnificent panorama of green slopes sliding down to sere, brown plains spreads below you.

The descent can be via the Naro Moru route or down the eastern side of the mountain to Hall Tarns and then on to Minto's Hut (14,075 feet) where you spend the night. From Minto's Hut you drop down into Nithi Gorge with a stunning view of Vivienne Falls and the sheer rock faces towering above you. The final night on the mountain is spent at the Uramandi Hut.

The last full day on Mount Kenya is spent walking through the cedar forest and open glades to the Meru Mount Kenya Lodge, where you spend the night in a wooden chalet and enjoy a hot shower and good food.

Tour operators:

Above the Clouds Trekking
Africa Adventure Company

Exodus Adventure
Explore Worldwide

Kimbla

Mountain Travel/Sobek
Expeditions

Nature Expeditions
International

Safaricentre

Mount Kilimanjaro Climb

Transportation: hiking

Accommodations: lodges/mountain huts

Land cost: $2,675-$3,690

Duration: 5 to 8 days

Seasons: year-round, except for rainy April and May; best months are January, February, and June through September.

The Chagga people believe that the angry gods who dwell on the Kipoo and Kimawenze peaks of *Kilemieiroya* will punish anyone who dares climb the "mountain that cannot be conquered." Take heed when embarking for a summit of Mount Kilimanjaro.

Kilimanjaro is known as the "shining mountain," or "Mountain of Greatness." Kilimanjaro's base is 37 miles long and 25 miles wide, making it the world's largest freestanding mountain.

You should be a strong, experienced hiker in top physical condition to successfully reach the Uhuru Peak (19,340 feet), the highest point of the mountain, located on the outer caldera of the Kibo volcano. Hikers as young as eleven years old and as old as seventy-four have made the climb. Children under ten are not allowed on the mountain's higher slopes. No technical climbing skills are necessary, but the summit approach is very strenuous. A guide is required.

Kilimanjaro consists of three major volcanic craters: Shira (13,650 feet), Mawenzi (16,893 feet), and, in the middle, snow-capped Kibo (19,340 feet), the newest formed. Kibo is a dormant, not extinct, volcano vent. Fumes and smoke rising from the caldera, which you can climb down into, attest to the volcano's active life.

The Mount Kilimanjaro National Park covers 292 square miles of the mountain above 8,856 feet. Six climbing corridors pass through the forest reserve to the peaks. The mountain rain forests contain many species of old African vegetation. The Marango route is the most popular with tour operators, although the Machame route is also used.

The Marango route—not too easy, not too hard—has the best hut facilities en route. The more scenic Machame route takes longer, allowing greater time for acclimatization. Hiring a porter to carry your sleeping bag and heavier gear is highly recommended. (Spending money to help support the local economy is a tenet of eco-tourism.) You need a daypack for on-trail necessities, such as water, high-energy food, a camera, raingear, and extra socks. Bring cooking kerosene to minimize deforestation.

The hike starts at the Park Headquarters at Marangu Gate. You leave in the morning to avoid the expected afternoon rains. The often muddy trail climbs from 6,000 feet to 9,000 feet during an easy four- to five-hour hike through tropical forests. Black-and-white colobus monkeys, olive baboons, blue monkeys, buffalo, and elephants live in the forests.

You spend the first night on the Marangu route at the Mandara Huts, a small village of wooden cabins clustered around a central lodge, which serves as a dining hall and social center. A dormitory with two hundred beds is above the dining area. The cabins are divided into two sections, each accommodating four persons on small platform beds. Foam pads, kerosene lamps, and cooking stoves are provided. There is no shower, only cold water from a central tap. Each hut has a long-drop pit latrine.

The second day you climb 3,346 feet through the forest zone of giant heath (tree-sized heather) to the moorlands with tussock grasses and giant lobelia. You leave the forest to follow a gentle path through an alpine meadow. Once clear of the trees, you get good views of Mawenzi. The five- to seven-hour hike ends at the Horombo Huts (12,205 feet), a camp similar to Mandara.

Many tours pause at Horombo for a day of acclimatization. You take day hikes to the saddle between Kibo and Mawenzi peaks or to bogs where forests of giant senecios grow. Mist often hangs in the trees, giving the mountain a moody atmosphere. Days are chilly, and nights are very cold. Expect to get your last good sleep for the next couple of nights here; sleeping, walking, and normal functioning suffer in the thin air of the higher altitude ahead.

In the morning you cross the desert saddle between Kibo and Mawenzi. You see little wildlife as you cross open grasslands. The thin air makes flying too difficult for most birds, and the only mammals that high up are your fellow hikers. The windchill can be bitterly cold—close to arctic conditions—so dress appropriately.

You may also feel some effects of altitude sickness—shortness of breath, nausea, insomnia, and headaches caused by the body working hard with less than one-half its usual oxygen supply. Do not ignore these symptoms. They can signal the beginning of pulmonary edema, which can lead to coma or death. When hiking above 15,000 feet, take measured, slow steps; breathe deeply; and drink more water than you think necessary.

After a five- to six-hour climb up 3,225 feet you come to Kibo Hut (15,500 feet), a stone hut with a dormitory. Get to sleep early because the push to the summit starts by 2 A.M. the next morning. You want to reach the summit by sunrise before the sun melts the frozen scree. When the snow covering the steep rocky slope becomes too soft, you sink down to your knees, making the climb even more demanding.

You reach Gillman's Point after four to five grueling hours up seemingly endless switchbacks. But the view from the point as the sun rises behind the jagged peaks of Mawenzi is worth all the effort. It is then another moderate hour's climb (705 feet) to Uhuru (Freedom) Peak, the highest point in Africa at 19,340 feet.

It is all downhill from there.

Tour operators:

Africa Adventure Company
Exodus Adventure
Himalayan Travel
Journeys International

Kimbla
Mountain Travel/Sobek
 Expeditions

Nature Expeditions
International

Safaricentre

Special Interest Tours &
Travel

Voyagers International

Wilderness Travel

Wildland Adventures

Woodswomen Adventure
Travel

World Expeditions

NAMIBIA

Transportation: motor vehicle/hiking

Accommodations: lodges/tents

Land cost: $1,945-$3,000

Duration: 16 to 22 days

Seasons: year-round; best months May to September

The eclectic combination of German neatness and African wilderness works well in Namibia. The former German colony, larger than California and Arizona combined, lies along the Atlantic Coast in southwest Africa, just north of South Africa.

You can enjoy the wildlife and stark beauty of the country on drives to various wilderness areas. Stops include the Swakopmund on the Skeleton Coast and the Etosha National Park. You camp in the Namib Desert, the Sesriem and Kuiseb canyons, and the dramatic Damaraland Wilderness Reserve.

At Sossusvlei in the southern part of Namib-Naukluft National Park you walk down the giant sand dunes, some up to one thousand feet tall. Your campsite in Sesriem Canyon is a few minutes drive from the dunes.

In Damaraland you camp near "Klein Serengeti," rugged country accessible only by four-wheel drive vehicles or on foot. You drive cross-country to hidden water holes and gorges searching for black rhino, desert elephants, giraffe, and zebra.

At Okaukuejo, in the Etosha National Park, you camp on the edge of the huge Etosha Pan, an alkaline depression where animals come to drink at water holes. Floodlights at the established campsite allow excellent night game-viewing.

You also go to the Caprivi Strip, Namibia's panhandle bordered by Angola, Zambia, and Botswana, to walk through the area's three reserves looking for wild animals. The Mudumu and Mamili national parks are much like Botswana's Okavango Delta. You paddle canoes on the Kwando and Linyanti rivers to see hippos in the shallows and herds of plains animals along the shore.

Seventeen percent of Namibia's land is preserved as wildlife refuges. But the country's environmental awareness goes beyond merely establishing national parks. Its innovative conservation programs are setting the pace for the rest of Africa.

The Himba and Herero tribes, who used to hunt elephants, both legally and illegally, are now the herds' protectors for the same reason they killed the animals: economics. Namibia wants to build its tourist industry, and a strong foundation block is wildlife. Himba and Herero men are hired as wildlife guards to assist the government's rangers under the Auxiliary Game Guard program. Tourists who come to see elephants spend money on traditional crafts in the tribes' villages. It is a win-win situation.

Another conservation effort to protect the dwindling rhino population in some areas is the removal of the animal's horns, thus eliminating the very reason for poaching. While this may seem a bit extreme, the rhino apparently survive just fine without them.

For more details on Namibia, see COMFORTABLE WILDERNESS: Africa/Namibia.

Tour operators:

Africa Adventure Company
Exodus Adventure
Explore Worldwide
Journeys International

Special Interest Tours & Travel
Tusker Trail & Safari
Wilderness Travel

RWANDA/ZAIRE

Transportation: motor vehicle/hiking
Accommodations: hotels/lodges/mountain huts

Land cost: $1,584-$2,400

Duration: 4 to 15 days

Seasons: mid-June to September; December to March

The main attractions of tours to Rwanda/Zaire are the gorillas.

"Don't stare, don't touch, don't be aggressive, don't run, don't point, act submissive," instructs the Hohatu guide. He then casually waves his hand at the Virunga Volcano and motions you and your fellow gorilla voyeurs to follow. The Virungas, a range of dormant volcanoes straddling Rwanda, Zaire, and Uganda are covered with dense, wet forests and are home to about three hundred and twenty mountain gorillas. The guide hopes to introduce you to a couple of gorilla families.

While you crawl up muddy slopes and haul yourself up hand-over-hand on roots and vines for three hours, the entire time desperately trying to avoid stinging nettles, the porters negotiate the mountains while successfully carrying your lunch on their heads.

The guide follows gorilla signs, such as trees stripped of leaves, matted grass, or uprooted bamboo. Suddenly he squats and motions you to do the same and be still. He cautiously creeps forward, silently parts the bushes, then motions you forward. You peer through the leaves. A huge male silverback, perhaps six feet tall and six hundred pounds, turns his head and stares at you.

The gorilla nibbles on a bamboo shoot as his family of twelve sits around the clearing. The guide makes gorilla noises deep in his throat to announce you and steps into the open.

You timidly follow. The gorillas do not acknowledge you as you approach very slowly, bent over so as not to appear threatening. If a gorilla charges, the guides tell you to kneel, turn away, and perhaps mimic eating leaves. The guide keeps a watchful eye on you more than on the gorillas. If there is to be danger, your clumsiness will start it.

The female rushes just as you take her picture. You want to become invisible, to have no smell. You try not to make direct eye contact or stare, but it is very difficult to ignore a gorilla in front of you beating its chest.

When viewing a gorilla family, you are in effect a guest, tolerated in the gorilla's home. Only eight visitors are allowed to visit a gorilla family for one hour each day. When the gorillas tire of you they move off. If you follow, the group's dominant male strongly tells you to leave.

Tours to the mountain gorillas' homes go to four national parks: Parc National des Volcans in Rwanda; Virunga National Park and the Kahuzi-Bienga National Park in Zaire; and the Gorilla Sanctuary in Uganda's Impenetrable Forest. You go to at least two of the four on a typical tour.

The gorillas are valued as economic saviors and peacekeepers, especially by Zaire and Rwanda. Their presence generates eight to ten million tourist dollars annually. Their presence has established a peace zone in the running battle between the Rwandan Patriotic Front and government forces. The fighters avoid the gorilla sanctuaries so they won't scare off tourists—but incidents do occur; one silverback male became a battlefield casualty.

Poachers killed many gorillas before a few dedicated conservationists/researchers, most notably George Schaller and Dian Fossey, set off an international protest. In 1950, about five hundred gorillas lived in Virunga. The population was reduced by nearly half within ten years through shrinking habitat and poaching. Then Fossey set up her Karisoke research base, which you can visit, and started her relentless effort to save the gorillas. Some years later she was murdered at her camp. Poachers were suspected.

In 1981, the gorilla tourist program was established. Poaching has declined dramatically since then, and the gorilla population has stabilized.

Accommodations vary from first-class hotels to a couple of nights in mountain huts, depending on the tour. Many tours use the Djomba Gorilla Camp in Virunga National Park. You stay in wooden cottages furnished with traditional decorations, each with two double-occupancy bedrooms, a private bath, a central living room, and a veranda.

After an exhausting day climbing in rain up muddy slopes and hacking your way through dense forest, a hot shower and a good meal at a hotel are welcomed. You rough it by day and rest in comfort by night.

Some tours take you searching for chimpanzees in Zaire's Tongo National Park, near Lake Kivu. Finding chimpanzees is more difficult than locating gorillas. The chimpanzees are less approachable than gorillas and do not sit around a clearing munching bamboo while you take pictures. They prefer to stay in the trees and on the move.

Viewing chimpanzees has been made easier through the efforts of Annette Lanjouw, who habituated several chimpanzee groups in this newly established park. Guides lead tours of no more than six visitors in search of the groups.

Tour operators:

Abercrombie & Kent
    International
Exodus Adventure
Explore Worldwide
Guerba Tours and Safaris
Journeys International
Kimbla
Oceanic Society Expeditions

Overseas Adventure Travel
Safaricentre
Trek Africa
Tusker Trail & Safari
Wilderness Travel
Wildland Adventures
World Expeditions

ZAMBIA

Transportation: hiking/canoe
Accommodations: lodges/tents/thatched huts
Land cost: $1,125-$2,590
Duration: 5 to 16 days
Seasons: June to October

These walking trips have two components, one by land and one by water. By land, you hike in the 3,500-square-mile South Luangwa National Park. By water, you shoot the Zambezi River cataracts.

In the Luangwa, called the "Crowded Valley" for the highest

concentrations of elephants in Africa, you hike from bush camp to bush camp. You hike three to five hours daily across the wide, relatively flat valley of scrub. Trails go through grassland and along the Luangwa River on the park's eastern border. An armed park ranger accompanies you.

An expert naturalist guide shows you how to track animals and explains the interrelationship of the various savanna, riverine, and woodland ecosystems. Children under twelve are not allowed on the trails.

You leave camp early to walk in the morning coolness, take a midday break, and walk again in the late afternoon. Most tours use permanent camps with thatched huts, laundry service, and hot showers. A resident cook prepares the meals. When going from camp to camp, your gear is carried by porters or transported by vehicles. Other tours offer basic camping, where you pitch a two-person tent and participate in camp chores.

On the hikes across the grasslands you see elephant herds, antelope, hyena, impala, giraffe, and lions. Crocodiles, hippos, puku (small antelope), waterbucks, and a wide variety of birds congregate along the riverbanks.

When the hiking part is over, you canoe or raft down the Zambezi River. You launch canoes on the Kafue River and paddle to the Zambezi confluence. The wide river with a steady current carries you along without paddling. You pass thatched-house villages of the Chiawa, who have lived along the river for generations as farmers and fishermen. You camp on the riverbank opposite hippo pools at the Lower Zambezi National Park. Large herds of elephants, buffalo, and antelope graze on the river's floodplain.

Below Victoria Falls, the end point for the tours, you raft the Zambezi's white water rapids. The green-colored river, almost a mile-and-a-half wide as it tumbles over the falls, is compressed in places into a gorge only twenty yards wide, causing turbulence that stands your twelve-foot rubber raft on end.

The professional river-running crew launches the rafts in a foaming pool below the falls called Boiling Pot, a graphic description. From then on, the fun really starts. On the six-day, thrill-filled trip, you plunge down a forty-five degree slope into a frenetic froth.

You carom between steep basalt walls through seven gorges of twisting S-turns as the river bounds down a series of rapids. At the Upper Mowimba Falls, you nearly free-fall over a series of cliffs. You portage the Lower Mowimba Falls, two waterfalls over 20-foot cliffs.

You camp along the river, taking care not to step on hidden land mines left over from the war of independence. The nights are surprisingly cold. Forget ecology for a moment; this trip is sheer, fun-filled terror.

For more details on Zambia, see COMFORTABLE WILDERNESS: Africa/Zambia.

Tour operators:

Africa Adventure Company
Exodus Adventure
Explore Worldwide
Guerba Tours and Safaris
Mountain Travel/Sobek
   Expeditions

Nature Expeditions
   International
Safaricentre
Trek Africa
Tusker Trail & Safari
Wildland Adventures

ZIMBABWE

Transportation: motor vehicle/hiking/canoe
Accommodations: lodges/tents
Land cost: $1,500-$3,800
Duration: 5 to 16 days
Seasons: year-round

Chizarira National Park best fits the image of wild, untamed Africa. Humans have barely scarred the 740 square miles of thick forest, bushveld (savanna covered with scrub and brush), and floodplains cleaved by deep gorges. A ferocious wildness lends the land an aura of independence. The land, although beautiful, makes no attempt to appear friendly. Adventurers relish the park; tourists complain.

Walking this area—the most remote and least developed wild-life area remaining in Africa—puts you as close to the heart of African wilderness as you are likely to get.

You ascend the 1,000-foot-high Chizarira escarpment after a six-hour drive from Victoria Falls through the Zambezi River Valley. For one to eight days, depending on the tour, you explore the park with the required, fully licensed guide and a tracker, one of whom carries a high-powered rifle. Expect to see black rhino, elephants, buffalo, and lions—and very few other people in this seldom-visited national park.

You have to work to find the animals. Big herds do not placidly graze like extras in a movie, as they do on the Serengeti Plain. Elephants hide out in the forest, and lions keep to rocky lairs. You follow rutted, ancient game trails and lie in wait at water holes for buffalo to appear. The tracker must really track, using skills disappearing in modern Africa. He shows you tricks of his trade—how to tell how old a trail is, where to find certain animals at certain times, and why.

The very real possibility of a sudden encounter with a rhino in the dense forest sharpens your alertness. This is not a "wannabe" experience. You are in the wildest part of Africa, on foot, camping along dry riverbeds, trying to look a wild animal in the eye.

You have a good chance of seeing a black rhino. Zimbabwe has about 1,700 black rhino, about half of the world's total. According to the African Wildlife Foundation, there are only about 3,000 black rhino left in all of Africa and another 170 in zoos. The black rhino and the white rhino, the other African species, are threatened with loss of habitat as the human population grows. Approximately 4,800 white rhino exist in the wild in Asia and Africa.

The more immediate threat to rhino in Africa, though, is poaching. In 1960, Kenya had 20,000 black rhino. By the end of the 1970s, fewer than 300 remained.

In the 1980s, Kenya established eleven black rhino protected re-serves, and the animal's population began to revive. Presently 400 black rhino live in Kenya. Namibia, South Africa, and Zimbabwe have also managed to stabilize their rhino populations, and numbers there are slowly increasing.

Rhino are killed chiefly for their horns, which are considered a powerful aphrodisiac in many Asian countries and are used in Chinese medicine. Kenya considers the rhino economically important in another way —they help attract tourists. One-third of Kenya's national economy comes from tourism. But the government in Zimbabwe views rhino slightly differently. Writing in *New Scientist* magazine (September 28, 1991) Colin Tudge quotes Rowan Martin of Zimbabwe's National Parks and Wildlife Management as saying, "The black rhino is a species with no legal economic value which is nevertheless very expensive to protect. Sustainable utilisation of rhino and rhino products offers a promising conservation alternative."

Zimbabwe conservation officials are pressing the Convention on International Trade in Endangered Species of Wild Flora and Fauna (CITES) to allow limited, strictly government-to-government trade of elephant ivory and rhino horn, reports Tudge. For more information on black rhino, see NOT ORDINARY TRIPS: Africa/Zimbabwe/Black Rhino Watch.

To the government of Zimbabwe, wild animals have an economic role other than just as a lure for tourists. Wild game is sold to zoos and private owners. So lucrative is the trade that land is being taken out of cattle and goat farming to give back to wild animals. Presently, about one-third of Zimbabwe is under wildlife management.

Walking tours to Zimbabwe also go to Hwange National Park, the country's largest; Matusadona National Park; and Mana Pools National Park. Some include a several-day canoe trip down the Zambezi River. For details on these areas see COMFORTABLE WILDERNESS: Africa/Zimbabwe.

Tour operators:

Above the Clouds Trekking

Africa Adventure Company

Exodus Adventure

Explore Worldwide

Guerba Tours and Safaris

Journeys International

Nature Expeditions
    International

Safaricentre

Special Interest Tours & Travel

Tusker Trail & Safari

Antarctica

Transportation: icebreaker ship

Accommodations: on-board

Land costs: $4,500-$16,475

Duration: 13 to 21 days

Seasons: October to April

"The risk one runs in exploring a coast in these unknown and icy seas is so very great that I can be so bold to say no man will ever venture farther than I have done and that the lands that may lie to the South will never be explored."

Captain James Cook, 1774

Captain Cook's view from the wooden, 462-ton ship *Resolution* certainly justified his opinion. Fierce wilderness attacked, clawed at, bashed against, and slashed his fragile ship. Icebergs threatened to ram and sink the *Resolution*. The sea could have frozen the ship in a deadly embrace.

Today, you sail to the Antarctic on specially built icebreakers appointed with the comforts of a luxury cruise ship. A deluxe cabin adds thousands of dollars to a tour's basic fare. Still, the journey is formidable. Force ten gales can and do blow, although more often the seas are moderate—but never placid. Cold is a constant companion. The weather determines how your trip will develop.

Antarctica, the world's fifth-largest continent, is drier than the

Sahara Desert, higher on the average than the Indian subcontinent, windier than Patagonia, and its days and nights longer than in the Arctic. There is less soil and more fresh water on Antarctica than anywhere else on earth. An estimated 40 percent of the earth's fresh water is frozen in the ice sheets that are about 7,000 feet deep. Not one tree grows in Antarctica.

However, writes Sanford Moss in his book *Natural History of the Antarctic Peninsula* (Columbia University Press, 1988) "the Antarctic is one of our most ecologically important wildernesses and scientifically one of the most valuable. The native plants and animals constitute one of the least complex webs of ecological interrelationship found on earth."

A record of the Earth's atmospheric composition dating back tens of thousands of years is locked in the Antarctic ice sheet. It was Antarctic studies that first alerted scientists to the hole in the Earth's ozone layer and that lent credence to the greenhouse effect theory.

Where you go in Antarctica depends on the point of departure, either from South America or South Africa. South American-based trips explore the western Antarctic Peninsula, South Georgia Island, and the Falkland Islands. Trips from South Africa, through Innerasia and Quark Expeditions, voyage to several sub-Antarctic islands and eastern Antarctica, nearly circumnavigating the continent.

The South American-based trips, leaving from ports in Argentina and Chile, wind through islands and pass glaciers from the Beagle Channel out to Drake Passage. The Antarctic Peninsula lies 600 miles to the south.

After three days at sea, the South Shetland Islands hove into sight and then the Antarctic Peninsula. You sail along the Danco Coast and through the narrow, ice-choked Le Marire or Neumeyer channels, where you can spot whales, sea birds, penguins, and seals. The twenty-four hours of daylight allow ample time for taking photographs.

The ship anchors off Port Lockroy in a bay surrounded by 8,000-foot-high mountains. Icebergs calve from glaciers with a resounding boom and splash as they hit the water. On shore you visit an Adelie penguin rookery.

The penguin is the unofficial symbol of the Antarctic. Only five of the eighteen species of penguins are truly Antarctic, meaning they breed in the region. Penguin fossils dating back to the Eocene epoch, forty million years ago, have been found on the Antarctic Peninsula. Although they are flightless birds like ostriches and emus, most experts agree that the penguins' ancestors were flying species.

The Adelie, the most abundant of the Antarctic penguins, lives in colonies composed of up to hundreds of thousands of breeding pairs. The birds return to the same breeding area, and often to the same nest, year after year. To reach those sites in Eastern Antarctica the birds may walk sixty miles over ice and land, traveling single file, covering about five miles a day.

Penguins are an unending source of amusement with their rolling gait and pudgy bodies so awkward on land. But in the water they are extraordinarily graceful and agile. Their 4:5 length-to-width ratio is ideal for drag reduction. Sleek, dense feathers streamline them for maximum hydrodynamic efficiency.

Paradise Bay at the Antarctic Peninsula is a usual stop on the tours from South America. The bay, ringed by 5,000-foot mountains with hanging ice cliffs and snow-filled aràtes (sharp-crested ridges), is perhaps the most beautiful site in the Antarctic. Leaving the mother ship in an inflatable Zodiac, you dodge icebergs on the short ride to shore, where you visit large Adelie and gentoo penguin rookeries. A climb up the hill behind the abandoned Argentine research station gives a sweeping view of the bay, weather permitting.

Other stops include King George Island, Half Moon Island, and Hope Bay before turning north toward South Georgia Island and the Falklands.

The 120-mile-long South Georgia Island is a mass of rugged, glacier-covered mountains. From a distance, they resemble spikes of crystals rising 9,500 feet out of the sea. Four species of penguins and four different types of albatross breed on the cliffs of this deeply indented coastline.

On seven-day cruises around the island, you stop at numerous bays and inlets and hike the Salisbury Plain. These stops are often offered by tour operators as a stand-alone trip. History buffs rush to a small cove at King Haakon Bay where, in 1916, the Antarctic explorer Ernest Shackleton and his men landed. They reached the cove in a canvas-covered whaleboat after escaping from their ship, which was frozen in the Weddell Sea ice pack 600 miles away. They landed on the uninhabited side of South Georgia Island and crossed the island to the then-active whaling station at Stromness Bay on the north coast. A close-up look at the intimidating mountains behind King Haakon Bay gives a vivid picture of the difficulties the men must have faced.

Later, on a walk along the shore of Stromness Bay, you see the 2,000-foot cliffs and glaciers Shackleton and his companions descended. You pass king and gentoo penguins on the beach and explore by Zodiac the face of a glacier as it noses into the bay.

On the island's Salisbury Plain you walk through thousands upon thousands of multicolored king penguins nesting in the tussock grass. Two glaciers and rugged, snowcapped peaks rise above the rookery.

At the Falkland Islands, 300 miles east of Argentina, tours stop at two remote islands off the coast of East Falkland and at three more accessible islands.

On Bleaker Island the tour naturalist explains the loves and lives of the large colony of gentoo penguins. Orca whales are often seen cruising just off the beach, a popular spot for their favorite foods: elephant seals and sea lions.

Large numbers of striated caracaras, one of the world's rarest birds of prey, nest on Sea Lion Island. Known locally as "Johnny Rock," the caracara only breeds on the Falkland Islands and off Cape Horn. You also see elephant seals, sea lions, and colonies of cormorants, and rockhopper, gentoo, and Magellanic penguins.

The tours disembark at Port Stanley, capital of the Falklands, perhaps best remembered as a battleground between Argentina and Great Britain in 1982. You fly to Santiago, Chile, from the Port Stanley airport.

Highlights of the voyages leaving from Cape Town, South Africa, include landings on sub-Antarctic islands, walks on ice shelves, and visits to the continent's inland hills via helicopter. The tours terminate in Australia or New Zealand.

The sub-Antarctic islands of Crozet, Kerguelen, and Heard lie east of Antarctica approximately equidistant from Africa and Australia. Scientists at the research station on French-owned Crozet helpfully explain aspects of Antarctica's ecology. You then walk to large colonies of king penguins and nesting albatross.

Kerguelen Island, the largest of the three islands, is a mecca for sub-Antarctic wildlife. You spend two days exploring the fjords in inflatable Zodiacs and walking on the permanent ice cap.

Heard Island, a true Antarctic island, lies just below the Antarctic Convergence, the boundary where the mass of cold Antarctic water meets warmer sub-Antarctic water. North of the shifting convergence line the surface temperature is 8 degrees Celsius; south of the line the temperature drops to less than 2 degrees Celsius. The heavier cold water sinks to about eight hundred feet and travels northward, influencing weather and marine life in the North Atlantic Ocean. The convergence zone teems with marine wildlife feeding on the rich nutrients welling up from the depths.

At this point you enter the Southern Ocean, one of the world's windiest and roughest waters.

Heard Island, dominated by Big Ben, a 9,005-foot glacier and snow-covered mountain, is home to hundreds of thousands of penguins, albatross, and petrels, as well as fur, leopard, and elephant seals. You land at several places to observe the wildlife up close.

Within two days of leaving Heard Island, your vessel, the *Kaptain Khlebhikov*, manned by a Russian crew and equipped with two helicopters, starts smashing through ice packs up to six feet thick. Helicopter rides give a great view of the ship surrounded by awe-inspiring wilderness.

You stop at the seldom-visited Oygarden island group to see large colonies of Adelie penguins and Weddell seals. A helicopter takes you—weather permitting—to the nearby mainland where you can explore inland glaciers on foot.

You may spot a rarely seen Ross seal, which prefers to live in the most inaccessible regions of the inner ice pack's dense ice floes. Six species of seals live in the Southern Ocean. Man first came to the Antarctic to hunt seals for their pelts and whales for their oil.

Man's greed nearly drove the Antarctic fur seal to extinction. In the 1930s, only a hundred or so remained. But when the market for their fur dropped, the seal populations recovered. An estimated nine hundred thousand Antarctic fur seals thrived in 1982. According to Moss, at the current growth rate, the population could reach four million by the year 2000.

Farther south of the Oygarden islands you visit the Australian Mawson Scientific Base on the mainland. The scientists give you a crash course in their projects on the peculiarities of the Antarctic and its wildlife. Weather permitting, you take a helicopter flight over the nearby Mawson-Masson Range and Fang Peak.

Tabular icebergs, huge floating ice plateaus, appear as your ship approaches the Amery Ice Shelf. You go ashore to the ice shelf with 100-foot-high cliffs to see penguin rookeries.

Near Bowman Island to the south you venture on to the Shackleton Ice Shelf, formed by the huge Scott and Denman glaciers. Whales are often seen feeding along the edge of the ice shelf. The ship rounds the end of the continent and heads for the Russian scientific base at Mirny.

You next sail along the West Ice Shelf past ice cliffs that calve huge tabular icebergs. Next is the Ross Ice Shelf, the largest in the Antarctic, where the explorers, Scott and Amundsen, set out for the South Pole. You stop at the Italian research station at Terra Nova and the American and New Zealand stations at McMurdo Sound. The raucous large Adelie rookeries at McMurdo Sound can be heard from as far as 30 miles downwind.

A helicopter ride takes you to the Dry Valleys, one of the few snow-free places on Antarctica. It was once a tropic land according to fossil findings. The narrow, barren, wind-sculpted valleys of hanging glaciers contain one of the continent's rare rivers, which flows into Lake Vanda.

From McMurdo Sound your ship turns toward Australia where you disembark.

Purists argue that tourism should be banned from the Antarctic. The mere presence of humans pollutes the pristine wilderness. Cruise ships have been known to foul the water with oil by bilging their pumps near sensitive habitats. Even though the tours take care not to pollute, the ships themselves discharge some inevitable pollutants.

On responsible tours, shipboard waste is not dumped into the sea. Visits to rookeries are arranged so as not to disturb nesting birds or disrupt ongoing research. You are repeatedly reminded to treat the fragile environment with extreme care and respect.

Unfortunately, Antarctica is marred by humans' thoughtlessness.

Ross writes, "Humans in Antarctica have a rich history of irresponsible trash disposal. Solid wastes, in particular, are enduring features of the Peninsula landscape." The governments responsible for the research stations have declared the intent to clean up the trash.

Antarctica wildlife and habitats are supposedly protected by the Antarctic Treaty, agreed to by twenty-nine nations, including the United States. However, conservationists fear the treaty is not ironclad in protecting the region.

Copper, zinc, silver, gold, molybdenum, and other valuable minerals probably lie beneath Antarctica's icy mantle, given its geological history and formation. Traces of oil have been discovered by test drilling in the Ross Sea. If world demand for these natural resources becomes great enough, the pressure to exploit the continent may override all other considerations.

"It is only a matter of time, many observers think, before the commercial exploration for and exploitation of possible gas and oil reserves takes place," Moss warns.

Environmental groups such as Greenpeace, Antarctica Project, and the Southern Ocean Coalition advocate an Antarctica Environmental Protection Agency and moratoriums on krill fishing (a major food source for Antarctic marine life) and on mineral exploration. No action has been taken on these issues yet.

Tour operators:

Abercrombie & Kent International
Innerasia Expeditions
International Expeditions
Mountain Travel/Sobek Expeditions

Quark Expeditions
Victor Emanuel Nature Tours
Wilderness Travel
Wildland Adventures

Asia

BORNEO

Transportation: plane/boat/motor vehicle/hiking
Accommodations: hotels/longhouses/lodges
Land cost: $1,474-$2,740
Duration: 14 to 21 days
Seasons: year-round

In the million-year-old jungle of Borneo, pigs and fish climb trees, snakes and frogs fly, giant spiders swallow mice whole, flowers grow three feet wide and trees glow in the dark, and native peoples wage a desperate battle against the loggers to save their forest homes.

Borneo, the world's third largest island after Greenland and New Guinea, is divided unevenly between Malaysia and Indonesia. The southern two-thirds of the island is Kalimantan, a province ruled by Indonesia. The northern third consists of the independent oil-rich state of Brunei and the Malaysian states of Sarawak and Sabah. Tours go to Sarawak, Sabah, and Kalimantan.

In Sarawak, tours start in the capital city, Kuching, where you stay in the Hilton Hotel. Before heading up the rivers to visit the Iban, Sarawak's largest indigenous tribe, you go to several wildlife reserves and national parks in the Kuching area.

At the Semengoh Wildlife Reserve, a rehabilitation center for orphaned orangutans, young orangutans are nurtured and prepared to be returned to the wild. Many of the babies were orphaned when their mothers were either killed by poachers or died as a result of logging in the forests. Honey bears, gibbon monkeys, hornbills, and other birds also live in the semi-wild park.

You drive out to the Bako Islamic village and take a motorized longboat across a bay of the South China Sea to the Bako National Park. The park's habitats of lush tropical jungle, sandy beaches, rocky headlands, and mangrove swamps are home to proboscis monkeys, leaf-eating langurs, and long-tailed macaques. Magpie robins, tailor birds, pied trillers, and kingfishers are among the birds you will see. You stay overnight at the park's bungalows.

To reach the Iban people, you drive from Kuching to the Batang reservoir and take a motorized longboat ride up a river to their Nanga Sampa Longhouse. A longhouse is a horizontal apartment building. Some longhouses can house twenty-eight or more families. The size of a longhouse is expressed in "doors." Each door represents a family. A village population is often counted in the number of doors rather than the number of individuals.

The Nanga Sampa Longhouse is equipped for tourists with bunks, mosquito netting, running water, bath facilities, and a dining area. Longhouses in poorer villages are a series of single rooms, one per family, furnished with only mats and blankets.

The Nanga Sampa Longhouse serves as a base for exploring farther up the river into a jungle that equals the Amazon in density and flora and fauna diversity. The jungle itself is quite different from the Amazonian rain forest. In Borneo, 65 percent of the rain forest is a wide variety of modified palm trees disguised as vines, bushes, shrubs, and rattan, the cane used for weaving furniture. But like the Amazonian jungle, the topsoil is very thin and lacks the nutrients to support cultivated crops.

Some tours take you to the Lemanak Dayak village on the banks of the Lemanak River. The former headhunters welcome you to their Ser Ubak Longhouse with traditional dances and songs. You share dinner with them and stay overnight in the guest longhouse.

A flight from Kuching up the eastern coast takes you to Miri, an oil-and-timber boomtown near the Brunei border. Local trips go to the Niah National Park and the Lambir Hills National Park. In the Niah park a 3-mile-long gangway through primary jungle goes to the Great Niah Caves. The limestone caverns comprise one of the most important archaeological sites in the Far East. Upright bipedal hominids inhabited the caves about thirty-nine thousand years ago. Studies are still being done at the caves, and you can visit a dig site with special permission.

The trip to Bunung Mulu National Park and to villages farther in the jungle starts from Miri. An air-conditioned river taxi takes you up the Baram River to Marundi.

Marundi, the last major trading post on the edge of the vast rain forest, is a tidy little town and the administrative center for the area. Cars and motorcycles are plentiful, although the one road from town goes only 9 miles before it ends in the rain forest. The vehicles are brought upriver by boat. Shops along the four-block main street sell Coca-Cola, T-shirts with English slogans, plastic buckets, plastic shoes—the type of merchandise found in stores in any small rural town. The Chinese restaurants—the Chinese dominate the town's retail trade—serve the same chicken, fish, and pork dishes found in Chinese restaurants the world over. The people, even those coming from nearby jungle villages to buy goods, dress in Western-style clothing.

Not until you go much farther up river do you meet people who still live in the traditional manner.

A motorized longboat delivers you to Bunung Mulu National Park. Caves big enough to drive a tractor-trailer into are the main attraction. Wind Cave is the longest cave system in Southeast Asia. Deer Cave boasts the world's longest cave passage. In the evening, thousands of bats stream out of the caves on their nightly feeding forays.

Farther up river you come to a Penan village. Stan Sesser, in the *New Yorker* (May 27, 1991), describes the Penan as "the shiest, least aggressive, and most isolated of the Borneo peoples—the last of the hunt gatherers. They are one of the few tribes on earth that still depend for survival on what is to be found in the forest rather than on crops grown or animals raised. A gentle people, they are always quiet-spoken, they never punish their children…"

In his book *Stranger in the Forest* (Penguin Books, 1988), Eric Hansen, an American who walked across Borneo in 1982, asked two Penan what would be a serious crime in the Penan community. "They conversed for a minute, as though they were having difficulty thinking of any crime. Then Weng explained the concept of see-hun, which means to be stingy or not to share."

The shy, gentle, nonaggressive Penan actively sabotage logging operations that threaten their forest. And they have served jail time for their "crimes." Most of the Borneo rain forest, one of the largest, oldest, and richest in the world, could be gone in five to eleven years at the current rate of logging, reports Sesser. More than two-thirds of Sarawak's remaining forest is licensed for logging.

After spending the night in the Penan longhouse, you return by express boat to Marundi and fly to Kota Kinabalu, the capital of the other Malaysian Borneo state, Sabah.

From Kota Kinabalu you drive two and a half hours through a lush countryside of rubber plantations and rice paddies to the Kinabalu National Park. The summit of Mount Kinabalu (13,455 feet) is your goal. The park's habitat, ranging from tropical lowlands to subalpine zones, supports three species of deer, bearded pigs, gibbons, honey bears, orangutans, and moon rats. An estimated three hundred species of birds live in or visit the park, including the rare Kinabalu friendly warbler. The park is also home to the atlas moth, the world's largest moth, and the parasitic rafflesia, the world's largest flower.

You cross the Crocker Range (5,000 feet) and check into park cabins. Above the range rises Mount Kinabalu, the highest peak in Southeast Asia. The mountain looks like a huge tower of vegetation, and the summit is always hidden in clouds, except at dawn. The local Kadazan people call the mountain "akinabalu," which means "the revered place of the dead." They believe the mountain will be the final resting place of their spirits.

On the two-day hike up the mountain you pass through rain forest, montane cloud forest, and subalpine ecological zones. The first day's five- to seven-hour hike to Laban Rata Hut is a strenuous 5,400-foot altitude gain. The steep trail has a series of steps and handrails, but they make the climb no less taxing. You stay overnight at Laban Rata Hut.

Laban Rata is more like a small hotel than a mountain hut. Private rooms contain six bunk beds with sheets, blankets, and electric room heaters. The bathrooms are clean and the showers warm. Chinese and Western food is served in the dining room.

The final hike starts at 3 A.M. If you do not leave this early, you may not reach the summit before the clouds close in. You reach Low's Peak (13,455 feet) in three to four hours. The trail traverses granite slabs that are quite slick when wet. Cairns and fixed ropes lead you to the summit. The summit plateau can be cold, windy, and foggy. In stormy weather, the climb cannot be safely accomplished.

The descent to Laban Rata Hut takes two to three hours. From there you hike down 4,800 feet to the road and drive back to Kota Kinabalu.

In the Kalimantan part of Borneo you take a seven-day hike to Dayak villages in the interior. This trip starts in the bustling oil town of Balikpapan, East Kalimantan. You drive 125 miles inland to Samarinda, the provincial capital on the banks of the Mahakam River. A twin-otter plane flies you to a landing strip on the Kayan

River. From the landing strip, you follow a path along the river and cross a suspension bridge to Long Ampunq, a Dayak village. There you spend the night in the chief's house.

Long Ampunq is a traditional village. Ritual carved-and-painted masks hang on the walls of the longhouses. The masks are said to appease the ancestors and win their goodwill. The longhouses themselves are often intricately carved and painted. They are complexes built on stilts complete with sacred herb gardens and ancestral stone images.

The Dayak villagers wear traditional sarongs, colorful cloth hats, and ear plugs to elongate the earlobe. The women carry their babies in the typically elaborate Dayak carriers decorated with intricate bead designs, old coins, animal teeth, and claws. The carriers are the communal property of several families, all of whom have contributed to the decorations over generations.

The Dayak decorate everything—utilitarian objects, longhouses, their bodies. Beadwork, basket-making, and tattooing are practiced with consummate artistic skill. Doors, railings, and house posts are carved with dragon, snake, bird, and demon motifs.

You hike and travel by dugout canoes from Dayak village to Dayak village for the next seven days. The paths lead deep into the jungle paths and cross rivers on suspension bridges made of vines and logs. Porters carry your gear, although the day hikes are only two to three hours. You may stay in a village overnight or perhaps for a couple of days. Accommodations are guest longhouses, a villager's home, or a two-person tent.

The jungle is park-like rather than dense with vegetation. The tall, shallow-rooted trees create a fragile ecosystem. Secondary growth of thick tall grass and scrub quickly takes over the jungle floor when the primary trees are cut. New tree growth is unable to compete, and the once-magnificent rain forest is reduced to weeds and brush. Sabah's primary forests will be completely cut down by 1995, estimates the World Rainforest Movement. Only a small area of the forest cut by logging companies has been replanted. Many illegal loggers make no effort at all to replant.

At Lidung Payau, a village of Lepo Tau Dayak, you spend a couple of days participating in the village life. The children crowd around to see the strange visitors. The men take you on a two-hour hike to their favorite fishing spot, where you help them catch dinner. In the evening traditional dances are performed and Dayak beliefs and legends explained.

You return to Lidung Payau by foot and dugout, then take another river to Long Nawang, home of the Lepo Tau Kenyah. They are aristocrats thought to be direct descendants of the first people of Borneo. Long Nawany is the administrative center of the Apo Kayan district. You stay overnight at the schoolteacher's house and meet several of the *paran bui*, or noblemen.

The Dayak are descendants of Mongolian immigrants who arrived in the area around 5,000 B.C. Seven principle Dayak tribes live on Borneo, one of which is the Klementan, for which Kalimantan is named. In premissionary times headhunting and taking skulls was an integral part of their religion.

A half-hour walk from Long Nawang is Nawang Baru, a large village on the Nawang River. The Adat Lama Dayak villagers left Long Nawang in the 1950s to avoid the influence of Christian missionaries. You spend a day and night in the village seeing Dayak life in perhaps its purest form.

You hike and travel by dugouts back to Long Ampunq for a final dinner and a celebration with traditional dancing. In the morning, you cross the suspension bridge and walk back to the grass landing strip, where the small plane awaits to fly you back to Samarinda.

Tour operators:

Exodus Adventure
Explore Worldwide
Innerasia Expeditions
Mountain Travel/Sobek
    Expeditions

Nature Expeditions
    International
Turtle Tours
Wilderness Travel

INDIA

Ladakh and Zanskar

Transportation: hiking
Accommodations: hotels/tents
Land cost: $1,595-$2,395
Duration: 17 to 24 days
Seasons: June to mid-October

Ladakh, in the high desert of the western Himalayas, represents the largest living remnant of Tibetan civilization. Tibet is currently under strict Chinese control, but traditional Tibet lives on in Ladakh, also known as "Little Tibet," which is technically part of the Indian states of Jammu and Kashmir. The clothes, architecture, and religion—Tibetan Mahayana Buddhism—of the Ladakhis are very similar to those commonly found in Tibet before the Chinese invaded.

For centuries little has changed in remote regions of Ladakh, which was opened to the world in 1975. Most Ladakhis live in small, isolated villages as farmers, traders, and craftspeople. Everyone joins in communal tasks, often sharing material resources. Fields scratched out of the desert and irrigated by melting glacier water provide sufficient food for the population of 100,000. For centuries the people have used the few resources with maximum efficiency and without destroying the environment.

Tours to Ladakh focus on learning from the people and their culture. The Ladakhis are not a poor people. Poverty, starvation, homelessness, class exploitation, and economic injustice do not exist, for the most part, in the country. Ladakh offers an escape from the modern twentieth century.

However, the traditional society is disappearing. Young people are leaving the villages for the city. Religious monuments in this strongly traditional Buddhist society have fallen into disrepair. In recent years Muslim Kashmiri merchants and businesses have weakened many of the traditions. The traditional Tibetan social fabric is becoming endangered.

Getting to Ladakh is an adventure in itself. The rough, narrow road across the mountains from Kashmir is closed eight or nine months each year due to heavy snow or landslides. The other road, from Manali, in India, is passable only by four-wheel-drive vehicles. Air connections to Leh, the capital of Ladakh, are infrequent and erratic. You may endure delays, dust, and difficult conditions just reaching your trek's starting point.

Trekking in Ladakh, at an average altitude of 11,000 feet, is moderately strenuous. You cross a 17,500-foot pass, ford rivers on foot, and carry all your provisions with help from the small Ladakhi staff. Your effort is well-rewarded by the friendship and generosity of the people, sights of dramatic landscapes, and visits to monasteries. Outside the capital city of Leh accommodations are primitive.

Leh (11,500 feet), located in a side valley of the Indus River Valley, is the highest inhabited city on earth. The city used to be a trade hub for camel caravans heading to Lhassa and Samarkand. The city's bazaars are full of Tibetan jewelry, cloth, brassware, and spices attesting to its trading tradition.

The eighty-room Stok Palace, where the queen of Ladakh lives with her four children, is built on a small rock outcrop in Leh. The palace's museum contains some of the finest *thankha* paintings (symbolic Buddhist paintings) in the world. You may be able to visit a *thankha* painter in his studio. The once-splendid palace is now being restored in preparation for when the young regent takes over his duties as king. The most visible feature of the palace is the two-story, copper-and-gold statue of the sitting Buddha.

Hemis Gompa, the richest and most powerful monastery in Ladakh, and Tikse Monastery, the largest in Ladakh, are both perched on a hill overlooking Leh. These monasteries—cities within themselves, lavishly decorated with detailed artwork—are the repositories of rare books and seats of learning. In this function, they resemble the monasteries of medieval Europe.

Another notable monastery on the trekking route is Ridzong, where the scholarly traditions and rituals are strictly maintained. You spend two days camping at the monastery observing monastic life and contributing however appropriate, such as collecting firewood or helping with repairs. You may be allowed to see the three-dimensional wheel-of-life (a graphic representation of physical and spiritual progress through life) at the top of the monastery and visit the adjacent nunnery.

At the Likir Monastery, where 150 monks live, you watch the ceremonial construction of an elaborate sand mandala (a graphic symbol of the universe). Your campsite, in a meadow with views of high peaks in every direction, is adjacent to a stream warm enough to bathe in. Only after days of trekking in Ladakh do you realize the rarity and luxury of a warm stream in that land of cold waters.

The famous tenth-century Alchi Monastery, hidden off the road near the Indus River, contains some of the best Buddhist wall paintings in existence, and exquisitely painted statutes of Buddha.

Most of the tours include two treks, one to Markha Valley and the other to Zanskar Valley. The main trekking route to Markha Valley starts from the village of Stok. You walk across the high, barren valley and start up a scree slope to the Stok La Pass (14,500 feet). You reach the summit four hours later via a series of switchbacks. From the top you look across the Indus Valley to the Karakoram Mountains.

After the descent, you pass the tiny hamlet of Shingo and enter a narrow gorge with 1,000-foot-high walls. In contrast to the usual stark landscape, the gorge is filled with thick scrub—and is very hot. A gently flowing stream offers cool relief. Eventually you emerge at the confluence of the Markha and Zanskar rivers, where you pitch camp along the riverbank at the village of Skiu.

The coppersmiths of Skiu are known throughout Ladakh for their fine work. The village has two simple but beautiful temples.

On the easy walk up the valley you pass patches of brilliant greens and yellows: crops nursed from the parched high desert and irrigated by glacier melt water. The trail zigzags back and forth across the river and up across steeply banked scree. You pass an ancient ritual site of red-painted shrines and yak horns, dating perhaps back to the pre-Buddhist Bon period. Buddhism replaced Bon, an ancient animistic faith, in the beginning of the eighth century. The older religion lingers only in a few isolated regions of Ladakh, Nepal, and Tibet.

You wade the knee-deep Markha River to reach Markha itself, a cluster of fifteen houses above the river. The next day you start the climb out of the valley. On the horizon looms the 21,000-foot-high Kang Yase to which you are headed. The trail climbs steadily, and in places steeply, to Nyimaling (16,200 feet), a shepherds' summer camp. Here you rest for a day watching the women making cheese and yak butter while the children play. Men drive flocks of sheep, goats, and yaks to distant grazing pastures.

The next day you cross Gongmaru La Pass (17,500 feet), the highest point on the trek. You descend past a couple of villages perched on the steep slopes on the way back to Leh.

The Zanskar trek begins after a two-hour drive from Leh up the Suru Valley to Panniker in a region known as Little Baltistan. You hike over the 13,124-foot-high Parachik La Pass, descend into the Stod Valley and drive to Padum (Spadum), Zanskar's administrative center. Some Zanskar-only treks enter from Manali, India, after a ride over the Ratang La Pass (13,050 feet) to Darcha in Zanskar.

The trek down the Zanskar Valley passes through several small farming villages. When you camp near the houses the people often invite you to a drink of *chang*, homemade barley beer. On the trek, you climb several passes, including the 16,500-foot-high Shingkuna Pass, which has a marvelous view of the Himalayan Range. Several monasteries are on the route.

You visit the 530-year-old Karcha Monastery, the largest and richest in Zanskar. Located in the village of Karcha, the monastery is the home to over one hundred monks. You get a panoramic view of the valley and mountains from the roof of the monastery.

On the last day of the northbound trek you visit the famous 1,000-year-old Gompa (temple) of Wanla, built by Rinchen

Zangpro, who also built the Alchi Monastery in Ladakh. You cross two final passes on the way to Lamayuru, from which you make a five-hour drive to Leh.

Tour operators:

Exodus Adventure	Turtle Tours
Explore Worldwide	Wilderness Travel
High Adventure Travel	Wildland Adventures
Journeys International	

NEPAL

Transportation: trekking
Accommodations: hotels/guesthouses/tents
Land cost: $1,330-$2,750
Duration: 8 to 32 days
Seasons: April to May; September to November

Gods, goddesses, and mountains are inescapable when trekking Nepal. You meet the gods and goddesses first in Kathmandu, the capital of Nepal. The city is one of three former medieval city-states in the Kathmandu Valley.

The city is filled with temples. Kathmandu's name is derived from Kasthamandap, a temple built from a single tree, which you visit before starting your trek. You also pay respects at the Temple of the Living Goddess and at Swayambhunath ("Monkey Temple"), located on a small hill west of the city. And again at Pashupatinah, the most sacred of Hindu temples in Nepal, dedicated to Lord Shiva.

And you also should not miss the Royal Palace, Durbar Square, Freak Street, the bazaar, or Bkatapur, the valley's most medieval-styled city designed in the ninth century in the shape of the Hindu god Vishnu's conch shell. Also try to visit Bodhnath, a short distance away, the largest Buddhist stupa in Nepal and the center of Tibetan Buddhism with a thriving Tibetan refugee community surrounding it.

If you visit Nepal in September and October you can participate in Dasain, Nepal's largest national festival. It is a ten-day celebration of the Goddess Durga, the embodiment of supreme energy over evil. There is another festival Tihar (also called Laxmi Puja), which is celebrated on the evening of the new moon following Dasain. The party—with fireworks and shops and homes and temples brightly lit—is for Laxmi, the goddess of wealth, who, it is said, enters only those dwellings that are clean and well-lit.

Then comes the trekking. You can take an easy eight-day trek or a strenuous month-long trek east, west, north, or south. You can hike around Annapurna, or you can climb into the Annapurna Sanctuary, or up the valleys leading to Mount Everest. You can also hike the Langtang National Park (see COMFORTABLE WILDERNESS: Asia/India/Nepal)

On all the treks you hike through tropical zones of bamboo forests up to temperate zones of rhododendron and oak forest and up over 16,000-foot passes in the high alpine zone where no trees grow in the thin air. You stop in Brahmin, Chettri, Newar, Tamang, Sherpa, Tharu, Gurka, and Gurung villages where you drink tea and perhaps *rakshi*, a home brew white lightning. The friendly villagers may teach you local traditional dances or how to play Nepalese card games.

"*Namaste, namaste*," (NAH-mah-stay) everyone calls out, the traditional greeting derived from Sanskrit meaning, "I salute the spirit within you." They clasp their hands together in a prayer gesture and touch the fingertips to their forehead, bowing slightly. You return the salute.

Accommodations in the cities are hotels. On the trails you stay in tents or guesthouses. However, inns and guesthouses should be avoided whenever possible because your presence requires the burning of more wood to prepare food. Deforestation with its attendant ills is Nepal's greatest environmental problem. Responsible tour operators, aware of this, carry cooking kerosene.

A typical trekking day begins around six in the morning with a cup of hot tea served to you by a porter while you stay snug in your sleeping bag. Camp is struck after a hot breakfast. Porters carry the heavy foodstuffs and gear. You carry only a daypack for on-the-trail necessities. The porters are usually young men and women from the areas you trek through.

At midday you break for a two-hour lunch followed by a three-hour hike. Camp is set up in the late afternoon, allowing time for you to relax or visit a nearby village before dinner is served. The average daily trek is five to ten miles.

A *sirdar*, the major *domo* who oversees your well-being, has overall responsibility for not getting the group lost; for finding food, accommodations, and camping sites; and for supervising the Nepalese staff. The *sirdar* speaks English and local languages and often has friends along the trekking route who introduce you to a community.

Most trekking routes are well-traveled by local people and traders, since there are few roads in the Himalayas. The unmarked trails follow the contours of the land and the river valleys. Rivers are crossed on suspension or log bridges, but occasionally you must ford one on foot.

Trekking requires no special skills or mountaineering equipment, but you should be an experienced camper and in good physical condition.

Immediately north of Kathmandu are the Langtang and Jugal Himals (ranges), a popular trekking area in the central Himalayas about 15 miles from the Tibetan border. The narrow Langtang Valley is classical Nepal trekking country hemmed in by the main Himalayan chain and a subchain of snow-covered peaks. To the north, glaciers glisten on peaks reaching 23,000 feet. To the east, the Rolwaling Himal peaks, including Mount Everest (29,028 feet), stand out dazzling white against the blue sky. Lush foothills of terraced farmland roll behind you to the south toward India.

Langtang Valley, site of the national park bordered by the Langtang Khola (river), was discovered by a monk searching for his yak. "Lang" means yak and "tang" means to follow. One camping site is at the Buddhist monastery Kyangjhin Gompa (12,075 feet).

The treks start at lower elevations in forests of oak, birch, and pine hung with Spanish moss and orchids. In the middle hills, where rhododendrons grow 60 feet tall, you meet the Tamang and Helambu Sherpas people. The Helambu Sherpas are traders and farmers with very different dress, language, and lineage from the famous mountain-guide Sherpas of the Khumbu area.

You hike up to the holy lakes of Panch Pokhari, where many Nepalese make pilgrimages. Streams tumble down from the glaciers above you. The trail climbs along the Trisuli River to Ganja Pass (16,300 feet), where you experience the grandeur of the high Himalayas.

Some treks start from Gorkha, a bumpy, dusty, six-hour drive north from Kathmandu. From the road you see views of thirty Himalayan peaks over 21,000 feet, including the massif of Dhaulagiri in the west.

Gorkha is as fascinating as Kathmandu in its own right. The bazaar bustles with farmers, townspeople, and merchants bargaining for everything from sheep, spices, and brass, to blocks of salt and vegetables. The small city has the atmosphere of a fourteenth-century market town.

The trek starts from the King of Gorkha's old palace on a hill overlooking the bazaar. In the 1760s King Prithvi Narayan Shah united the regional feudal kingdoms into the state of Nepal. The present King of Nepal is the eleventh grandson of this unifying monarch. A temple within the palace, accessible only to the king, is one of the holiest sites in all of Nepal.

The trek is only moderately difficult with no steep ascents, but you are constantly walking either up or down. The Jugal Himal section is somewhat demanding, especially if you encounter snow. But anyone in good physical condition can make the trek.

The Annapurnas, six peaks surrounding Annapurna (26,545 feet) itself, provides another popular trekking route. Pokhara, 100 miles northwest of Kathmandu, is one starting point for the trek. Depending on the tour, you make a fifteen- to thirty-day loop to the north, either clockwise or counterclockwise, around the Annapurnas.

The village of Dumre, an eight-hour drive on a dirt road from Kathmandu, is another starting point for treks around the Annapurnas via Thorong La Pass (17,770 feet). You follow the Manang Valley, created by the Marsyandi River. The architecture and the people in the valley have a strong Tibetan flavor.

You hike through meadows and forest, cross rivers on swaying bridges, and meet caravans of ponies led by traders coming from Tibet. Bells worn by the ponies send playful fairyland music echoing through the valleys. Herds of blue mountain sheep clamber along the cliffs. You may also see a lammergeyer, a large vulture with a wingspan up to twelve feet.

You follow a steep yak trail along a rock ledge to a notch in the mountains at 15,350 feet, then continue to climb over an old glacial moraine another 2,000 feet to the summit of Thorong La Pass. On the ascent you see the Annapurna Range to the south, with Manasula Range and the Gorkha Himal in the background. The glaciers and unexplored peaks at the head of the Jargeng Khola (river) lie to the northwest. From the pass you see the desolate summits of the Mikut Himal, bordering the politically restricted Dolpo region. On the 5,000-foot descent to the town of Muktinath you have stunning views of Dhaulagiri (26,811 feet) and Tukuche Peak (22,703 feet) to the west.

Muktinath, mentioned in the Indian classic epic *Mahabharata*, is one of the most important pilgrimage sites for Nepali Hindus. Worshippers bathe in the holy water trickling from 108 carved spouts surrounding the Vishnu Temple in a grove of sacred poplars. The town is also holy to Buddhists. You can visit their temple in which fire burns in a stream of water.

The trek includes the Annapurna Sanctuary (11,900 feet), a glacier-covered amphitheater formed by a circle of the principal peaks of the western Annapurna Range—Annapurna South (23,814 feet), Fang (25,089 feet), Annapurna I (26,545 feet), Gangapurna (24,458 feet), Annapurna II (24,787 feet), and the spire of Machapuchare (22,958 feet).

Other treks into western Nepal that also start at Pokhara go to the Dhaulagiri Range, one of Nepal's most impressive. Summer monsoon rains encourage verdant forest growth on the mountains' southern slopes, but the isolated valleys to the north comprise one of the country's driest regions. You follow the Kali Gandaki River, which cuts between Annapurna and Dhaulagiri, forming one of the deepest gorges in the world.

The trail ascends through rock scree and snow to the top of French Pass (17,650 feet). It is not a difficult technical climb, but the rocks and snow can make it treacherous. You dip into Hidden Valley, a barren place where you camp, and then cross Thapa Pass (17,225 feet) for the final descent to the town of Jomosom.

The trek takes you through the habitats of the snow leopard (do not expect to see one), the Himalayan tahr (a large antelope), musk deer, large grey langur monkeys, and steppe eagles.

Another western trek goes to the Rara Lake National Park, a relatively unexplored region. The trip leaves from the city of Jumal and climbs through meadows and forests of spruce, birch, and rhododendron to Danphe Lagna (10,266 feet). You spend a day walking through river valleys and climbing steep switchbacks over ridges to gain the high valley, where you camp near the tiny village of Chautha.

The wooded valley narrows before flaring out into an immense treeless meadow of fields leading to Bhulbule, the park's entrance station. You follow a trade route to Churchi Lagna Pass (11,316 feet) and through the Mandu Khola valley. The dress and the customs of the people in this remote region are strongly influenced by nearby Tibet.

It takes another day of hiking to reach the Rara Lake (10,000 feet). With a diameter of 8 miles, the lake is Nepal's largest. The homes of a few park wardens and the ruins of the deserted Rara and Chapra villages are the only signs of humans. But there are plenty of birds, flowers, and wildlife. Himalayan tahr, serow (a long-haired goat), goral, musk deer, red pandas, Himalayan bears, and rhesus and langur monkeys live there. The 550-foot-deep lake, with fish and otters, is an important resting place for migrating birds.

On the four-day trek back to Jumal you stay at the Brahmin and Chettri village of Sinja on the banks of the Sinja Khola.

In eastern Nepal, the trekking routes tend to follow the Arun River Valley toward Mount Everest and Makalu, or up the Tamur River farther to the east to the Kangchenjunga base camp.

The Arun River valley has, generally, wetter climate and steeper terrain than other areas of Nepal.

Brahmin, Chettri, Rai, Limbu, Tamang, Magar, and Gurung peoples live in the valley, so you get a wide sampling of cultural variations and of local food.

Unlike other parts of Nepal, this region has few local people who speak English, and the villages have no facilities that cater to trekkers. You meet few travelers and encounter fewer villages on the higher trekking routes, enhancing the sense of a wilderness adventure.

The footpath along the valley floor is a major trade route designated to be converted to a road. A dam on the upper Arun to produce electricity is also on the drawing board. If the hydroelectric project is built, some of the most extraordinary stretches of the trail will be wiped out. Such progress jeopardizes the character of the valley; but the local people want the convenience of electricity and the lifestyle improvements it will introduce.

The best winter trekking is in eastern Nepal. Interesting places can be reached without climbing high passes. When you get above the 10,000-foot cloud level, you see only snowcapped peaks floating on a sea of fluffy white clouds. Be prepared for snow from December to February above 10,000 feet, even though the treks start in subtropical regions warm enough for swimming in the Sabhaya Khola.

The eighteen-day trek toward Mount Everest and Makalu begins at Tumlingtar, which you reach by plane from Kathmandu. Makalu is 27,790 feet in elevation, only 1,237 feet lower than Everest. The Arun River bisects the town in the warm Sabhaya Khola Valley. On the way to the big peaks you stay in Chainpur, which many people consider the most attractive hill bazaar town in Nepal. You get the first great views of Everest, Makalu, Kangchenjunga, and Chamlong peaks five days into the trek.

The route to Makalu passes through the upper portions of the Arun Valley. This area is sparsely settled by the Bhotia people, who practice Bon, the ancient animistic faith of Tibet. Snow may be encountered in the high passes. You cross the Barun Valley, which is designated to become part of a large international protected area to preserve the Mount Everest ecological zone (see NOT ORDINARY TRIPS: Asia/Nepal). Barren slopes replace conifer forests and meadows as you near Makalu's base. Weather conditions at the 16,000-foot base camp are subarctic. A short distance up the southeast ridge of Makalu you get superb views of Mount Everest, Lhotse, and the Makalu summits.

The trek to Makalu base camp is not to be casually undertaken. Whenever you reach altitudes above 15,000 feet the conditions become demanding. Snow, fog, and hard storms can blow in unexpectedly. The thin air can induce altitude sickness. It is always cold. Experience in wilderness camping and physical fitness are prerequisites for the trek. The trail, although not particularly difficult and requiring no mountaineering skills, does ascend and descend steeply–and there are no handrails.

The other popular trek in eastern Nepal goes to Kangchenjunga (28,156 feet), the world's third highest peak. The mountain marks Nepal's eastern border with the Indian territory of Sikkim. Darjeeling, the hill country famous for its tea, lies only 46 miles south. The white crown of Kangchenjunga rising above the rolling green foothills is one of the Himalaya's most impressive sights. "Kangchenjunga" in Tibetan means "Five Great Treasures of the Snow."

The trail to Kangchenjunga leads through beautiful and largely unspoiled countryside. In the lowland foothills you pass terraced fields and villages. The trail climbs in the middle hills through forests and meadows before reaching the Kangchenjunga Glacier. You pitch a base camp in barren but beautiful canyons. From the base camp you explore the area and local Tibetan communities with old Buddhist temples.

Tour operators:

Above the Clouds Trekking
Exodus Adventure
Explore Worldwide
High Adventure Travel
Himalayan Travel
Ibex Expeditions
Innerasia Expeditions
Journeys International
Mountain Travel/Sobek
   Expeditions
Nature Expeditions
   International
Third Eye Travel
Wilderness Journeys
Wilderness Travel
Wildland Adventures
WomanTrek
Woodswomen Adventure
   Travel
World Expeditions

PAPUA NEW GUINEA

Transportation: riverboat/dugout canoe/hiking
Accommodations: lodges/village guesthouses
Land cost: $2,600-$4,000
Duration: 11 to 18 days
Seasons: year-round

In Papua New Guinea the native people are as colorful as the tropical birds. They paint their faces and bodies with elaborate designs in yellow, red, white, and ochre. Their headpieces and wigs are large, flamboyant affairs of feathers, shells, flowers, and jungle plants. They wear necklaces, bracelets, earrings, nose hoops, arm bands, and headbands of silver, brass, beads, bone, shells, and gold. Thorns resembling tiny rhino horns are often embedded in the end of their nose.

Tours into the interior of Papua New Guinea take you to the villages of the Arambak, Chimbu, Asaro (mud men), Huli (wig men), Megabo, Wahgi, and Iatmul clans. The routes are nearly identical: up the Sepik, Tagari, and Karawari rivers and into the highlands.

The tours begins in Port Moresby, the country's capital. Within a day you are cruising down a river and trekking the highlands.

Every tour goes on the Sepik River in the Western Highlands. The Sepik rises in the Victor Emanuel Range, crosses into Irian Jaya (which shares the island with Papua New Guinea), twists back in great loops, and flows east into the Bismarck Sea. The river is a mile wide when it enters the sea.

The river trip often starts at the village of Timbunke after a drive across the small Sepik River plain. The four- to five-hour drive in a van or an open-back covered truck over the rough road is dusty in the dry season; in the wet season, floods often close the road.

The Sepik Basin is divided into tribal areas, each having its own distinctive art forms, cultural traditions, and dress. Many of the tribes do not even speak the same language. Approximately 738 vernaculars are spoken in Papua New Guinea—over one-third of the world's total languages. Pidgin English is the most commonly shared means of verbal communication.

The people are of Melanesian stock, although their exact origin is unknown. They have lived on the island for at least thirty thousand years in small tribal communities, each clan developing its own lifestyle in isolation.

On the two- to three-day river trip you stop at various villages, especially those of the Iatmul clan, the most prolific and diversified carvers of the Sepik. The ceremonial house of each village is decorated with huge gable masks and intricate carvings rivaling the stonework of European medieval cathedrals. Accommodations are special guesthouses that do not differ much from the villagers' dwellings. You sleep on mats in a communal room beneath mosquito netting strung between the support poles.

In many of the clans the men and women do not regularly share sleeping quarters. Within the societies duties and roles are strictly divided between the sexes. The men are warriors, hunters, and keepers of the ritual traditions and spiritual ceremonies. Only men are allowed in the *haus tamaran*, the ceremonial houses where rituals connected to warfare, magic, and sorcery are conducted.

These imposing "spirit houses" are often sixty feet high. In the downstairs, men sit, smoke, carve, and discuss village matters.

Only initiated men, those who have endured the skin-cutting ceremony, are allowed upstairs, where sacred totems, flutes, and clan masks are stored. In some clans women also undergo the painful skin-cutting ceremony as an initiation into the adult world. During the skin-cutting ceremony, shallow cuts of varying lengths are made in patterns on the body. Next, ash is placed in the cuts, or the skin around the cuts is pinched, so that the wounds heal in raised ridges.

There are no hereditary chiefs or other formal leadership positions in the clans, although only men make decisions affecting the community. Men rise to positions of power and influence because of their skills, leadership ability, personal wealth, and generosity in gift-giving. Through gift-giving they build a network of people beholden to them.

The women have no opportunities to obtain positions of power or influence. They raise and collect the food. The children are their responsibility. The men often live permanently in men's longhouses, while women live in single houses with their children.

Vessels for the river trips are either motorized dugout canoes, "river trucks" (covered, flat-bottom aluminum boats), or the riverboat *Sepik Spirit*. Used by many tour operators, *Sepik Spirit* is a 98-foot, steel-hulled ship with an air-conditioned dining room, a bar, an observation deck, and twin-bed cabins with private facilities. The boat draws only three feet, allowing it to enter shallow waterways.

At the junction of the Sepik and Karawari rivers you turn up the Karawari. The dense jungle lining the river is occasionally broken by a small cluster of huts. Sago, betel nut, breadfruit trees, banana trees, palms, and other jungle plants compete for space and sunlight in this hilly, riverine country.

Approximately 70 percent of Papua New Guinea is covered by primary rain forest. Well over half of the world's plant families are found on the island. In two acres of Sepik Basin rain forest an average of one hundred and fifty different species of trees may be found.

Your destination is the Karawari Lodge on a ridge overlooking the Sepik Basin. The lodge sits on six well-maintained acres with a swimming pool. Sepik blue orchids and other plants found in the nearby jungle grow in the gardens. The thatched main building, designed in the style of the local *haus tamaran*, is made of local material. It houses the dining room, bar, library/lounge, and a museum, featuring a fine collection of local carvings and crafts. A long verandah overlooks the Karawari River and the jungles of the Sepik Basin. The rooms, in separate buildings similar to village dwellings, have twin beds, private baths, ceiling fans, mosquito nets, and a verandah.

Trails from the lodge lead to the surrounding primary forest. Eclectus parrots, sulphur-crested cockatoos, and gloriously colored birds of paradise are among the birds seen in the forest. Thirty-six of the thirty-eight species of birds of paradise are indigenous to Papua New Guinea, which has approximately 720 species of birds.

You may also see a Goodfellow's tree kangaroo, a flying fox, or a long-beaked echidna. Papua New Guinea and Australia, once linked by a land bridge, are the only countries with representatives of all three kinds of mammals: the primitive egg-laying monotremes, the marsupials, and the placental mammals. Papua New Guinea also has 2 species of crocodiles, 110 species of snakes, 170 species of lizards, and numerous species of turtles and tortoises.

From Karawari you take a domestic flight to Mount Hagen in the Central Highlands, home of the Wahgi clan. The clan was first seen by outsiders in 1933. You drive through the Wahgi Valley, an idyllic setting of tea and coffee plantations and tidy villages surrounded by peaks reaching 14,924 feet.

The Wahgi people often dress in their traditional tribal costume, especially at a "sing-sing." A "sing-sing" celebrates an event, such as an exchange of gifts, a marriage, or any other reason to have a party.

You visit an Asaro village where "mud men," so called because they cover themselves in mud for decoration, perform a dance and play traditional flutes. Later you visit a Mindima village where villagers dressed in traditional attire mime and dance reenactments of "recent" tribal battles. They perform ceremonies invoking the spirits to make their crops bountiful and to ensure that their pigs have many offspring.

From Mount Hagen you fly by domestic airlines to Tari in the south.

In the Southern Highlands you trek for three days in the Tari Basin. The hikes average four to six hours a day along well-used footpaths and jeep tracks. You pass through the intensively cultivated valley and cross streams on logs or suspension bridges. The trail goes through forests of bamboo and fruit trees where rare orchids grow. You dip in and out of valleys with views of the surrounding mountains. On the last day the hike becomes more strenuous as you cross a mountain range on steep and muddy trails.

The hike goes through the territory of the Huli people, often called the "wig men." The young Huli men grow their hair long and then cut it and weave it into a bamboo frame to make a wig hat to be used as part of their initiation rite. The "wigs" are decorated with bird feathers and beaks, pig tusks, cus cus (possum) skin, and blooms of flowers cultivated especially for this purpose. Wild pig tusks and large, crescent-shaped kina shells are worn as necklaces.

The Huli clan is one of the largest ethnic groups in the Southern Highlands. They have kept their culture the most intact of all the Papua New Guinea tribes. The Huli are proud people whose traditions and ways of life are still governed by their belief in ancestral spirits and sorcery.

The Huli were once much feared by the other highland tribes. Now, for the most part, they are at peace with their neighbors. On the hike you see huge interconnecting trenches, up to fifteen feet deep, dug by hand with wooden paddle-like shovels. The trenches were used as secret passageways for warriors during clan fights. Now they delineate clan boundaries and control the movement of pigs.

The Huli are subsistence farmers who grow sweet potatoes, taro, and sugar cane in scattered garden hamlets.

Porters carry your gear on the hikes. At night you stay in village guesthouses, sleeping on woven bamboo platforms. You cook on open fires and wash in the streams. In the Central Highlands you stay at the Ambua Lodge when not on the trail. The lodge features a restaurant and modern cabins with private bathrooms and electric blankets. Evening are pleasantly cool at the lodge 7,000 feet up the side of a mountain. Terrific views of the Tari Valley and the surrounding mountain peaks reaching 9,500 feet can be seen from your cabin window. The Tari Gap is an easy day hike from the lodge.

Tour operators:

International Expeditions
Journeys International
Mountain Travel/Sobek
   Expeditions
Nature Expeditions
   International

Safaricentre
Wilderness Travel
WomanTrek

RUSSIA

The Kamchatka Peninsula

Transportation: hiking/raft/helicopter
Accommodations: hotels/tent
Land cost: $4,190-$4,366
Duration: 12 to 13 days
Seasons: August to September

The Kamchatka Peninsula has been open to tourists only since 1990. Not many visitors have seen its volcanoes, geysers, cauldrons of boiling mud, forests, and wild rivers.

The size of California, Kamchatka has 127 volcanoes—of which 29 are active—and calderas. This is more than any place in the Pacific Ring of Fire except Java. On this trip you hike among the geysers and hot springs of the Valley of Geysers, part of the Kronotsky Nature Preserve, and raft the wild Zhupanova River. The Valley of Geysers was not discovered until 1941.

The trip starts from Petropavlovsk, the peninsula's only major town. The small city is named for two of Vitus Bering's ships, the *Peter* and the *Paul,* which he used when discovering the Bering Strait and Alaska. In 1741, Bering set sail from Petropavlovsk for his second voyage to discover if Russia and America were joined or separated by water. He reached Alaska, confirming that the strait separates the two land masses.

Your accommodations are 18 miles outside Petropavlovsk at Yelizovo, an old spa with a sauna and swimming pool. The sauna is useful, since the average temperature on the peninsula is in the low 50s even in the summer.

The peninsula has few roads and no facilities set up for tourists.

From Yelizovo you fly by helicopter north to the Valley of Geysers, or travel by cross-country vehicle to the Kronotsky Nature Preserve. The helicopters are Russian military surplus, very dependable and noisy. However, if overcast or rainy weather sets in, as is often the case, the pilots do not fly. You may be stuck for a day or two.

The Kronotsky Nature Preserve was founded in the last century to protect sable and its habitat. The preserve is now part of the United Nation's worldwide network of biospheres. To help preserve the nature of the pristine wilderness only 100 permits for foreign visitors to Kronotsky are issued each year.

On the REI Adventures tour, you spend an afternoon exploring Kronotsky's multi-tiers of geysers along the slopes of a small valley dotted with cauldrons of boiling mud, hot pools blue with algae, and steam vents. A helicopter takes you to the preserve's boundary for a three-day hike to the Zhupanova River. You carry all the camping gear, but the rafting equipment is delivered to the river by helicopter.

The hike away from the preserve passes through dense forest and across highlands. You hike an average of seven miles a day. The terrain is not difficult but certainly interesting. You walk across nearly barren plateaus studded with small lakes. The alpine tundra is carpeted with wildflowers and blueberries, where bears like to feed. The first night's camp is on the rim of the Uzon caldera.

The trail down to the upper reaches of the Lugovaya River descends through birch forests with cedar brush. You camp along the river, then hike to the convergence of the larger Zhupanova River, where the rafts wait.

The three-day raft trip is relatively calm with only one set of small rapids. You have plenty of leisure time to enjoy the wilderness and watch out for Pacific and White-tailed eagles, endangered species common along the river. You may sight caribou or a brown bear on the river's banks.

At the conflux of the Zhupanova and Gavanki rivers, you pull in at the Cedar Lodge for a long soak in the *banya*, a steam bath. The helicopter ferries you back to Yelizovo.

The vehicle trip, by Innerasia Expeditions, goes 50 miles southwest from Petropavlovsk to the 7,619-foot Mutnovsky Volcano, where you set up a base camp. You make day trips to the active Gorely Volcano, the Zhirovsky Hot Springs, and to the seashore. You may go up to the Valley of Geysers, but there are plenty of geysers and thermal activity where you are.

A helicopter takes you to another base camp on the Plotnikov River, west of the volcanoes. For two days you take day hikes through glades of rhododendron, rock birch, alder, and pine. The hiking is very pleasurable through the park-like setting. You return by helicopter to Petropavlovsk.

The tour operators emphasize the need for a tolerant attitude, patience, and a good sense of humor for this trip—qualities more important than good physical condition. There is little tourist infrastructure in the Russian Far East. You can expect problems with plumbing, mediocre meals, indifferent service, and difficult schedules.

Tour operators:

Innerasia Expeditions   REI Adventures

THAILAND

Transportation: motor vehicle/hiking/elephant/bamboo rafts
Accommodations: hotels/lodges/village guest houses
Land cost: $2,230-$2,450
Duration: 14 to 16 days
Seasons: November to December; February to March

On tours to northern Thailand you hike between villages of the various tribes, Hmong, Yao, Akha, Meo, Karen, Lisu, and Lahu; walk through the Phu Kradung National Park; take an elephant excursion along the Nan River; and raft down the Mae Taeng River gorges through dense jungle. In southern Thailand, you spend time on the islands and beaches of Phuket Bay.

Visiting the hill tribes of the "Golden Triangle" where Thailand, Burma, and Laos meet—an area notorious for its opium trade—is the most fascinating part of the tours.

The hill tribes are slash-and-burn farmers, opium poppy growers, hunters, and craftspeople. They live without electricity or running water. They have not adapted the wheel to grind rice, preferring to use the traditional pounder. They trade in the lowland city of Chiang Mai, know about the wide world, send their children to school, including to university, and have fought long, hard armed battles, often without success, to keep their territories. Many of the people are refugees from Laos, China, and Burma.

Chiang Mai is Thailand's second largest city, a bustling university town and commercial center of 150,000. Here you stay at a complex of five traditional teak houses in a small village a half-mile from town. A couple of days are spent seeing the city sights, such as the ancient temples. Some of them are eight hundred years old, most notably Wat Chiang Meng and Wat Doi Suthep. You get your first sight of the hill people at the night bazaar, where they come to trade their crafts. This bazaar is unrivaled in Thailand, and perhaps Asia, for the ethnic crafts, textiles, Asian antiques, and unique collector items for sale.

To reach the hill villages you drive north from Chiang Mai on an asphalt road that becomes gravel, then dirt, then a rough, narrow track as it climbs into the mountain jungle. The track ends near the village where you start a three-day trek visiting the hill tribes in their homes.

You walk two to four hours each day, carrying only a light daypack. Sleeping bags, food, and heavier gear are ferried for you. You sleep in guesthouses in the villages. The tour's cook prepares your meals, a blend of Western and Thai tastes. An interpreter who speaks the local languages, and may be from one of the tribes, guides you along the jungle paths from village to village.

The Hmong village of Cheng Meng is typical of the ones you visit. The village sits on the lee side of a hill for protection from monsoon storms and overlooks neat squares of rice and vegetable fields. The thatched houses of bamboo or hardwood face downhill in a horseshoe pattern. No two houses are aligned. Good spirits enter a house in a straight line and nothing must obstruct their path. A single well serves the community of three hundred. The headman, dressed in a shirt and slacks but without shoes, welcomes you. The men and boys dress in Western style, but the women and young girls retain tribal dress, which varies from tribe to tribe. The Meo wear black turbans and silver jewelry; the Akhas dress in bright colors; the Yao decorate their clothes with fine embroidery.

The headman and interpreter exchange smiles, bows, and handshakes. The prolonged and profuse greeting includes compliments on the village, inquiries about the headsman's children and wife, and the family lineage of the interpreter.

The complex etiquette ritual can take a good twenty minutes. Knowing a person's genealogy is important to Hmong men, who must marry a woman from another clan or sub-clan. It would not do to have a village maiden fall for the interpreter, or vice versa, if their clans were not compatible.

The hill tribes believe every living thing has a spirit, on whose good side they take great care to stay. The people do not intend to conquer nature but rather to balance their needs and wants with the resources. Otherwise, their rice might be taken away.

In actuality, the tribes are not particularly environmentally conscious. They farm land until the soil is depleted and then move on. Irreparable destruction has been avoided so far because there has been plenty of land to absorb the growing tribal population. Nearly 500,000 people live in the hill region.

But trouble is brewing. A growing birth rate and immigration from Laos and Burma in recent years has dramatically increased the hill tribes' populations. Competition for land on which to grow crops is heating up, sometimes resulting in conflicts between tribes or villages. Marginal land has been cleared and the critical fallow period essential for a field's recovery drastically shortened to meet the growing demand for food.

Thai farmers, also facing significant land shortages, are pushing into the hills. Logging companies clear-cut acres of valuable teak and mahogany, trees the tribes use to build houses. The threat to the hardwood forests became so great the Thai government declared a logging ban. But outlaw loggers and the hill people continue to cut down trees.

After leaving the hill tribes you rest in a mountain resort. Some tours go to Phu Kradung or Khao Yai national parks in the northeast. Asiatic black bears, gibbons, tigers, serow, tapirs, giant hornbills, and seldom-seen wild elephants live in the forest. For more information, see NOT ORDINARY TRIPS: Asia/Thailand.

You can also take a trip down the Mekong River (known as the Nam Khong in Thailand) with Turtle Tours. The trip starts with a drive from Chiang Mai to Thaton on the banks of the Kok River at the Burmese border. A pirogue, the local version of a dugout canoe with an outboard motor, takes you 12 miles through mild rapids beneath steep jungle hillsides. You stay overnight at Chiang Rai, a market town for the hill tribes. In the morning you take a minibus drive on a dirt road to the mountain town of Chiang Sang, where a larger pirogue takes you down the Mekong itself.

For ten days you journey down the Mekong, stopping in the Laotian capital Vientiane. The final stop is Bangkok.

Most tours also fly down to Phuket, the fabled resort town in southern Thailand. Most tours leave Phuket quickly, because it is a modern Western-style resort area with beautiful beaches where tourists are seen as easy marks.

You go to more peaceful regions of Phuket Bay, such as Koh Phi Phi, or the Koh Hang islands, or snorkeling among the islands in Krabi Bay. On one of the islands you climb down to a small lake surrounded by 1,000-foot, jungle-covered cliffs. You can take an inland excursion to the Phanom Bencha National Park and visit a forest temple in a valley surrounded by 2,000-foot limestone mountains.

On a rain forest safari offered by Boulder Adventures, you stay in bungalows built 50 feet up in the forest canopy where gibbons, monkeys, and hornbills and other birds live.

Thailand's rain forest has existed in its present state, more or less, for 70 to 100 million years. But the forest habitat for Thailand's wildlife is fast disappearing: 45 percent of the country's forest was lost between 1961 and 1985. Sixty percent of the remaining rain forest will disappear by the year 2000, estimates the Rainforest Action Network. When the forest disappears, so will the hill tribes and much of the wildlife.

Tour operators:

Above the Clouds Trekking
Adventure Tours of Asia
Boulder Adventures
Exodus Adventur
Explore Worldwide
High Adventure Travel
Ibex Expeditions
Lost World Adventure

Mountain Travel/Sobek
   Expeditions
REI Adventures
Sierra Club Outings
Turtle Tours
Wilderness Travel
World Expeditions

Central America

BELIZE

Transportation: kayak/horseback/inner tube
Accommodations: hotel/ranch/tents
Land cost: $1,865-$3,195
Duration: 9 to 26 days
Seasons: year-round

Belize is a working vacation: some physical effort is required to make your vacation work. Sea kayaking 100 miles along the barrier reef from Belize City to the Guatemala border, a jungle excursion on horseback, tubing down a jungle river, visiting a jaguar reserve, exploring Mayan ceremonial caves—these things all require work.

Belize's barrier reef is the most extensive coral reef system in the Western Hemisphere. It is a friendly playground of technicolored fish and coral. The calm sea passage between the reef and the shore is ideal for kayaking; although infrequent squalls can liven up your day. You paddle for half of the day, traveling seven to fifteen miles. In the afternoon you set up camp on a small island (or cay) and then go snorkeling. Meals are prepared by the tour's staff. Daytime temperatures range between 73 and 86 degrees, going up into the 90s during March and April.

The object of the tour is to have fun while discovering the reef, mangrove swamps, and jungles. The undersea world of the living reef is home to angelfish, parrot fish, spotted eagle rays, and other marine creatures. The biologically rich mangroves expand your appreciation for "swamp life."

You spend eight days paddling down the length of the Sapodilla Cays. Located some distance out in the Gulf of Honduras, the cays are out of sight of the mainland. The trip is leisurely. Sometimes it takes an entire day to get from one cay to another. The two-person expedition-quality kayaks are stable and easy to handle. They are rigged with sailing equipment so you can catch the trade winds. No prior kayaking or sailing experience is necessary.

At the end of the Sapodilla segment a motor launch takes you to cays located closer to the coast. You continue paddling south to Punta Gorda, Belize's southernmost town. From there you head inland to the jungle mountains.

Your guide into the mountains may be a local Mayan, as on the Ecosummer trips. You spend two nights with him and his family at their modest farm. He shows you the local wildlife, especially the birds, and tells about the reality of living in the jungle.

Then it is back in the kayaks for a trip down Monkey River to the coast. For two days you are immersed in a lush tropical world where parrots, toucans, black howler monkeys, and other jungle animals live. You camp along the riverbank completely isolated from the outside world.

The river emerges at Monkey River Town, a fishing village. From there you paddle along the mangrove coast to Placencia. A van takes you inland along the Hummingbird Highway to the Mayan Mountains, where you set up camp along a river. The area is honeycombed with caves, many used by ancient Mayans as spiritual, ceremonial, and burial centers. Special permits are needed to visit some of the protected and remote underground caverns. In many caves you find stalactites, stalagmites, cave pearls (round limestone stones), and Mayan petroglyphs.

You are then back on the water; this time in an inner tube for an extraordinary trip. You float down the small River of Caves through limestone caves.

When you reach Mountain Pine Ridge you trade your inner tube in for a horse and spend a day exploring the jungle and pine forest. You visit one of the few truly traditional Mennonite villages. Mennonites are masters of low technology, as exemplified by their horse-powered saw mill.

Visits to the Mayan site of Xunantinich, whose main temple is Belize's highest structure, and to Tikal in northern Guatemala, are part of the tours.

For more details on Belize, see COMFORTABLE WILDER-NESS: Central America/Belize.

Tour operators:

Ecosummer Expeditions   Sierra Club Outings

COSTA RICA

Transportation: hiking/raft/kayak/horseback
Accommodations: lodges/tents
Land cost: $1,325-$2,445
Duration: 10 to 15 days
Seasons: year-round

On camping safaris in Costa Rica you hike dry tropical forest and lush tropical jungles, kayak the shores of a national park, walk up the slopes of an actively exploding volcano, and explore the rain forest of an Indian reservation.

In Palo Verde National Park in the northwest province of Guanacaste, you hike through fourteen different habitats. You explore marshes, grasslands, and forest on foot, by boat, and on horseback. Herons, wood storks, ducks, and numerous forest birds are frequently seen, as are white-faced and howler monkeys, deer, and coati, which resemble a raccoon but with a longer body and a long, flexible snout.

The campground in the park has clean water, tables, outhouses, and shady trees. The tour's staff sets up the walk-in tents and prepares the meals.

On the Wildland Adventures tour you hike and camp by special permission in the private Los Tigres premontane forest reserve. The dense, lush rain forest in a saddle between the Tenoiro and Miravalles volcanoes is surrounded by open forest canopy. Sloths, several species of monkeys, agouti, iguana, colorful tanagers, toucans, parrots, and multitudes of tropical birds live in this mixed forest habitat.

Walking the rolling hills is easy, but the rain forest is thick with heat and humidity. Fortunately, a stream with a small waterfall suitable for bathing runs near your camp.

A couple of hours' drive south takes you to Lake Arenal, not far from the active Arenal Volcano. On a hike in the forest along the lakeshore you find anteaters, jaguarundi, howler monkeys, toucans, and hawks. You stay overnight at the Arenal Observatory bunkhouse on a hilltop facing the volcano. You have a great view of the volcano spewing red-hot rocks and smoke into the air every few hours. The volcano last really erupted in 1968, sending rivers of lava down its sides. On an all-day hike to a waterfall and natural hot springs near the base of the volcano, you see the effects of the 1968 eruption.

Tours in the northwest also go to the dormant Rincon de la Vieja volcano, near the city of Liberia. You stay at a hacienda and go by horse to "Las Pailas," an area of abundant wildlife, hot springs, small geysers, and mud pots. You hike to the top of the volcano or to the Azufrales pools to bathe in thermal mineral waters. Posh spas charge big bucks for a dip in the healthy waters.

On Ecosummer Expeditions' trips you explore by sea kayak the coast of Guanacaste's northernmost peninsula, which is tucked in just under Nicaragua. The six-day trip takes you past the steep 2,300-foot-high peridotite cliffs that mark the boundary of Santa Rosa National Park. The rare, dark, heavy peridotite is the oldest rock in Costa Rica. You camp at Nance Beach, where mass nestings of Olive Ridley sea turtles occur during September and October.

You meet no other people on this remote coastline. The only light you see is from your campfire. The only sounds you hear, besides your own, come from the surf and the wild animals at your back. The trip ends at the fishing village of Cuajiniquil in the Gulfo de Santa Elena, where a vehicle takes you to the Arenal Volcano.

Tours continue to the Caribbean watershed region, reached by a van ride over the central mountains. You take a one-day raft trip down the Pacuara River coursing down the eastern slopes of the mountains. The river has some big rapids that can be thrilling but are not dangerous. Densely packed rain forest grows in every direction, waterfalls splash into cool swimming holes, and tropical birds add an exotic soundtrack.

After the river trip, you drive down the Caribbean coast south of the city of Limon to the Talamanca region. English-speaking people of Jamaican descent live along the coast. Great music, piquant food, and outgoing people make the towns festive. Several native groups, the Bri-bri Indians being the most notable, live in the rugged interior mountain range.

You stop at Cahuila National Park on the way to Puerto Viejo, just north of the Panamanian border. Here you snorkel the coral reef, or take a day hike to the Bri-bri reservation or a night hike into the rain forest. Maurico Salazar, a local Bri-bri Indian, guides you on a difficult—and muddy—five- to six-hour hike through the cocoa plantations and primary rain forest of the Cocles Indian Reserve.

On the Pacific coast, you start a two-day sea kayak trip from Isla Damas near Manuel Antonio National Park. Sea kayaks are the perfect way to slip into the mangrove tidal zones and observe the wildlife, particularly birds. You spend the night at a bed and breakfast in the small town of Manuel Antonio and hike the nearby park with a naturalist guide.

From Manuel Antonio, you follow a gravel road farther south to the Osa Peninsula, which dips nearly down to Panama. You then take a boat 15 miles down the Sierpe River to a jungle lodge, where you stay for three nights. Here you explore the estuaries, rain forest, beaches, and jungle bays.

You hike the peninsula's Corcovado Park, internationally recognized as a vital research area for the study of tropical rain forest ecology. Costa Rica's largest population of scarlet macaws, jaguar, tapir, crocodiles, ocelots, and jungle birds live within the park. A naturalist guide accompanying the tour explains the interrelationships of the various ecosystems of the park.

You also visit two island reserves off the Osa coast, Isla Violin and Isla del Cano. The islands, covered with evergreens and surrounded by white sand beaches, are archaeologically important for their pre-Columbian artifacts.

Other stops on the tours include Rara Avis Reserve and Monteverde Cloud Forest Reserve. For more details on Costa Rica see COMFORTABLE WILDERNESS: Central America/ Costa Rica.

Costa Rica has an enviable environmental record. National parks, wildlife refuges, and biological reserves occupy 12 percent of the land in this country, which is less than half the size of Ohio. Yet, the environment is still threatened by agricultural expansion, a growing population, and the need for inexpensive sources of fuel. The government is under pressure to offset the growing national debt by selling the country's natural resources.

The forests have been the hardest hit. Approximately 50 percent of Costa Rica's forests have been lost in the past fifty years—and the cutting of trees continues. Conservationists are concerned that no original forest will remain outside the parks and reserves. And the parks and reserves are considered too small and physically dissociated to ensure viable populations of many wildlife species.

Tour operators:

Above the Clouds Trekking
Adventure Associates
Ecosummer Expeditions
Exodus Adventure
Innerasia Expeditions

International Expeditions
Sierra Club Outings
Turtle Tours
Wildland Adventures
World Expeditions

North America

CANADA

Transportation: kayak/hiking/raft
Accommodations: lodges/tent
Land cost: $1,199-$4,300
Duration: 7 to 20 days
Seasons: June to September

Tours in Canada concentrate on three general areas: Vancouver Island and Queen Charlotte Islands on the west coast; the Yukon's Far North; and the Ellesmere and Devon islands in the Arctic.

Vancouver Island

The west coast of Vancouver Island, popular for kayaking and hiking, is remote yet accessible with fjord-like clefts, forests of fir and spruce, and cliffs broken by broad expanses of sandy beaches.

Kayak trips around Nootka Sound are typical of what you can expect. The base camp is a lodge in Strathcona Park, where for a day you practice—or learn—kayak paddling techniques on the Upper Campbell Lake. You then head for the coast. The *Lady Rose*, a vintage 1930s cargo and passenger vessel, takes you from Gold River along Muchalat Inlet to Bligh Island. There you disembark and paddle to your first campsite on the Spanish Pilot Islands.

Four days are spent exploring coves and bays inaccessible except by water. You stop at the sites of old Indian villages where totem poles, relics from the 10,000-year-old Haida culture, still stand. Seals, otters, porpoises, and fifteen different species of whales share the water with you. On land, you may spot black bears, black-tailed deer, and mink. Eagles, osprey, and waterfowl are also often seen.

No previous kayaking or camping experience is necessary. The flat-bottomed, two-person sea kayaks are stable, unlike the whitewater kayaks. The trip leaders are certified wilderness guides. You rendezvous with the *Lady Rose* for the return trip to Gold River.

Other kayak trips go to the Johnstone Straits on the northern tip of the island where orca whales congregate. For more information on this area, see FAMILY: Canada/Vancouver Island/Orca Whale Watching.

A week-long hike along the west coast of the island starts at Thrasher Cove across from Port San Juan. At low tide you walk the beach and a sandstone shelf of bluffs and caves. Eventually you go inland, climbing wooden ladders to the top of bluffs covered with rain forest.

Wooden ladders are placed at difficult, steep places. A board-walk crosses a bog of spruce, cedar, and stunted cousins of hemlock. Platforms suspended from a cable save you from wading across several creeks. Logan Creek even has a suspension bridge. However, you still have to contend with enough mud, fallen logs, mosquitoes, and creeks for this to definitely qualify as a wilderness hike.

You set up tents every night. You carry your own gear and a portion of the group's food and camping equipment. You should be in good physical condition to carry the forty-pound backpack.

Just past Tsuquadra Point, along the section of trail set aside as a Native Reserve, you find petroglyphs on rock walls and in caves. The caves are burial sites for the ancestors of the local Indians and are considered sacred. Past the caves is Tsusiat Falls, where you spend a few hours resting and washing off trail grime.

After crossing the Klanawa River by a suspended cable car, you follow Trestle Creek and then go into the forest again. From the trail you see the rock shelf where, in 1906, the *S.S. Valencia* went aground in a violent storm. One hundred and twenty-six passengers and crew were lost before help could arrive. This tragedy was the catalyst to establishing the Life Saving Trail, which later become the West Coast Trail you are hiking.

At Pachena Bay, the end of the trail, you take a taxi into Bamfield. Here you board the *Lady Rose* for the four-hour voyage to Port Alberni.

Queen Charlotte Islands

North of Vancouver Island lie the Queen Charlotte Islands, an archipelago of small islets and two large islands 100 miles off the coast of British Columbia. Moresby Island, the southerly of the two large islands, is the center for kayaking trips in the Queen Charlottes. Graham Island is the more populated of the two.

The Queen Charlottes, known as the "Northern Galapagos," are a biological treasure chest full of sitka spruce and red cedar, bonsai bogs, and alpine areas where endemic plants that survived the glacial retreat live. The islands are a haven for bald eagles, 25 percent of British Columbia's nesting seabirds, and a third of the area's peregrine falcon population. Seals, whales, porpoise, and the largest population of Stellar sea lions in British Columbia live in the waters around the islands.

The heritage of the Haida Indians is the islands' cultural treasure. As far back as ten thousand years ago, the Haida created a sophisticated society supported by the abundance of the land and the sea. The large-standing totems on Anthony Island, just off the southern tip of Moresby Island, attest to the culture's richness.

Haida elders referred to Moresby as *Gwaii Haanas*, the place of wonder. The Haida Indians were a presence on the island until a hundred years ago when a smallpox epidemic spread through the tribal populations. Missionaries urged the Indians to leave their villages and move to Skidegate, on neighboring Graham Island, where they would be cured at the hospital. Many villages were abandoned and the Haida culture declined.

The South Moresby area has been made a national park. The rich feeding grounds of the Temperate Pacific Marine Zone attract a great deal of marine wildlife. You may see orca or humpback whales, seals, and a variety of sea birds as you paddle the convoluted shoreline.

The bays and small islands protect you from the worst weather blowing in from the Northern Pacific. While no previous experience is necessary—the sea kayaks are stable and easy to handle—large tides and strong currents demand alertness. You quickly get the knack of moving with the sea. The mornings are spent paddling and the afternoons snorkeling, beachcombing, or hiking in the high mountain ridges of the San Cristoval Mountains, Canada's densest eagle nesting area.

You camp each night, sleeping on the ground in tents either on a beach or under the shelter of forest trees. The guides prepare meals over a campfire, but you are expected to help with camp chores, including washing the dishes.

Trips also go along the east coast of South Moresby National Park Reserve to the Haida heritage village of Tunu. You paddle around Bumaby Island with its long beaches and old growth forest. You go through the Bumaby (Dolomite) Narrows, which has one of the densest concentrations of marine life on the west coast. Once you round the southern tip of Moresby Island, you get a taste of open sea kayaking. For a break, you stop at Hotsprings Island for a soak in outdoor hot pools.

Anthony Island, with a provincial park cared for by the Haida, lies off Moresby Island's southern tip. In a grassy clearing between the sea and the forest stand the ruins of an abandoned Haida village, Ninstints, which is a United Nations World Heritage site. About twenty-five totems, the largest remaining collection, are standing, leaning, or lying in their original places, but the natural process of decay is having its inevitable effect. Experts estimate the totems will be indistinguishable from other decaying logs in about twenty years.

Kayaking is the only way to observe colonies of rhinoceros auklets, puffins, and fork-tailed petrels in the islets around the Anthony Island. Bald eagles and peregrine falcons nest in the trees. Seals; Stellar sea lions; minke; and humpback, fin, and orca whales are often sighted in the waters.

Hiking trips usually start on Graham Island, the northern and larger of the two main islands. The first part of the ten-day trek follows the Tlell River down to the coast through rain forest. You walk the beach of Naikoon Park and camp at the Meyer River.

You carry all your own gear and pitch camp on beaches or in the forest. The terrain is not difficult and the daily hikes not particularly tiring. The hike is a very pleasant way to see the varied wilderness of the Queen Charlottes.

You pass several Haida sites on the hike. Cape Ball, where you walk beneath 330-foot-high white cliffs, was, and still is, believed by the Haida to be the home of the greatest of all the ocean spirits—"Great-Swashing-of-the-Waves." You camp at the mouth of the Oeanda River, home at various times to numerous Haida clans.

At Rose Spit you set up a base camp and take day hikes without a backpack. The Haida call Rose Spit "Nai-kun," meaning "long-nose-of-Nai," an ocean spirit. It was here they believe that the Haida were born as a people.

The hike goes seaborne when you take a two-day exploration of the Moresby Islands' eastern coast in inflatable Zodiacs, visiting many of the places on the kayaking itinerary.

Yukon

Kluane National Park in the Yukon offers a very different hiking experience. The park is located along the Alaskan border, 500 miles north of the Queen Charlotte Islands. Kluane, Canada's largest mountain park, contains the country's highest peaks, largest ice fields, and biggest glaciers outside the polar region. The eight- to twelve-day hike through arctic, glacial, and alpine ecosystems will give you an appreciation for these environments.

The park is located north and east of the Saint Elias Mountains, the highest coastal mountains in the world. The range forms a 400-mile-long barrier causing Pacific storms to dump their moisture on the western side, creating ice fields and glaciers. The Hubbard, Seward, Malaspina, and Kaskawalsh glaciers, which are up to 70 miles long and 12 miles wide, flow from the mountains into the ocean or north into the Yukon.

The eastern side of the range is desert-like. This environment, similar to the steppes in Tibet and China, has many features that were evident over the rest of North America during the great ice ages. Arctic, alpine, and taiga (coniferous forest) ecosystems mingle with glacial refugia and Eurasian plant species not found anywhere elsewhere in North America.

The wildlife is equally diverse. Moose graze in the valleys; caribou roam across the tundra; and the world's highest concentration of Dall sheep stay on the high mountainsides. Grizzly bears and wolves range over the whole area. Birds include the Eurasian wheatear, arctic species such as jaeger and snow bunting, and coastal species such as rufous hummingbird.

The hike covers 60 miles. You travel off-trail through grassy meadows along game routes. You scramble up steep rocky gorges and scree slopes, cross spongy tundra, and wade creeks. You carry a pack weighing approximately forty pounds containing sleeping bag, food, camping equipment, and personal gear. Halfway into the hike an airdrop supplies you with more food. Since you do not follow established trails, you meet no other hikers.

To begin the hike, you drive two hours east of Whitehorse until the dirt track, used mostly by gold miners, becomes impassable. You then start walking up to the Burwash Uplands and the snow-capped Mount Hoge. You climb through an alpine meadow to Hoge Pass and descend a steep, rocky gorge cut by a swift mountain creek to the Donjek Valley—where the 7-mile-wide Donjek Glacier looms.

You camp several days in an alpine valley to explore the glacier, the spruce forest, and the high tundra. The Donjek is a surging glacier, moving down the valley at approximately twenty-five-year intervals. When it surges, it diverts the Donjek River and blocks the valley, forming a lake upstream.

There are two ways to get out of Donjek Valley: a one-day raft trip down the river or a climb over Atlas Pass (6,500 feet). The climb gives a stunning view of the Saint Elias range and large valley glaciers. After a steep descent down scree slopes to Duke Valley, the hike is easy going along game trails through spruce forest.

You finally emerge at the Alaska Highway, where a van awaits to take you back to Whitehorse, the capital of the Yukon Territory.

High Arctic

High Arctic kayaking and hiking trips go to the Admiralty Inlet and Somerset, Ellesmere, and Devon islands, approximately five hundred miles south of the North Pole.

Ellesmere and Devon, the northernmost of the destinations, are "arctic oases" created by heat from the twenty-four-hour sun reflecting off the surrounding ice caps. This climate quirk causes the sea ice to break into large floes and the land to bloom. The area is a popular "summer resort" for up to thirty species of nesting birds, including arctic terns, red-throated loons, eider ducks, and snow geese. Bearded seals and walrus ride the ice floes. Musk-ox with long shaggy coats graze on the hills.

During the brief thaw (July to August) you paddle the rugged coastlines cut by deep fjords. Around polynias, upswells that keep the sea open for much of the year, you see a wide diversity of marine life. On land, you hike to lush oases in the polar desert scattered throughout the High Arctic Islands.

You reach the islands by flying to Resolute Bay, a small native settlement that serves as the logistic center for the High Arctic. There you meet researchers at the Arctic Research Institute of North America station. They explain their scientific studies and take you on a walking lecture to familiarize you with the lowland ecology. You will explore a similar ecology on Devon Island. The lowlands are a series of raised beaches, small ponds, and lakes created by the retreat of an ice cap. They provide ideal grazing environments for musk-ox and nesting sites for migrant birds.

An hour's flight from Resolute Bay takes you to Devon Island, where the institute has a research base. Your camp on a peninsula in the Truelove lowlands is made up of portable structures flown in and assembled on the spot. You sleep in a dormitory-type room on cots. Two-person dome tents with foam floors and deluxe Therm-a-rest mattresses also serve as sleeping quarters. Privy facilities are outhouses. The dining-cooking facilities are heated and insulated structures specially design for arctic conditions.

Truelove lowlands consists of 17 square miles of oasis on Devon's northeast coast. The lowlands were released from under an ice cap approximately ten thousand years ago and have been raising significantly ever since. The ponds and numerous lakes are prime breeding grounds for arctic birds. Herds of musk-ox and an occasional a polar bear may wander through the area.

Since Jones Sound does not have predictable open water for kayaking, your time on Devon Island is spent exploring the arctic landscape. You also visit Grise Fjord, Canada's most northerly Inuit settlement.

Ellesmere Island, on the north side of Jones Sound from Devon

Island, is considered the best kayaking destination in the High Arctic for two main reasons: plenty of arctic wildlife and good weather. The island's continental mountain range blocks the cold, moisture-laden air from the west. A profusion of plants flourish under the long hours of sunlight.

Kayak trips start in Buchanan Bay, 30 miles west of Greenland's coast. Ice in the bay breaks up early because of polynias, where local currents and upswellings keep the water open. You explore the bay's numerous islands, many with village and campsite remains of the Thule and Dorest native peoples, who hunted and fished the water as long as four thousand years ago. In the deep fjords you see some of the most extensive and best preserved prehistoric sites of the Arctic. You paddle the southern coast for a couple of days, perhaps spotting ring seals, bearded seals, and walrus with their young on ice floes.

You paddle along the island's north coast and visit offshore islands. Exactly where you go is largely dependent on the ice conditions. The ice prevents the sea from becoming too rough and often makes for glassy smooth conditions.

No previous kayaking experience is necessary. The guides show you how to handle the stable, flat-bottomed kayaks designed for ocean travel. The trips are graded at level four (difficult), not so much due to physical difficulties but because of the weather. Daytime temperatures vary from 39 degrees to 64 degrees and that can flip-flop in minutes when a cloud obscures the sun or the wind blows up. There is always the possibility of a gale or a snowstorm. Nighttime temperatures may hit freezing, but the midnight sun keeps the temperatures somewhat moderate. It may actually be hot at midnight.

On kayak excursions out of Buchanan Bay to small islands you pitch tents wherever you decide to make camp. The guides prepare the meals, but you are expected to lend a hand with camp chores, including loading, unloading, and launching of the kayaks.

The camp at Buchanan Bay is a former Royal Canadian

Mounted Police outpost built in the 1950s. Or you may set up a base camp on the shoreline of the Alexandra lowlands, a north-facing valley about three miles long and a mile wide. The valley acts like a giant solar heater. This good summer weather helps create a microclimate where arctic flora grows profusely, especially in July and tapering off in August.

The northern end of Ellesmere is a national park. The hub of this park, created in 1988, is the Hazen Plateau, a rolling upland plain bordered by the Grant Land Mountains, Chandler Bay, and the Tanquary Fjord. The topography creates a natural east-west corridor, which was formerly used by the Paleo Eskimo and the Inglefiedland Eskimo from Greenland who came to hunt musk-ox.

The hiking is terrific. The large mountain ranges, ice fields, and smaller hills effectively block the cold air from the Arctic Ocean, creating a summer climate similar to Juneau, Alaska.

The twelve-day hiking route goes northward from Tanquary fjord, round the Ad Astra ice cap, past the Air Force glacier, and into the Ekblaw Basin. Here glaciers drop straight off the ice cap into a lake. You climb through a narrow notch between Charydbis and Schylla glaciers, descend through a gentle valley to Lewis Lake, pick your way beneath the ice streams on the southern flank of the Viking ice cap, and circle back to Tanquary Fjord.

In tundra meadows you see herds of musk-ox, and perhaps a few Peary caribou, or a pack of arctic wolves. The plant life is rich, creating meadows of color against the grey-black-white arctic landscape.

You follow no defined trail for the most part. You hike eight to fourteen miles a day carrying a fifty- to sixty-pound pack. The ground is often rough and uneven, and you ford fast and deep streams. Good physical condition and a mental attitude for cheerfully accepting wilderness difficulties is essential for enjoying this rugged backpack trip.

Tour operators:

Arctic Edge

Black Feather

Canadian Recreational

Canoeing Association

Ecosummer Expeditions

Exodus Adventure

Great Expeditions

Mountain Travel/Sobek
   Expeditions

Outer Edge Expeditions

Sea to Sky Trails

Sierra Club Outings

Special Interest Tours & Travel

Sunrise County Canoe
   Expeditions

Whitewolf Adventure
   Expeditions

Wilderness Inquiry

Wilderness Journeys

MEXICO

Baja

Transportation: sea kayak/hiking

Accommodations: tents

Land cost: $600-$2,600

Duration: 5 to 15 days

Seasons: January to April

A sea kayak provides the most intimate means of approaching a sixty-foot grey whale in the waters of the Mexican Baja.

Blue, grey, fin, humpback, Bryde's, sperm, and minke whales all swim in the waters surrounding the Baja Peninsula, a rugged, mountainous desert finger of land stretching eight hundred miles south from California. Each species seeks out the perfect set of environmental conditions of survival: the right food, the right water temperature, and safe breeding sites. The type of whale you see depends on which Baja coast you paddle, east or west.

The east coast fronts the Sea of Cortez (also called the Gulf of California) between the peninsula and the Mexican mainland. The sea supports the largest and most varied year-round population of whales in the world for any body of water of comparable size. It is one of the world's last sanctuaries for the globally decimated great blue and fin whales, the largest mammals in existence. Baleen whales also feed on the vast blooms of plankton along the east coast.

Over six hundred and fifty species of marine life are found in the Sea of Cortez's rich feeding ground. You see dolphins, sea lions, seals, and tropical fish. Frigate birds, brown pelicans, blue-footed and brown boobies are your frequent companions.

The east coast's landscape is barren, jagged mountains, basalt escarpments, and granite-carved arroyos created when two crustal plates began separating nearly two million years ago. The mountain ranges were thrown up by volcanic activity and movement along the San Andreas Fault. The landscape continues to change as the peninsula moves toward Alaska at the rate of several inches per year.

On tours to the east coast you launch two-person sea kayaks from the town of Loretto, 600 miles south of the U.S. border. It is the oldest town in the Baja.

The tours, covering 40 miles, make a week-long loop to the south. Along the way you stop at Danzante and Carmen islands, uninhabited wildlife sanctuaries. Some tours, such as those of Sea Quest Expeditions, are accompanied by a biologist or a trained naturalist so you learn the intricacies of the ecosystems you pass through.

Some tours start at La Paz, approximately one hundred miles south of Loretto. From there you paddle around Espiritu Santo Island. You spend four days exploring the island's 25-mile shoreline of sandy coves, seaside caverns, and towering volcanic cliffs. A sea lion rookery is found on Los Islotes, three rocky islets off Espiritu's north end.

You camp along the shore. A hike into the inland canyons and desert of elephant trees, giant cardoon cactus, and wild figs offers a break from the sea.

Baja's west coast is a gently sloping landscape with an extensive system of shallow lagoons. Long, narrow islands of shifting sand dunes shield the lagoons from the Pacific Ocean. The lagoons are a favorite breeding ground for grey whales, which migrate 5,000 miles from the Bering Strait. Here they feed, play, mate, and give birth in these warmer waters in January, February, and March.

The lagoons are popular sites for whale watching. The San

Ignacio Lagoon and Magdalena Bay farther to the south are major breeding and calving grounds for the grey whale. The whale, now a protected species, was nearly exterminated by whalers. They have since made a strong comeback from the estimated one hundred living in 1937. You camp by the lagoons on flat, featureless scrubland unprotected from strong winds and frequent, chilly fog.

Conservationists are concerned that whale-watching traffic has become too excessive. In recent years, fewer whales have returned to the lagoons, perhaps in favor of a place with less noise and fewer distractions.

Unthinking, uninformed, insensitive, and perhaps uncaring, tourists have been known to swim to a seal rookery and climb on to the rocks, causing panic among the animals. Even the most well-meaning visitor can cause grievous, possibly even lethal, harm to the wildlife. When people venture too close to a pelican nest, the pelicans abandon their nests, leaving their eggs exposed to opportunistic yellow-footed gulls. This can happen even when humans think they are a safe distance away.

In addition, drift nets—called "ghost nets" because the curtains of thin monofilament fiber cannot be seen underwater—used to catch fish are great threats to the seals, sea lions, sea turtles, and sea birds in the area. The animals can fatally injure themselves trying to escape the nets. Shreds of nets imbedded in the animals' bodies or wrapped around their necks can weaken or restrict their ability to feed.

Another serious danger to the marine life is habitat pollution and destruction. The Sea of Cortez is a major breeding ground for the blue whale, whose population is in serious trouble. There are perhaps only twelve to fifteen hundred blue whales alive worldwide, according to a 1989 study by the International Whaling Commission.

Motorized tourist boats are one cause of the habitat pollution. On some tours the heavier gear—tents, food, personal duffle bags—are transported from campsite to campsite by motor-driven boats. Other tours shun these gasoline-powered supply boats as a noisy, smelly intrusion into the wilderness experience.

Normally you paddle two to four hours a day. No previous kayaking experience is necessary. Sea kayaks have flat bottoms and foot-operated rudders, which make them much more stable and easier to maneuver than white-water kayaks. You do need a lightweight wet suit, which can be rented, and snorkeling equipment.

No special physical skills are required but you must be in good physical condition. A couple of weeks of swimming, push-ups, or weight work will help build your upper body strength.

A more land-oriented trip to northern Baja goes to the Blue Palms canyons. The desert canyon complex lies near Tecate, a few hours drive south of San Diego. You backpack and camp for four days where the canyon, mountain, and desert ecologies meet. On the Sierra Club's trips a naturalist explains the ingenious survival techniques of the plants and animals as you visit a hidden waterfall in Cloudburst Canyon and walk through a blue palm "forest."

The pace is light to moderate over hilly terrain with elevation ups and downs that are never more than one thousand feet. You walk no more than six miles a day carrying a light pack in temperatures from ranging from 70 to 90 degrees. You must be confident in moving over rough, boulder-strewn land and must not be deathly afraid of rattlesnakes. They do live here.

Tour operators:

American Museum of Natural
   History/Discovery Tours
American Wilderness
   Experience
Avant Garde Travel
Ecosummer Expeditions
Mariah Wilderness Expeditions
Mountain Travel/Sobek
   Expeditions

Oceanic Society Expeditions
REI Adventures
Sierra Club Outings
Wilderness: Alaska/Mexico
Wildland Adventures
WomanTrek

Copper Canyon

Transportation: train/hiking/motor vehicle
Accommodations: tents/lodges
Land cost: $1,125-$1,285
Duration: 10 to 12 days
Seasons: October to March

Copper Canyon, or "La Barranca del Cobre," located in the Sierra Madre in Mexico's state of Chihuahua is often called the "most spectacular canyon system in all of the Americas." Six times larger than the Grand Canyon complex, the 1,000-square mile canyon system encompasses unexplored mountains, rivers full of rapids, sawtoothed ridges with steep trails, hot springs, waterfalls, and hundreds of uncharted archaeological sites. The canyon complex is also home to the Tarahumara Indians.

Good physical condition is essential for this strenuous hike. Trails over the rugged, rocky, and steep terrain are barely more than goat paths. Once down in the canyon, you must climb 3,000 feet back out. You cover 7 to 10 miles a day carrying only a day-pack with water, lunch, and personal gear. Burros haul the camping equipment, food, and other supplies.

The trip starts from El Paso, Texas, with a seven-hour train ride through the Sierra Madre. The train crosses thirty-nine bridges, goes through eighty-six tunnels, and makes one 270-degree turn on the trip through mountains, canyons, and gorges.

The actual trek begins from Mansion Tarahumara with a 9-mile descent, which takes about seven hours, to a secluded warm spring where you pitch camp. In the morning you hike down another 1,000 feet before reaching the Rio Urique, which carved the 4,000-foot-deep canyon.

Unlike the Grand Canyon, Copper Canyon is not just a single big cut in the earth's crust with side canyons. The canyon complex includes a fruit-producing region, mines, logging operations, and entire towns. One town you visit in the canyon is Batopilas, which has a Wild West feel about it. You also visit Cerro Colorado and Santa Rita, a Tarahumara village.

The Tarahumara is the second largest Indian tribe north of Mexico City; the Navajo in the American Southwest is the largest. More than 50,000 Tarahumara live in the canyons of Sierra Tarahumara, which includes Copper Canyon. They have maintained many of their traditions because the rugged land has kept outside influences at a distance.

They actively worship their ancestral gods, particularly Raineari, the sun god and protector of men, and Mecha, the moon god and protector of women. Consumption of peyote plays an important part in their spiritual life, as it does in the practice of some Southwestern U.S. tribes. Since the time of the Spanish conquest, Catholic missionaries have been moderately successful in influencing the Tarahumara, whose sorcerers are as important as priests in the villages.

Timber cutting in the Copper Canyon region threatens the area's potential as a world-class wilderness area. Clearing the pine forest from the steep canyon sides, resulting in erosion and loss of wildlife habitat, degrades the canyonland's environmental integrity. One percent of the Copper Canyon land has been set aside as a national park, but the boundaries are not marked. No rules to protect the environment are posted, and there are no guards to keep loggers out. All the mature trees in some areas have been cut, destroying critical wildlife habitat.

Tour operators:

Adventure Associates
American Wilderness
    Experience

Wilderness: Alaska/Mexico
Wildland Adventures

Rio Usumacinta

Transportation: motor vehicle/raft/hiking
Accommodations: hotels/tents
Land cost: $2,000
Duration: 10 days
Seasons: February

A raft trip down the Rio Usumacinta ("river of the sacred monkey") is the only way to penetrate deep into the Lacandon jungle, North America's most significant remaining tropical rain forest.

The river is not a Sunday float trip. You run narrow gorges, big rapids, and skirt whirlpools. Professional guides row the 12-foot inflatable rafts, but you must throw yourself about to counter the force of big waves that threaten to tip you over. This is particularly true in the Gran Canon de San Jose, where 1,000-foot vertical walls are only thirty feet apart.

The trip starts in Villahermosa, the capital of the state of Tabasco in southeastern Mexico. From there you drive 90 miles to Palenque, a 1,000-year-old complex of Mayan temples and pyramids on the edge of the Sierra de Chiapas rain forest. After staying overnight in a local hotel you drive to the trailhead at Bonampak and hike a short distance before pitching tents on the outskirts of Lacanha Chan Sayab, a Lacandon Indian village.

After each day of rafting you set up camp along the river wherever you are. One night you camp at the Mayan ruin Yaxchilan. A cook prepares the meals, but otherwise you participate in loading and unloading the rafts and pitching the tents. You spot howler and spider monkeys, scarlet macaws, toucans, and parrots in the jungle. After five days on the river you run the final canyon and pull into shore. A vehicle takes you back to Palenque or Villahermosa. On the final day you visit the Agua Azul National Park near Villahermosa and take a raft trip down the Rio Shumulha, if the water level is high enough.

Rio Usumacinta was a major trading route in Mayan times. The river forms part of the Mexican-Guatemalan border midway between the Yucatan Peninsula and the west coast of Mexico.

The Rio Usumacinta is threatened by a government plan to dam the river to produce electricity. Three Mayan ruins would be submerged and hundreds of acres of wildlife habitat drowned if the dam is built. Conservationists question the practicality of damming this seasonally active river. In the summer dry season, the water flow nearly disappears. In the winter wet season, the river becomes a nearly unmanageable raging torrent.

The Lacandon people are also in danger. In the 1940s, the tribe's population was estimated to be two hundred and fifty. Today, an estimated eight hundred to nine hundred Lacandons live in this area, mostly in three villages. However, it is not a healthy population. The small gene pool has resulted in albinism.

The rain forest in which the Lacandons live has not fared much better. As much as 30 percent of the forest has been cut down to create croplands, coffee plantations, and cattle ranches. However, over 6,000 square kilometers of the forest have been declared a forest reserve, and nearly half of that is a UNESCO biosphere reserve.

For more information on the Mexican tropical forest, see NOT ORDINARY TRIPS: Vanishing Rain Forest of Mexico.

Tour operators:

Mountain Travel/Sobek Expeditions

UNITED STATES—WEST

ALASKA

Hiking and Rafting the Arctic National Wildlife Refuge
Transportation: bush plane/hiking/raft
Accommodations: tents
Land cost: $2,150-$2,255
Duration: 10 to 20 days
Seasons: June to September

The Arctic National Wildlife Refuge is 30,000 square miles of tundra, mountains, rivers, and sea coast on the northern edge of Alaska, 200 miles above the Arctic Circle. The refuge is larger than ten of the lower states.

Tour operators run various combinations of hiking/rafting trips into different areas of the refuge: the Brooks Range and the numerous rivers—Hulahula, Jago, Kongakut, Canning—being the most popular.

All tours start in Fairbanks, where you take a bush plane to

Arctic Village, a Gwich'in Indian (Athabascan) settlement 250 miles to the north. From there you take another small plane to the Kongakut or Jago rivers, or to the slopes of the Brooks Range.

The Kongakut trip is an eleven-day hike combined with a 50-mile raft trip down the river. The Kongakut is called the "river of the caribou" because 180,000 caribou cross it at several points on their annual migration. On this trip you can expect to see herds swimming the river.

On the Jago River trip you backpack 60 miles over rugged mountain terrain to the river's source and then spend twelve days shooting rapids to the Beaufort Sea.

The Brooks Range/Hulahula River trip typifies what you can expect on these trips. A four-seat bush plane flies you from Arctic Village to the Hulahula Valley on the north slope of the desolate Brooks Range. You land on a flat grassy place, unload the camping gear, and watch the plane take off.

You immediately set up camp while the guides make dinner. In the morning you load your tent and your sleeping bag into your backpack, which weighs about thirty pounds, and begin a ten-day hike to the headwaters of the Hulahula River. The group, maximum of twelve, fans out across the tundra rather than walk in single file so as not to create a path others may follow. The fragile tundra scars easily and takes years to heal.

The route goes along the ridge separating the Hulahula and Jago rivers. The landscape is sparse. The hike is much the same. There are no trails, or established campsites, or signs pointing the way.

The valley route climbs into Dall sheep territory. Brown and black bears live here, too. You gain about 1,200 feet in altitude as you hike 7 to 9 miles daily for the next five days. On the two rest days you hike without packs to the higher ridges to photograph Dall sheep, 400-pound white mountain sheep with swept-back horns ending in a flip curl.

On the seventh day you climb a gentle pass leading to the wild tributary of the Hulahula and camp on a butte with a superb view of sere mountain peaks and glacial valleys. Night hikes under a full moon are a special treat. The land is coated with a silver wash so you can see your way quite clearly. In the distance loom Mount Michelson and Mount Chamberlin (9,020 feet), their glacial caps glowing in the moonlight.

On the tenth day you walk down into a little valley split by a stream puffing itself up to be a river. A red-and-white Cessna mysteriously arrives with four rubber rafts and more food. You spend the day preparing to run the Hulahula River to the Arctic Ocean.

The first day on the river you run "ruffle rapids," the little kind that barely splash. Then you hit a stretch of white water that gives you a shot of adrenalin and puts a sharper edge on the adventure. Between the rapids you gaze at mountain ranges with glaciers dripping off the peaks.

The next day you paddle through 10-foot-high frozen blue walls of canyons of ice carved by the river. On the rest day, you wander about the vast tablelands covered with wildflowers right up to the base of a large glacier nosing down Mount Michelson. Far in the distance you see the Arctic Ocean. But between you and the ocean are the real white-water rapids. The river drops off the plateau and begins its run to the ocean.

It takes most of a day to paddle five miles. The guide thoughtfully scouts each rapid, picking the fall line, pointing out traps, and instructing you how to avoid them. You do not want to get dunked in the frigid water. Besides, grizzly bears frequent this stretch between the foothills and the mountains, and it would be a shame to have one mistake you for a salmon.

The river calms down once on the coastal plain of the Arctic National Wildlife Refuge. You float along watching herds of grazing, shaggy musk-ox, their heavy horns lying flat across their skulls, survivors of the Ice Age. The coastal plain, the "Serengeti of North America," is the core calving area for the porcupine caribou and the main hunting ground for bears and grey wolves.

The Arctic National Wildlife Refuge comprises "the only conservation system unit that protects, in an undisturbed condition, a complete spectrum of the various Arctic ecosystems in North

America," according to a U.S. Department of Interior environmental analysis.

The refuge is currently at the center of a national energy debate between conservationists and the government. Congress designated only 8 million acres of the refuge as wilderness. The remaining 1.5 half million acres of coastal plain and 8.5 million acres south of the Brooks Range are opened by the U.S. Fish and Wildlife Service. Conservationists are nervous that the land may someday be approved for oil and gas drilling. Exploration wells have already been drilled. Environmentalists and their allies in Congress fought hard to block further drilling. The Natural Resources Defense Council brought suit in federal court to prevent oil development in the refuge. The government backed off but did not abandon its development plans.

Only 25 miles of the refuge's 125-mile-long coastline are designated as wilderness. That small protected piece of coast, known as 1002 Area, is the only section on the entire 1,100 miles of arctic coast on the north slope closed to oil and gas development. The Department of Interior steadfastly claims that oil development in the 1002 Area is a matter of national security.

A full-scale drilling project would require a 150-mile-long elevated pipeline connected to numerous feeder lines, according to the Department of Interiors' 1002 Area report. A parallel haul road would link with 160 miles of spur roads fanning out to different parts of the oil field. Four airfields, sixty drilling pads, and eleven gas-oil processing factories would also be built. Construction would require up to 50 million cubic yards of gravel to be excavated from the area's rivers and plains.

The report frankly admits that full development would destroy the present wilderness character of the entire 1.5-million-acre 1002 Area.

You camp in the 1002 Area. On a hike you see arctic and red-throated loons, flocks of Canadian geese, whistling swans, sandhill cranes, and hundreds of caribou.

On the trip's final day you paddle the remaining 5 miles

through 1002 Area to the Arctic Ocean and set up camp on the shore. A bush plane will pick you up in the morning.

Tour operators:

ABEC	Wilderness: Alaska/Mexico
Alaska Discovery	Wilderness Journeys
Sierra Club Outings	

Gates of the Arctic
Transportation: hiking/raft
Accommodations: tents
Land cost: $1,795-$2,295
Duration: 5 to 15 days
Seasons: July to August

When Robert Marshall, founder of the Wilderness Society, explored the Brooks Range in 1929 he named the two massive portals flanking the North Fork of the Koyukuk River the "Gates of the Arctic." Today that area of the central Brooks Range is known as the Gates of the Arctic Park and Preserve.

The park is working land, not a natural museum, where humans and the environment dynamically cooperate. Native peoples hunt and fish in the territory as they have done for centuries.

The park contains no trails, campsites, roads, or structures of any kind. This backpack trip is strenuous, covering roughly forty-five miles. On the rafting segment you go about sixty-five to one hundred miles down the Koyukuk or Noatak river. You carry a fifty-pound backpack over tundra of bogs and tussocks—it is slow, wet, uneven walking. It is a physical feat to hop from tussock to tussock (clumps of grass) to cross the bogs. In the river valleys, you follow game trails through dense willow and alder thickets.

No helpful hints, like trail markers, point the way. You and the guide must invent a route each day, and it may require wading icy streams. This trip is not for beginners.

The trip starts with a 200-mile flight from Fairbanks to Bettles, a small village on the south slope of the Brooks Range, originally settled by Athabascan Indians. Your route through the wilderness park depends on the tour operator. You may spend a week circling Mount Doonerak, the highest peak in the central Brooks Range, or take a floatplane to one of the lakes in the Oolah Valley, just south of the Continental Divide. From there you follow the Itkillik River to the North Fork of the Koyukuk, walk down the valley, and make a river crossing near the north face of Mount Doonerak.

The hikes last from five days to two weeks. Fresh supplies and rafting equipment arrive by plane at the headwaters of the Koyukuk or the Noatak. Both rivers rate Class II. You paddle and drift along for four to seven hours daily. You may see Dall sheep, grizzly and black bears, wolves, wolverines, lynx, and a wide variety of migratory birds. The river occasionally becomes braided with shallow channels. Then you must pull and lift the rafts over the gravel bars. No rafting experience is necessary.

On the Noatak River, which means "the river from deep within" in Eskimo, you may witness the caribou migration, one of the greatest mass herd movements outside Africa's Serengeti Plain. The herd crosses this river at several places. The animals organize the crossing with near military precision. The lead cow, other cows, and young bucks cross first finding the surest route. Then come the young calves led by a cow. The older bucks remain on the bank to protect the herd at this vulnerable time.

These trips traverse the 150-mile width of the central Brooks Range. You are well north of the Arctic Circle, in the land of the midnight sun. Deep in the wilderness, you must rely on your own resources. The weather is an unpredictable blend of fair and foul, sunny and rainy, warm and cold. On the best days the temperature never reaches over 70 degrees. On the worst days you encounter rain and near freezing temperatures.

Tour operators:

ABEC   Alaska Discovery

Arctic Treks

Wilderness: Alaska/Mexico

Sierra Club Outings

Wilderness Journeys

Glacier Bay, Admiralty Island, Icy Bay, and Misty Fjords

Transportation: kayak/canoe

Accommodations: tents

Land cost: $1,100-$1,650

Duration: 5 to 10 days

Seasons: June to September

Glacier Bay is both old and new. Two hundred years ago glaciers filled the entire bay. When Captain George Vancouver found Icy Strait in 1794, Glacier Bay was a barely indented glacier up to 20 miles wide and 4,000 feet thick. It extended more than one hundred miles to the Saint Elias mountains due west. In 1879, naturalist John Muir found that the ice had retreated 48 miles up the bay. By 1916, the ice had retreated another 17 miles.

The astonishingly rapid retreat of the glaciers left "new" land, which was quickly reoccupied by a variety of marine and terrestrial wildlife. While kayaking you meet seals, porpoise, an occasional whale, and a variety of seabirds. Bald eagles, mountain goats, moose, and bears may be seen on hikes along the shoreline and in the temperate rain forest.

Glacier Bay seems an unlikely place for a rain forest. But the continuous calving of glaciers sent ocean salt spray onto land scraped clear by retreating glaciers. The salt provided nutrients necessary for plants to grow. Since the climate is not arctic, and rainfall is heavy due to the ocean currents, seeds and spores of sitka spruce, hemlock, and alders took root. The Bartlett Cove rain forest, the oldest in Glacier Bay, originated more than two hundred years ago.

Three species of whale visit Glacier Bay: humpback, minke, and orca. With luck you may see a 50-foot-long humpback breaching or lifting its tail out of the water as it dives. Only about 7 percent of the now-endangered whale population survived the whaling slaughter of earlier centuries. Humpbacks are coastal feeders often found along the shoreline, in fjords or bays. Glacier Bay humpbacks have been observed hunting singly or in pairs by casting a "net" of bubbles around their prey.

You paddle for five to ten days around the bay, depending on the tour. On the longer trips, you cover a total of 50 to 60 miles, averaging 8 to 10 miles daily. Camp is set up on the shore each night. You sleep in two-person tents in a sleeping bag, which you provide. A couple of days are devoted to on-shore hikes through the forest and up to a terminus of a glacier.

Professional wilderness guides well-versed in the biology and ecology of the bay lead the trips.

No kayaking experience is required for the trip, but you must be in good physical condition. Each two-person kayak is loaded with personal gear as well as a portion of the group's camping equipment. You haul the eighty-pound kayaks over rocky beaches when making camp. If you have chronic back or knee problems, kayaking probably is not for you. Sitting for hours in a cramped kayak without room to shift around to relieve lower back pains or to stretch your legs is uncomfortable.

Other sea kayaking trips go to Admiralty Island, Icy Bay, and Misty Fjords.

Many tours combine the Glacier Bay kayak trip with an Admiralty Island canoe voyage through one of the richest estuary and island complexes in Alaska.

Admiralty Island is considered by conservationists as the "crown jewel" of the Tongass National Forest. Brown bears and eagles outnumber people on the island. On the tour you explore the Mitchell Bay complex for five days. You paddle through Kootznahoo Narrows (Kootznahoo is the Tlingit word for "Fortress of the Bears"), a region of rapid tidal flows and drops, tide pools, and many islands. Bears, eagles, mink, seals, and porpoises are frequently spotted. You paddle up the gentle Hassleborg River and camp on shore in the old growth spruce forest. The bear paths make excellent hiking trails.

The trip is easy. You paddle only two to four miles a day and spend plenty of time viewing wildlife, taking short hikes, and just plain relaxing. No canoeing or camping experience is necessary.

At Icy Bay, 120 miles north of Glacier Bay and west of Mount Saint Elias (18,008 feet), the mountains and glaciers of southeast Alaska and the Yukon Territory meet the sea. The remote and isolated area can only be explored by kayak or on foot.

The trip is rated strenuous, although the paddling and hiking are moderate. The heavy kayaks must be carried over rough terrain when establishing camp. Some days involve long paddles or difficult camping. Some kayaking and camping experience is recommended.

You start at Yakutat, a fishing village on Yakutat Bay bordered by the Chugach and Wrangell-Saint Elias mountains. You then take a small plane over Malaspina Glacier, larger than the state of Rhode Island, to Icy Bay. You paddle among icebergs watching for seals and small porpoise for four days. You explore glacial moraines on hikes. There is no set itinerary. The tides, winds, ice pack, and will of the group directs the trip.

The campsite changes each day. You help in loading and unloading the kayaks, cooking meals, and with general camp chores. Your personal gear and a portion of the group's camping equipment are transported in your kayak.

The weather is unpredictable. Storms off the Gulf of Alaska hit Icy Bay with strong winds and driving rain. Good raingear is essential. Since the weather is so unpredictable, a three-season sleeping bag is recommended. Summer temperatures range from 50 degrees to 70 degrees, dropping lower at night.

The Misty Fjords National Monument encompasses all the ecosystems of southeast Alaska. Hanging valleys, cirques (steep, deep-walled basins), lava flows, and thousands of waterfalls are hidden in the often mist-shrouded fjords. Old growth stands of Sitka spruce and western hemlock cover the mountainsides. Open muskegs and alpine meadows lie in the mountain valleys. Kayaking is often the only practical way to see the land and the wildlife.

Seals, whales, porpoise, and sea lions cruise the Behm Canal, the main route of your trip. Brown bears, black bears, Sitka black-tailed deer, wolves, mink, marten, and river otters are common onshore.

The trip begins by taking a two-hour ride on a 50-foot excursion yacht from Ketchikan to Princess Bay. From here you paddle for six days around the isolated and remote bay. No kayaking experience is necessary. The calm water of the protected bay is an excellent place to learn kayaking skills. You paddle an average of twelve miles a day and camp on the beaches. The daily trip starts in the early morning, and camp is set up by mid-afternoon, giving you plenty of time to hike the old growth forest.

In Manzanita Bay you stop at Eddystone Rock to watch seals. In Walker Cove you explore the 1,500-foot cliffs marked by continental and valley glaciation. In Punchbowl Cove, you camp under 3,150-foot vertical cliffs that hang over the water. On the final day, you paddle into Rudyard Bay, surrounded by cliffs, waterfalls, and stunning scenery. The excursion yacht picks you up at the head of the bay for a six-hour trip back to Ketchikan.

Tour operators:

Alaska Discovery
Alaska Wildland Adventures
Exodus Adventure
Mountain Travel/Sobek
　　Expeditions

REI Adventures
Wilderness Journeys
Woodswomen Adventure
　　Travel

The Tatshenshini River

Transportation: raft
Accommodations: tents
Land cost: $1,640-$2,200
Duration: 10 to 13 days
Seasons: mid-July to late August

Rafting the Tatshenshini River is for people who like calm stretches between their adrenalin rushes. The river bounces through Class III+ (intermediate to advance-intermediate) white water, calms down, then kicks along at a nice five- to seven-mile-per-hour clip before hitting big boulders in a narrow canyon.

The Tatshenshini begins its 160-mile coarse in the remote northwest corner of British Columbia and empties into the Pacific Ocean on the northern edge of Glacier Bay National Park. The river cuts through Kluane National Park in the Yukon, and Wrangell-Saint Elias and Glacier Bay national parks in Alaska. On this trip you see some of the highest peaks in North America, immense glaciers, ice fields of the world's largest nonpolar glacier system, ancient rock-strewn moraines, valleys of wildflowers and berries, and old growth forests of spruce, hemlock, fir, and tamarack.

You start at Haines, Alaska, reached by a flight from Juneau in a small plane up the Lynn Canal, which is flanked by glaciers. From Haines you drive 104 miles north to Dalton Post in the Canadian Yukon, the headwaters of the Tatshenshini. Be sure to bring proper identification for crossing the international border (birth certificate or passport). A driver's license is not sufficient.

Within two hours of launching the 18-foot rafts you slide into the 8-mile Tatshenshini Gorge. Class III waves splash 6 feet over you. Your job in the big white water is keep yourself and the raft upright.

You paddle through dense woodlands. Moose, beaver, wolf, bear, and deer tracks can be seen on the mud flats along the river. You spend four to five hours on the river daily, allowing time for afternoon hikes to ridges, meadows, and glaciers. On a clear day you can see eighteen glaciers glittering on the mountains.

You camp at the junction where the Alsek River rushes into the Tatshenshini from the largest ice field outside of Greenland and the Antarctic. Your tent is at the foot of Walker Glacier. At another campsite, ice-capped mountains that resemble Pakistan are on one side of the river and lush forest reminiscent of Hawaii's Na Pali Coast are on the other.

You drift down an avenue of glaciers. This is Ice Age country. The land was scraped barren by retreating glaciers, leaving behind dry valleys of rocky rubble. Literally dozens of large and small glaciers are everywhere you look. Near Alsek Bay you see the immense Noatak glacier, Mount Fairweather, and the Alsek glacier. On the last 11 miles of the trip you steer through ice flotsam and icebergs that calved off of the glaciers.

The trip ends at the Dry Bay Fishing Company outpost along an estuary of the Alsek River. A small plane ferries you to Yakutat, where you make connections on scheduled Alaska Airlines flights to Juneau or Seattle.

The wildness of the Tatshenshini is threatened. Toronto-based Geddes Resources wants to build the largest copper mine in Canada in the center of the publicly owned Tatshenshini Wilderness. The company proposes to shear off the top of Windy Craggy Mountain (6,000 feet) to reach the mineral deposits. The plan includes a 360-foot-high dam that would create a two-and-a-half-mile-long reservoir for acid-rock mine tailings. The proposal includes a 150-mile-long slurry and oil pipeline as well as a major access road into the heart of the area.

The pipeline would run through the only Dall sheep winter range in British Columbia and the Chilkat River Eagle Preserve, which supports 3,500 eagles. The Tatshenshini River and twenty-six of its tributaries would be bridged.

The Windy Craggy site is located in the most earthquake-prone area of North America—more so than the area around California's San Andreas Fault. In 1899, North America's largest earthquake, measuring 8.6 on the Richter scale, occurred 75 miles from Windy Craggy. The quake's aftershock lifted the mountain 50 feet in five minutes and caused its glaciers to surge forward a half-mile.

According to the Western Canada Wilderness Committee, which opposes the mining scheme, Geddes Resources is pressing the Canadian government for approval and wants to start mining construction in 1994. The United States government can stop the plan if the environmental risks to U.S. fisheries and the Glacier Bay National Park are deemed too great, or if mine concentrates are not allowed to be shipped through U.S. territory. No decision has been reached by either government.

Tour operators:

Alaska Discovery

American Wilderness
  Experience

Canadian Recreational
  Canoeing Association

Canadian River Expeditions

Ecosummer Expeditions

Exodus Adventure

Mountain Travel/Sobek
  Expeditions

REI Adventures

Sierra Club Outings

Wilderness: Alaska/Mexico

Wilderness Journeys

Umiaking the Beringia

Transportation: ship/umiak/helicopter
Accommodations: on-board/tents/hotels
Land cost: $3,200-$3,700
Duration: 10 to 12 days
Seasons: August

Beringia, the Land of the Bering Strait, consists of the Commonwealth of Independent States' (C.I.S.) Chukotka Peninsula and the United States' Seward Peninsula on either side of the strait. The land was designated to be the Beringia Heritage International Park in a proclamation signed by George Bush and Mikhail Gorbachev in 1990. The area may officially become an international park in 1992 if all the agreements and paperwork are completed, according to the U.S. National Park Service.

Depending on the tour operator, the trip to Beringia starts in either Anchorage, Juneau, or Nome. Each take different routes to reach the same places.

Innerasia Expeditions starts you with a trip to Kotzebue, on the northern side of the Seward Peninsula. You meet with a representative of NANA, the Eskimo corporation working for a strong economic future and community for the native people. You visit a local Eskimo fish camp and learn of the connections between the peoples on both sides of the Bering Strait.

The Chukchi and Eskimo natives share a common cultural history and traditional lifestyle. Ten thousand years ago people migrated east across the land bridge now covered by the Bering Strait and moved down the North American continent. Family links on both sides of the strait have been rediscovered with the thawing of the "Ice Curtain."

The United States' contribution to the international park is the existing 2.7 million-acre Bering Land Bridge National Preserve on Seward Peninsula. The Commonwealth of Independent States intends to contribute the entire Indiana-sized Chukotka Peninsula. They also proposed a 60-mile-wide marine sanctuary in the Bering Strait, but the U.S. Park Service balked at the suggestion. The marine sanctuary would lie outside the department's jurisdiction and might be in conflict with off-shore oil interests (with allies in Congress).

Returning from Kotzebue to Nome, you take a day trip to Cape Woolley, the summer subsistence camp of the King Island Eskimos. You join the Eskimos in gathering berries, fishing, birding, and other activities similar to those performed by the natives on the Chukotka Peninsula. A storyteller relates the early history of the people and tales about their culture.

Flying from Nome to Provideniya, 200 miles west, you stop at Saint Lawrence Island. The island is populated by the Yu'pik Eskimos, who originally came from Siberia, rather than the Inupiak Eskimos, who live in Alaska. The Saint Lawrence Islanders live a traditional coastal subsistence lifestyle similar to the natives along the Chukotka Peninsula. The Eskimos show you how to make an umiak, a boat you will paddle on excursions in the Senyavin Straits.

Umiaks are the traditional Eskimo sea kayak made from two walrus hides that are dried, split, and lashed over a strong wooden frame. They hold two to six passengers and are used extensively along the Chukotka coast, although they have been modified for an outboard motor.

Upon arrival in the C.I.S., you spend a couple of days at a hotel in Provideniya (population 5,000), Chukotka's largest town. You then drive to the outlying villages of New Chaplino and Yan-rakynot. At New Chaplino, the village troupe performs traditional Chukchi songs and dances.

You stow your gear in a *baidara*, the Chukchi umiak, and pad-dle with two guides across the Senyavin Straits to Yttygran Island. The guides, Chukchi, Eskimo, or Russian, serve as interpreters, as few of the local people speak English. Yttygran Island was used by Eskimo hunters for centuries. The island's Whale Alley, hun-dreds of bowhead whale jawbones and ribs standing vertically in the ground, marks a ceremonial site used in the sixth century by the hunters. You camp overnight on the island. Whale Alley is one of hundreds of archaeological sites on the Chukotka Peninsula yet to be studied.

The next day you paddle the *baidaras* two to three hours to Arakamchechen Island. Here you examine subterranean houses, typical of the Maritime Chukchi until the mid-19th century, and a line of whalebone arches. Walrus haul out on a nearby beach.

From Arakamchechen you paddle to the mainland and visit a reindeer camp. The nomadic Reindeer Chukchi live in yarangas, a tent made from reindeer skins, and share many traits with the Arctic Saami reindeer people of Finland, Norway, and the Kola Peninsula bordering Norway and Finland.

After spending time with the reindeer herders in an open-air hot springs, you paddle back to New Chaplino and return by road to Provieniya.

A cruise tour by Cheesemans' Ecology Safaris goes farther north through the Senyavin Straits to Uelen on the corner of the Chukotkan Sea and the Bering Sea.

Tour operators:

Alaska Discovery   REI Adventures
Cheesemans' Ecology Safaris   Transiberian Tours
Innerasia Expeditions

ARIZONA

Grand Canyon North Rim

Transportation: hiking/cross-country skiing

Accommodations: tents

Land cost: $630-$895

Duration: 8 to 13 days

Seasons: September to October (hiking); March (skiing)

The thirteen-day fall hiking trip is strenuous, made more so by the forty- to fifty-pound pack on your back. The trail is so steep in places that you must take the pack off and lower it down in order to negotiate the trail. The trip is not recommended for those with a fear of heights. Most of the hike is off-trail and intended for experienced backpackers.

You start down off the North Rim from Muav Saddle along Tapeats Creek. The trail follows the creek and the contours of Tonto Platform around Explorers Monument to Shiumo Creek and Bass Camp. You finish the loop by returning to Muav Saddle via the North Bass Trail.

The days are warm to hot, and the nights cool to cold, in the canyon bottomlands. Even in the desert it rains, so pack some type of sleeping shelter.

The winter cross-country ski/hike lets you experience a serene Grand Canyon undisturbed by sightseeing helicopters and hoards of tourists. You ski 43 miles and hike 23 miles during the trip, averaging eight or nine miles a day. The terrain is relatively flat so no technical cross-country skiing skills are needed. But you must be experienced enough to carry the fifty-pound pack and stay upright on skinny skis.

The tour meets in Page, Arizona, and travels by van to Jacob Lake on the north side of the Grand Canyon. You ski 9 miles into white space and set up tents. Winter camping can be quite comfortable if you have the right equipment and clothes. After two days of skiing, you arrive at the North Rim campground.

From the rim you hike, carrying the skis on your pack, down

the North Kaibab Trail to Phantom Ranch, a 13-mile trek. You stay a day at the campground then make an 11-mile hike up to the South Rim via Bright Angel Trail.

Hiking Canyon de Chelly

Transportation: hiking
Accommodations: tents
Land cost: $590
Duration: 6 days
Seasons: October

Canyon de Chelly (pronounced d'Shay) is home to numerous Navajo who have lived, farmed, and grazed sheep there for more than two thousand years. A Navajo guide takes you to places in this national monument not seen by the casual tourist. On the trip you meet local residents and learn the history of the region. The people explain the basis of mythological, cultural, and religious traditions. They show you which plants have medicinal properties and how they are used.

You hike an average of ten miles a day up two huge canyons, de Chelly and del Muerto. Red canyon walls smoothed by water and wind rise hundreds of feet above you. The trail passes fields of corn, beans, squash, fruit, and nut trees. The Kayenta Anasazi grew the same type of crops in the canyon as far back as 1000 B.C.

The trek takes you into the center of one of North America's most important archaeological regions. You see many ruins of grain storage bins, stone houses, and cliff dwellings. The guide explains the meaning of the petroglyphs and other rock art found on the canyon walls.

The demanding hike is mostly cross-country. You carry a backpack with personal gear—warm clothing, water, food, raingear. The heavier camping equipment is hauled by pickup truck to a different campsite each evening. You are expected to participate in all camp chores.

Tour operators:

Four Corners School of Outdoor
Education

Sierra Club Outings
Wild Horizons Expeditions

COLORADO

Hiking the Weminuche Wilderness

Transportation: train/hiking
Accommodations: tents
Land cost: $360
Duration: 6 days
Seasons: August

This trip is a regression through techno-time. You fly to Durango, Colorado, board a train pulled by steam engine, and finally walk into the wilderness.

You take the Durango & Silverton narrow-gauge railroad, formerly used to haul silver ore and miners, for a 37-mile trip along the Animas River into the San Juan Mountains. The train stops at the trailhead at Elk Park. You shoulder your pack and start walking into the Weminuche Wilderness.

The 36-mile loop hike starts up Elk Creek. You climb 1,300 feet in 4 miles past beaver ponds to a campsite in a stand of trees adjacent to a meadow. During the next five days you will hike over three passes topping 12,400 feet, loll in meadows of wildflowers along the Continental Divide, cool your feet in mountain streams, and breath clean air. The daily hikes average five to eight miles, usually all uphill. The steepest altitude gain is 2,900 feet in 5 miles.

You must be in good physical condition and be an experienced backpacker for this trip. Weather in the high mountains is unpredictable, but you can expect daytime temperatures in the 60s and 70s and nighttime temperatures near freezing. Afternoon rain showers are always a possibility.

Tour operators:

American Wilderness
    Experience
Mountain Travel/Sobek
    Expeditions

Sierra Club Outings

HAWAII

Hiking Hawaii, Kauai, and Maui

Transportation: motor vehicle/hiking
Accommodations: hotel/cabins/tents/bed and breakfast
Land cost: $1,200-$1,395
Duration: 7 to 13 days
Seasons: year-round

There are two ways to see the Hawaiian Islands: from a beach chair or exploring the nature preserves on foot. Exploring tours go to three islands: Hawaii, Kauai, and Maui.

On Hawaii, the Big Island, you hike the Volcanoes National Park down into the steaming crater of Kilauea Iki. A 5-mile trail begins and ends on the 4,000-foot summit of the volcano. You start along the crater's rim through an ohia/fern climax forest, where you see birds endemic to the island. Ninety-five percent of the islands' native birds, animals, and plants are found only on Hawaii.

The trail winds down 400 feet to the crater's floor, crosses to the other side, and goes back up to the rim. You pass through lush foliage on the crater rim to the blasted remains of trees and hardened lava flows on the crater floor. Acrid fumes and earth tremors remind you that molten magma still surges against the earth's thin crust underfoot. The easy hike takes about three hours.

On Kauai, a 4-mile hike goes along the Na Pali Coast Trail to Hanakapiai Beach. The trail is part of a 1,000-year-old system called the "King's Trail," which once served as a major travel route for islanders. The trail starts at sea level at Ke'e Lagoon but quickly climbs 600 feet to cliff tops. The trail winds in and out of tropical forest valleys and along windswept promontories. The last half-mile down to Hanakapiai Beach can be one, long slide, since the trail is often wet, muddy, and slippery. You can expect frequent rain: perhaps a drizzle, perhaps a full-blown ocean squall. The hike takes four hours round-trip, depending on the condition of the trail. Sections of the trail were wiped out by Hurricane Iniki in September 1992.

The Awaawapuhi Trail is another hike on Kauai. The trail begins near the Alakai Swamp in Kokee State Park atop the Waimea Canyon. You walk steadily but not steeply down three and a half miles through a mature ohia cloud forest to a koa dry forest. The trail ends at a meadow overlooking the Na Pali coast. You can walk back up the 2,000 feet to the canyon rim or continue an additional five and a half miles on the Naulolo Trail to the Kokee Lodge. Hiking time is approximately five hours round-trip.

On Maui, you start on Haleakala Volcano summit (10,000 feet) and hike down 4 miles to the crater's floor. You walk 4 miles across the caldera, a large green rolling meadow, and climb 1,000 feet of switchbacks to the crater's rim. The hike takes six or seven hours.

The volcano is the centerpiece of the Haleakala National Park that stretches to the southeast coast and includes the tropical rain forest of Kipahula Valley. Trails in the valley follow the Ohe'o Stream, which connects many pools and waterfalls in the rain forest. During heavy rains flash floods may turn the pleasant stream into a torrent. The Maui parrotbill, the honeycreeper, and the brilliant red I'wi are examples of the dozens of endangered forest birds that live in the rain forest's upper elevations. Rare and endangered plants, such as the silversword which blooms only once in its lifetime, thrive in the rain forest.

Humans have not marred this uninhabited valley of mango, kukui, and bamboo, but pigs and goats have caused serious damage. The now feral animals were introduced to the islands by the first European settlers. Pigs root in the soil, inadvertently sowing the seeds of pest plants. Goats can easily denude a hillside of its vegetation. The Park Service has fenced off some areas to keep out the wild pigs and goats.

A shorter hike goes to Waimoku Falls. Starting at sea level, the 2-mile trail parallels Ohe'o Stream through a grassy meadow for the first mile. On the second mile you hike through a bamboo and wetland forest to the base of the 420-foot Waimoku Falls. This part of the trail is always wet. A boardwalk covers some of the rougher, muddy sections. The trail crosses rocky and slimy areas at a modest 750-foot gain in elevation. On the hike you can experience sun, light showers, and a tropical downpour all within the three hours it takes to complete the hike.

For more information on these islands see COMFORTABLE WILDERNESS: North America/United States—West/Hawaii.

Tour operators:

Above the Clouds Trekking

American Wilderness
Experience

REI Adventures

Sierra Club Outings

Wildland Adventures

MONTANA

Doing "The Bob" on the Chinese Wall

Transportation: horseback/hiking

Accommodations: tents

Land cost: $175 to $210 per person per day; Sierra Club Outings $390 for entire tour

Duration: 6 to 12 days

Seasons: July to August

"The Bob," as the Bob Marshall Wilderness Area is called, lies just south of Glacier National Park in northern Montana. The 3,770-square-mile wilderness is twice the size of Rhode Island and larger than Yellowstone National Park. Here you find virtually every animal and plant, with the exception of bison, that existed in the area before Europeans arrived. The largest bighorn sheep herd and the most viable grizzly population in the lower forty-eight states thrive in "The Bob."

The area is named in honor of Robert "Bob" Marshall, who is personally credited with adding 3.4 million acres to the United States wilderness system. He was also the founder of the Wilderness Society.

The greater wilderness of Bob Marshall country has three sections: Great Bear Wilderness in the north; Bob Marshall Wilderness with the Chinese Wall in the center; and Scapegoat Wilderness in the south. Trips tend to concentrate on one or two of the areas. Scapegoat Wilderness and the Chinese Wall part of the Bob Marshall Wilderness are favorites. Which area you explore and exactly where you start varies with the tour operators.

The Sierra Club hike begins at Swift Reservoir west of Dupuyer, Montana. You climb nearly two thousand feet over Gateway Pass and cross the Continental Divide. After a 15-mile hike you camp at the Big River Meadows. You cross the divide four times. The next day you hike down the Gateway Gorge to the headwaters of the Flathead River, where you spend a day exploring Gooseberry Park.

A three-day hike covering 48 miles takes you to the Chinese Wall. The Chinese Wall is a 10-mile line of 1,000-foot cliffs that marks the Continental Divide. This is a very environmentally fragile area of highland meadows, nesting sites for birds, and grazing range for bighorn sheep. Moose, elk, bighorn sheep, deer, eagles, black bears, and grizzly bears also live in the area.

Between the Chinese Wall and the ramparts of the Rocky Mountain front lies a north-south running valley. This is a good place to camp within sight of the Chinese Wall without disturbing the wildlife. A stream flows through the alpine meadow shaded with pastel wildflowers.

On the return route you strike off cross-country, make an easy scramble up Trick Pass, and camp near Needle Falls, where the White River runs through a pipe-like rock formation. On the final day you cross the divide at White River Pass (7,600 feet) and make your last campsite along the headwaters of the Sun River.

Backpacking experience is preferable for this trip. You need to be in good physical condition, since you will carry a fifty-pound backpack. A waterproof tent, a good rain suit (not a poncho), and a supply of insect repellent are essentials. Daytime temperatures are in the 70s and 80s. Nighttime temperatures dip to the lower 30s.

Horseback trips in the area cover approximately the same territory. Individual tour operators have their favorite variations. When camping near the Chinese Wall you may go up to the well-hidden Lake Quite or climb Halfmoon Peak for a close look at the wall.

The horseback trips are suited for novices and experienced riders of all ages.

For more information on the Bob Marshall Wilderness, see NOT ORDINARY TRIPS: United States—West/Montana.

Tour operators:

American Wilderness
Experience

Montana Nature Conservance
Sierra Club Outings

NEW MEXICO

Hiking the Gila Wilderness

Transportation: hiking
Accommodations: tents
Land cost: $400-$500
Duration: 7 days
Seasons: April and May

On many maps the 500,000-acre Gila Wilderness is a blank space. The terrain in this southwest corner of New Mexico about eighty miles from the Mexican border ranges from mountains to deserts to canyonlands. In 1924, the area became the United States', and the world's, first designated wilderness area.

The Gila lies on the southern edge of the Rocky Mountains and the northern edge of the Chihuahuan Desert. Within an hour you can hike from barrel cactus in the desert heat to 10-foot snow drifts in the high country. Elk, mule deer, beavers, hawks, turkeys, rattlesnakes, and Gila monsters are commonly seen. Black bear, mountain lions, big-horn sheep, bobcats, and eagles also live here but are not frequently spotted.

You visit the Gila Cliff Dwellings and spend two days wading up the West Fork of the Gila River. Escaping the desert heat, you make a strenuous hike through forest and snow drifts to Mogollon Baldy Peak. Escaping the cold, you hike down into the Mogollon Creek Drainage and soak in Turkey Creek Hot Springs. The trek ends with a walk down the Gila River.

The daily hike averages ten miles or less. You carry a backpack with your personal gear, limited to twenty-five pounds. Cooking equipment is provided.

Despite this area being a long-revered wilderness area, logging and cattle overgrazing pose environmental problems. The habitat of the Mexican spotted owl is threatened as well as the potential of reintroducing the Mexican wolf and the grizzly bear into the wilderness area.

Tour operators:

American Wilderness
    Experience
Mountain Travel/Sobek
    Expeditions

Sierra Club Outings

UTAH

Escalante Canyons Wilderness

Transportation: hiking
Accommodations: tents
Land cost: $400-$500

Duration: 6 to 7 days

Seasons: April and May

Ringed by formidable cliffs and impassable canyons, the Escalante River was unmapped and unnamed until 1872. This region
of deeply eroded sandstone peaks, plateaus, and narrow canyons
remains one of the United States' most remote wildernesses. The
river tumbles off the 11,000-foot Aquarius Plateau. It cuts a vertical mile through Navajo, Kayenta, and Wingate sandstone formations of the late Triassic and early Jurassic ages. The river and its
tributaries carved a 1,000-mile maze of interconnected canyons.

The upper reaches of the river run through forests of aspen and
ponderosa. The Escalante carves glens and hanging gardens into
the desert sandstone and burrows slot canyons 100 feet deep and
no wider than ten inches in places. Grottoes, alcoves, and caves
honeycomb the cliff walls smoothed by the river.

You find arches, fins, domes, pinnacles, sinkholes, and natural
bridges on the hike. In the canyons' cool bottomlands you camp
near clear springs in groves of cottonwood. Daytime temperatures
reach into the 80s, with overnight lows in the 40s.

The canyonlands provide habitats for 270 species of mammals,
birds, reptiles, amphibians, and fish. Mountain lions, mule deer,
elk bears, coyotes, and antelope live in the high canyons. Wild
horses graze in the valleys and desert bighorn sheep scramble on
the cliffs. Two endangered bird species, the bald eagle and the
peregrine falcon, have been spotted, along with golden eagles and
Lewis's woodpeckers.

Some four hundred thousand acres of the Escalante wildlands
are protected within Capital Reef National Park and Glen Canyon
National Recreation Area. Yet the majority of the Escalante wildlands are unprotected. The U.S. Forest Service oversees 200,000
acres and the Bureau of Land Management (BLM) another
350,000 acres of the wilderness. The BLM land lies in the center
of the Escalante region linking national forest lands at the river's
headwaters to the deep, scenic canyons of Glen Canyon National
Recreation Area. The land provides critical winter range for deer

and elk. The majority of hiking routes are in the core area controlled by the BLM. Float trips down the river go mostly through BLM land.

The BLM and the Forest Service plan to open two-thirds of their roadless lands in the region for mineral exploration, timber cutting, and the construction of hundreds of miles of associated roads, according to the Utah Wilderness Coalition, a conservation organization that advocates that more of the Escalante wildlands be placed under protection. The BLM does recommend wilderness protection for the core of the Escalante Canyons Wilderness but leaves almost 200,000 acres of wildland open for potential development.

Tour operators:

American Wilderness
Experience
Mountain Travel/Sobek
Expeditions

Sierra Club Outings
Woodswomen Adventure
Travel

Dirty Devil Wilderness

Transportation: hiking
Accommodations: tents
Land cost: $525-$795
Duration: 7 days
Seasons: May

The Dirty Devil River region, just west of the Maze District of Canyonlands National Park, is one of the most rugged and remote landscapes of the American West. It is where the outlaw Butch Cassidy and his Wild Bunch hid out in the 1890s.

The Dirty Devil River winds for 90 miles through a 500-square-mile canyon system between Utah Highway 24 and Lake Powell southeast of Hanksville, Utah. Low reddish hills east of the highway conceal 40 miles of river canyon. Eight major side canyons up to 15-miles long with high, curved, sandstone walls, some as deep as 2,000 feet, lie in that seemingly empty landscape.

You hike old mining tracks high above the river. The horizon is filled with colorful cliffs, slickrock domes, spires, arches, buttes, and "The Block," a 1,000-foot fortress of a cliff. You hike along the "Chinese Trail" and climb down an adventurous set of natural steps carved in the sandstone. The weather varies from hot to rainy and windy. A tent and a rain suit are essential.

Herds of antelope roam the plateau country along the canyons' rims. Desert bighorn sheep climb the cliffs where golden eagles and peregrine falcons nest. A rare population of beavers lives in Beaver Wash, one of the side canyons.

Nearly five hundred thousand acres surrounding the lower Dirty Devil River canyon are part of the Glen Canyon National Recreation Area. The remainder of the wilderness canyonlands are under the jurisdiction of the BLM. The government agency proposed to open the land for uranium and tar sand development, creating a 100-square-mile mining and industrial zone at the heart of the canyon system, according to the Utah Wilderness Coalition, which continues to wage an eight-year battle to block new developments on the lands.

On the hike the guide discusses the environmental and ecological nature of the region and the impact of mining and the cattle industry.

Tour operators:

American Wilderness
Experience

Four Corners School of Outdoor
Education

Dark Canyon Wilderness

Transportation: hiking
Accommodations: tents
Land cost: $425
Duration: 7 days
Seasons: September to October

The descent into Dark Canyon passes through the 300-million-year-old Honaker Trail Foundation, one of the oldest rock layers exposed in southern Utah. The formation's mix of limestone, shale, and sandstone creates whorls and streaks of reds, oranges, sepia, and blues. Fossils and crystals are embedded in the limestone bedrock.

The hike starts among the pines and aspens on Elk Ridge Plateau (8,000 feet). For the first three days you descend Woodenshoe Canyon through forests that gradually change to a sparse savanna of piñon, juniper, and "oriental gardens" of cacti and other wildflowers. In the canyon bottomlands, you find streams connecting waterfalls, plunge pools, hanging gardens of ferns, and groves of cottonwoods that shade your campsites. The walls of the canyon are consistently 1,500 to 2,000 feet high for its 30-mile length from the forests of Elk Ridge to Cataract Canyon.

You walk generally downhill, except for the 1,000-foot climb up the talus slope of Sundance Trail, which takes you above the canyon's rim at the hike's end. The trail is on narrow footpaths, talus slopes, slickrock ledges, and streambeds. A few places are so steep they require handholds and footholds. There is no officially maintained, trail so you are on rough ground much of the time. The daily hikes averages less than ten miles, although one or two longer hikes are necessary to reach a water supply. You carry about forty pounds of necessary supplies and camping equipment.

Occasionally you pass Anasazi ruins, primarily cliff dwellings and granaries. "Because of the inaccessibility of Dark Canyon, this area potentially contains numerous pristine cultural resources," according to a BLM report. The BLM estimates that up to 2,658 archeological sites could exist within the Wilderness Area.

Tour operators:

American Wilderness
Experience

Four Corners School of Outdoor
Education

Labyrinth Canyon Wilderness
Transportation: hiking/raft
Accommodations: tents

Land cost: $525
Duration: 7 days
Seasons: April to May

"There is an exquisite charm in our ride today down this beautiful canyon. It gradually grows deeper with every mile of travel; the walls are symmetrically curved and grandly arched, of a beautiful color, and reflected in the quiet waters," wrote John Wesley Powell of his trip through Labyrinth Canyon in 1869.

Very little has changed since Powell first saw this canyon, now in the Glen Canyon National Recreation Area. The Green River runs through the canyon for nearly fifty miles of smooth water unbroken by rapids or falls. Labyrinth Canyon is the last vestige of what Glen Canyon was like before it was dammed.

The four-day hike starts at Horseshoe Canyon, which leads into the Maze District of Canyonlands National Park. The trail into the canyon is steep, until you reach the bottom of the canyon where the ground is fairly level. Deep within the 35-mile-long canyon you come to the Great Gallery, one of the finest examples of prehistoric rock art in the Southwest. Human artifacts nearly nine thousand years old have been discovered by archaeologists within the canyon complex. There is also evidence of mammoth, bison, camel, sloth, and an extinct species of horse.

The daily hikes average eight miles. You carry about forty pounds of personal gear and a portion of the group's supplies and camping equipment.

You camp on the beach at the Green River on the sixth day. There, an inflatable raft awaits to take you to Mineral Bottom, where you camp overnight before returning to Green River, Utah, by vehicle.

The Bureau of Land Management oversees the portion of Labyrinth Canyon not within Canyonlands National Park. The BLM has recommended wilderness designation for the area west of the Green River, leaving more than half of the Labyrinth Canyon Wilderness open to road building, mineral exploration, hydropower development, and indiscriminate off-road vehicle use, according to the Utah Wilderness Coalition. The coalition proposes designating the entire canyon system a protected Wilderness Area.

Tour operators:

American Wilderness Experience

Four Corners School of Outdoor Education

The San Juan-Anasazi Wilderness

Transportation: hiking
Accommodations: tents
Land cost: $545-$800
Duration: 6 days
Seasons: September to October

This hike goes into the enormous outdoor museum of Anasazi ruins within the Fish, Owl, Road, and Lime canyons system. The Anasazi Indians left the canyons about seven hundred years ago, yet the dry desert air has preserved their mud-and-stone cliff dwellings, shards of pottery, and stone towers. The concentration of archaeological sites in this region, up to several hundred per square mile, may be as great as anywhere in the United States.

Fish Canyon and its western tributary Owl Canyon are narrow with steep sides reaching up to eight hundred feet. They twist pass near-perfect ancient Anasazi cliff dwellings and kivas. This is a very popular hiking route, favored by people on day trips. The canyons provide habitat for mule deer and the endangered bald eagle. Petroglyphs on the canyon walls indicate that bighorn sheep once inhabited the area.

The narrow slickrock Road and Lime canyons form the south-central block of the Wilderness Area. Despite the name, there are no roads in Road Canyon. Far fewer people visit these canyons than Fish and Owl. There are well-preserved Anasazi and Basketmaker sites in the canyons.

The hikes average nine miles daily, much of it up and down on off-trail rough ground. The hikes on the mesa top and in the canyon bottoms are relatively flat.

One day's hike goes along Comb Wash near the mouth of Arch and Mule canyons. The Anasazi heavily populated the immediate area. The continuous series of sites has been likened to a prehistoric city. Some of the cliff dwellings rival those of Chaco Canyon in New Mexico.

However, unrestricted vehicle access to much of the Wilderness Area makes the ruins easy prey to pothunters (amateur archaeologists) and other vandals. The vehicles also tear up the fragile soil.

Tour operator:

Four Corners School of Outdoor Education

WYOMING

The Greater Yellowstone Ecosystem

Transportation: hiking

Accommodations: tents

Land cost: $415

Duration: 7 days

Seasons: August

The 14-million-acre Greater Yellowstone Ecosystem includes two national parks, Yellowstone and Glacier, three national wildlife refuges, and twelve wilderness areas. The ecosystem contains the world's most extensive geyser and geothermal features; the largest populations of elk, deer moose, bison, and bighorn sheep in the lower forty-eight states, and two hundred or so endangered grizzly bears.

This hike takes you into the Absaroka-Beartooth region of the Greater Yellowstone Ecosystem. This rugged area of canyons, glaciers, 12,000-foot peaks, and 10,000-foot tundra-like plateaus lies on the northern edge of Yellowstone National Park.

The Absaroka-Beartooth is the fourth most visited Wilderness Area in the United States. To avoid crowds, this hike goes to the

Beartooth Plateau in the austere northern section. Three-quarters of the plateau lie above timberline. The ragged white limestone cliffs, resembling bears' teeth, gave the region its name.

The trailhead begins at Hellroaring plateau speckled by dozens of lakes. You drop down the Lake Fork drainage through berry patches where you may encounter grizzly bears and black bears. Bald eagles, elk, wolverine, bighorn sheep, and moose live in this wilderness.

The trail leads to Black Canyon, where on your rest day you can explore Grasshopper glacier. Grasshoppers were frozen in the ice thousands of years ago. You hike over the 11,000-foot Sundance Pass from which you see rank upon rank of snowcapped peaks. The steep descent of fifty-six switchbacks takes you down to West Fork Creek, where you camp next to one of the many waterfalls.

The hike is strenuous with large elevation gains in the first couple of days. You must be physically fit to carry the forty-pound pack over rough terrain. Snow, heavy rain, and freezing temperatures are all possible.

The final segment of the hike takes you through Quinnebaugh Meadows, past Timberline and Gertrude lakes, and across the Silver Run plateau. The route may change due to the presence of grizzly bears.

This wild and remote area of biologically interrelated land is considered the world's largest intact temperate ecosystem. Yet the wilderness is not untouched by man's influence. Toxic mine waste, logging, oil and gas drilling, new roads, and the pressure of increased recreational use threaten the Greater Yellowstone Ecosystem. In Glacier country, the U.S. Forest Service has given oil companies permission to drill in the Badger Two-Medicine area. The companies want to cut 17 miles of roads into the region and drill twenty-two wells, according to the Sierra Club, which opposes the development.

Brooks Lake, in the heart of the Yellowstone ecosystem, is being leased for oil and gas, even though biologists say such development will harm the grizzly bear population.

Tour operators:

American Wilderness
Experience
Four Corners School of Outdoor
Education

Montana Nature Conservancy
Sierra Club Outings
Woodswomen Adventure
Travel

Cross-country Ski Yellowstone

Transportation: cross-country skiing
Accommodations: lodges
Land cost: $850-$1,599
Duration: 5 to 7 days
Seasons: January and February

Escaping the crowd is perhaps the most difficult part of finding a wilderness experience in the Yellowstone National Park during the summer. But in the winter the parking lots are empty (snowed over) and the roads closed, except for the northern entrance at Gardiner. Then you can easily find wilderness solitude on cross-country ski treks, the only environmentally conscionable method of seeing the park in the winter.

Most tours follow the same route. As a result you may see other groups and share the trails with snowmobilers. On the positive side, the wildlife can anticipate where humans may be during the winter and avoid them.

First stop is Mammoth Springs to ski Mammoth Terraces and the pine forests near the Gardiner River. The 4-mile Lost Lake Trail or an 8-mile loop on the Chittenden Trail or Tower Falls are other options. You ski to Lamar Valley or the 7-mile Blacktail Trail on the second day.

A four-and-a-half-hour snow coach ride (a large, specially appointed Snow-Cat) ride over the Continental Divide takes you farther into the park's interior to Old Faithful. Numerous trails in the Old Faithful area provide good backcountry skiing. The Continental Divide Trail, Biscuit Basin Loop, or Mystic Falls make for fine day trips. And, of course, you tour the area of steaming pools, painted mud pots, geysers, and ice-encrusted waterfalls for a couple of days.

Bison often hang out near the hot-water pools. Snow geese, coyotes, elk, and winter swans are among other wildlife you are likely to see.

Accommodations are the Mammoth Hot Springs Lodge, the Chico Hot Springs Lodge, and lodges at Old Faithful.

Trips by the Four Corners School of Outdoor Education are geared toward education as well as recreation. A geologist and biologist explain winter animal behavior, geology of the area, snow and avalanche conditions, and Yellowstone's ecology.

Many of the trails are suitable for novice skiers. The Continental Divide and other backcountry trails require skill and experience. The trips average four to eight miles a day, always returning to a lodge for the night.

The park's geysers have attracted geothermal developers. They purchased land just outside the park and want to tap into the underground thermal energy sources that connect with the geysers and hot springs within the park. The threat to the park's ecosystem became so great that U.S. Representative Pat Williams (D-Mont) drafted the Old Faithful Geothermal Protection Act that calls for a four-year prohibition on geothermal drilling.

According to Irving Friedman, a senior geochemist with the U.S. Geological Survey, tapping the underground thermal energy sources outside Yellowstone could result in "pulling the plug" on the underground source of the geysers in the park. Yellowstone has the largest concentration of geothermal features on Earth. It is one of three major geyser regions in the world that has not been drilled. Seven of the ten major geyser regions were stilled when drilling occurred.

The Yellowstone Park Preservation Council, an environmental group made up mostly of the park's employees, propose the creation of a 15-mile buffer zone around the park to restrict commercial, residential, and ranching development. Within the park, the proposal includes creating a 40-mile zone, encompassing

Old Faithful, Mammoth Hot Springs, and Norris Geyser Basin, in which all development would be prohibited.

The Secretary of the Department of Interior, Manuel Lujan, three conservative Western senators, and allies of the Bush administration oppose a complete ban on geothermal development. They cite potential infringement on private property rights.

"The area outside the boundaries of the park are more threatened now, and less protected by law, than they were just five years ago," Friedman was quoted in the *Denver Post* (7 June 1992).

Many of the park's pools contain tinted microscopic bacteria. The bacteria give the pools their varies colors. The bacteria are so important that samples have been used to pioneer DNA fingerprinting, which is on the cutting edge of genetic science, according to Friedman.

Geothermal developers are not the only threat to the integrity of the Yellowstone ecosystem. Mining, clear-cutting, and rapid development at the park's edges are squeezing the habitats of the wildlife. Six million acres of the national forest not designated wilderness have been opened to oil- and gas-leasing without environmental-impact assessment, charges Ed Lewis, head of the Greater Yellowstone Coalition, an advocacy group for the preservation of the park's ecosystem.

The coalition makes the point that cross-country skiers and snowmobilers alarm elk, deer, moose, and bison. The animals often flee, especially at the sound and smell of snowmobiles, expending calories hard to replace in the harsh winter conditions.

Tour operators:

American Wilderness Experience	Montana Nature Conservancy
Four Corners School of Outdoor Education	Sierra Club Outings
	Woodswomen Adventure Travel

NORTHEAST

MAINE

Sampling the Appalachian Trial

Transportation: hiking
Accommodations: tents
Land cost: $415
Duration: 7 days
Seasons: June and July

This hike goes through perhaps the most spectacular hiking country in the eastern United States. The trail leads you into the relatively secluded backcountry of Maine, where a naturalist accompanying the tour explains the workings of the various ecosystems. The entire 46-mile hike past lakes and along mountain streams is on a portion of 1,200-mile Appalachian Trail in western Maine.

You start just south of Rangely with a short and gentle 4.5-mile hike to Sabbath Day Pond lean-to, where you camp along the shore of the pond. The adjacent Long Pond has a little sand beach, ideal for an afternoon swim.

The next day you leave the lake country and climb 9 miles up the spine of the Bemis Range to the Bemis Mountain lean-to (3,000 feet). The hike is up and down, gaining 1,700 feet in altitude and losing 1,300 feet. It is not strenuous and has no steep climbs. You camp overnight at the shelter.

In the morning you hike through a stand of virgin red spruce, whose older trees date back to the early 1600s. The trail then climbs a few hundred feet to the summit of Old Blue. You camp 2,200 feet below Old Blue's summit at Black Brook Notch.

The following day begins with a steep climb up and over Moody Mountain. During the 7-mile hike you wade across Sawyer Brook and follow the trail up Wyman Mountain to Surplus Pond. Camp is pitched on the lakeshore. You are expected to help with all camp chores—cooking meals, pitching tents, general clean-up. You carry a portion of the group's food and equipment, plus your personal gear in a pack that weighs approximately forty pounds fully loaded.

From Wyman Mountain you descend to Dunn Notch and a 60-foot double waterfall. An easy 4-mile afternoon hike takes you to the Frye Notch lean-to, where you camp for the night. On the last day you hike above timberline to the twin peaks of Baldplate Mountain. You see New Hampshire's Mount Washington and all of western Maine's mountains from this perch. The trail leads down to Grafton Notch, where a vehicle takes you to Bethel for a celebration dinner.

Tour operator:

Sierra Club Outings

SOUTH

NORTH CAROLINA/TENNESSEE

Appalachian Autumn Hike

Transportation: hiking

Accommodations: tents

Land cost: $345

Duration: 7 days

Seasons: October

The Joyce Kilmer-Slickrock and Citico Wilderness contains the East Coast's only remaining climax forest. This stand of trees miraculously escaped the rapacious timber barons of the 1930s. Straddling the North Carolina/Tennessee border southwest of the Great Smoky Mountains National Park, the 32,904-acre Wilderness Area lies within the Unicoi Mountain Range.

The only true vestige of virgin forest in the East lies within the 3,840-acre Joyce Kilmer Memorial Forest, part of the Wilderness Area.

A 40-mile hike takes you into what was the homeland of the Cherokee until 1838. It was in 1838 that U.S. troops forcibly drove the tribe west along the infamous Trail of Tears. The hike starts from Rattler Ford campground, 60 miles from the nearest airport at Knoxville, Tennessee. You follow the Haoe Lead Trail up the narrow spine of Haoe Mountain. According to local legend, "Haoe" (Ha'o) is not a Cherokee word but an expression of exhilaration inspired by the beauty of the land.

On the hike you pass through rhododendron, stands of old growth hemlock, and sugar maple in the Slickrock Basin. Getting down Slickrock Creek Trail is a feat of agility as you scramble down a 45-degree slope. You use roots as handholds to check your slide. You camp a half-mile upstream of Wildcat Falls, a four-tiered falls that cascades into catch pools.

The next day you hike nearly nine miles up Big Stack Gap Branch Trail. The trail continues northwest along the ridgeline of Slickrock Creek to Stiffknee Trail. The trail leads down through tunnels of rhododendron and hardwood hollows and along an old logging railbed. You camp on a northern section of Slickrock Creek for two days. On a rest day you walk to Slickrock's Lower Falls, 1.5 miles from camp.

On the last day you hike 6.5 miles out of the Slickrock Basin to the top of the 5,200-foot-high outcrop Hangover, where you camp for the last night. The final day is an easy 5-mile stroll through old growth hemlock, Carolina silverbell, and red maple.

Rain is very common in the Smoky Mountains. A rain suit with hood is essential for the trip. A well-sealed tent is a necessity. Daytime temperatures are in the 60s with nighttime lows in the 30s.

You carry about forty pounds in your backpack: personal gear and a portion of the group's food and camping equipment. Although the route is not difficult or strenuous, you should be in good physical shape to enjoy it.

Tour operators:

American Wilderness
    Experience

Sierra Club Outings

South America

ARGENTINA/CHILE

Patagonia and Torres del Paine National Park

Transportation: motor vehicle/hiking
Accommodations: hotels/lodges/tents
Land cost: $1,595-$2,725
Duration: 10 to 19 days
Seasons: October to March

Situated at the extreme southern end of the Chilean Patagonia, just north of the Strait of Magellan, the Torres del Paine (Towers of Paine) is hundreds of square miles of lakes, rivers, rolling pampas, beech forest, ragged peaks, glaciers, and spires of black/grey slate —the *cuernos*, or horns, unique to this World Heritage Park.

On a hike through the park's mountains you visit Milodon Cave, where bones of a prehistoric ground sloth were found in 1895. You camp along lakes, hike to a glacier, and pass through the habitats of rheas (South American ostrich), flamingos, black-neck swan, condors, parrots, puma, and guanacos (see NOT ORDINARY TRIPS: South America/ Chile).

Horses carry the camping equipment and your gear, except when you hump it all over the 4,000-foot-high Gardner Pass and meet the horses two days later on the other side. The trek is moderate on trails not particularly rugged or difficult—just demanding. Weather is your main adversary. Wind and rain are the norm, although December and February (summertime) can be delightful. Daytime temperatures are commonly in the 70s—and daylight lasts eighteen hours during the summer months.

For ten days you circumnavigate peaks topped in height only by the highest in the Himalayas. Daily hikes average four to five hours, the longest being eleven hours to Grey Glacier in the heart of the Paine Range. On that day you walk along the ridge above Grey Lake at the foot of the glacier, then down through a beech forest to the lake. There you get the first view of the impressive glacier, which comes down from the huge Patagonian Ice cap. Icebergs that calved from the glacier's face float in the lake.

Completing the trek, you drive to Laguna Azul opposite the vast cirque beneath the actual Torres del Paine, a group of three vertical granite towers among the mass of lesser mountains. You are on your way to Argentina's Los Glaciares National Park (Glacier National Park), about 120 miles northeast, to hike among Argentina's Patagonian peaks. No air service operates between Chile and Argentina in the Patagonia region, so you go by van or bus.

On the ten-hour drive across the pampas (plains) over dirt roads you see buttes, bluffs, and open ranges resembling Wyoming. Flamingos, condors with 12-foot wingspans, rhea, and black jackrabbits live here. You stay overnight at the resort town of Calafate on the shore of Lago Argentino, the second largest lake in South America.

A morning's drive from Calafate takes you to Moreno Glacier. The 3-mile-wide Moreno is one of the few glaciers in the world that is still growing—at the rate of eighteen centimeters per day. Columns of ice over twenty stories high drop off the glacier's face into the lake with a resounding boom. A trail through evergreen and lengua forest (temperate forest of moss-covered trees) along the lakeshore leads to a prominent point from which you can see the entire glacier.

In Los Glaciares National Park proper, a long day hike through beech forest takes you to the base camp of Fitzroy Mountain (11,072 feet). From the camp, you hike 1,300 feet up to Laguna de Los Tres, a triangular lake reflecting Fitzroy and a glacier.

The final hike takes you to the slender obelisk of Cerro Torre (10,280 feet), where you pitch tents for the night. The overhanging mushroom of ice on top of the vertical pinnacle makes Cerro Torre particularly impressive.

A seven-hour drive along the Atlantic Coast takes you to Rio Gallegos where you catch a flight to Buenos Aires.

For more information on Patagonia, see COMFORTABLE WILDERNESS: South America/Argentina.

Tour operators:

Above the Clouds Trekking	REI Adventures
Exodus Adventure	Sierra Club Outings
Ibex Expeditions	Turtle Tours
International Expeditions	Wilderness Travel
Journeys International	Wildland Adventures
Lost World Adventures	World Expeditions
Mountain Travel/Sobek Expeditions	

BRAZIL

Transportation: motor vehicle/boat/hiking
Accommodations: lodges/riverboat/tents
Land cost: $1,795-$2,395
Duration: 14 to 16 days
Seasons: year-round

When the Portuguese came to Brazil in the 1500s, the vast mountain range paralleling the South Atlantic Ocean coastline from Rio Grande do Norte to Rio Grande do Sul was one of the Earth's richest ecosystems. Today, only about 5 percent of the original Atlantic coastal rain forest remains.

Still, Brazil has one-third of the planet's remaining rain forests, containing some of the world's greatest biodiversity and the highest level of endangered species: 40 percent of the endangered mammals, 50 percent of the endangered birds, and 55 percent of the endangered plants are found nowhere else on earth. But, a chunk of Brazilian wildlife habitat two-and-a-half times the size of Portugal will be lost by the year 2000, according to the 1978 United Nations State of Knowledge report.

Visits to Superagui National Park, Guaraquecaba Ecological Station, and the Pantanal and the Brazilian Amazon give you an appreciation of the rain forest's biological wealth. One-fifth of all the birds and plants on Earth evolved in the Amazon Basin. According to the National Academy of Science, a typical 4-

square-mile patch of rain forest contains as many as 1,500 species of flowering plants, 750 species of trees, 125 mammal species, 400 bird species, 100 reptile species, 60 amphibian species, and 150 different species of butterflies.

The Superagui National Park and the Guaraquecaba Ecological Station are in the Lagunar Estuary, which spans the northern coastline of Parana State, about two hundred miles south of Sao Paulo. From Curitiba, the capital of Parana, you take a bus to the village of Guaraquecaba on the shore of Paranagua Bay. After a short bus ride from the village, you hike two hours to the base of the 240-foot-high Marato Waterfalls.

On the boat ride to Superagui Island you poke around in mangrove swamps, home to some important Brazilian plant species and aquatic birds, including egrets, great blue herons, and spoonbills. The following day you visit Pinheiros Island, best known for its thousands of parrots.

You travel by boat through the coastal mangrove swamps on the fringes of Paranagua Bay. This estuarial complex of shoals and over three hundred islands covered by rain forest and marshland is called "The Atlantic Ocean's Nursery." Plants and animals already becoming extinct in other places are perpetuated in this ecosystem, considered the third most important in the world.

Biologists and ecologists from the research station explain the ecosystem and the work being done to preserve it.

Every tour goes to Iguazu Falls. Iguacu means "great water" in the Guarani Indian language. Over 2.5 miles wide, the waterfall divides into 275 cascades on its 260-foot drop. You hike the Macuco Trail into the canyon of the Lower Iguassu River.

For three days you hike the jungle around the Iguacu Falls viewing monkeys, sloths, woodpeckers, toucans, hummingbirds, tapir, caimans (alligator), and butterflies.

On a visit to the Xavante Reserve, home of the Xavante tribe, the Indians invite you to share their daily life. Approximately five thousand Xavante live in roughly thirty-five villages spread throughout the savanna region of the southern Amazon. The population of indigenous people inhabiting the Brazilian rain forest is steadily and drastically declining. In 1500, an estimated six to nine million native peoples lived in the rain forest. Today, less than two hundred thousand of the people survive, according to Catherine Caufield in her book, *In the Rainforest* (University of Chicago Press, 1984).

About half of the estimated original 230 tribes have been completely destroyed. The greatest threat to Brazil's tribal people, most of whom live in the Amazon rain forest, is the invasion of their territory by ranchers, miners, land speculators, and others, reports Caufield.

On the Xavante trip, arranged by Mountain Travel/Sobek Expeditions in partnership with the Rainforest Action Network, you stay in Xavante-style huts, sleep in hammocks, and share food prepared by the villagers. The men take you fishing. The women show you how to weave a basket or a straw mat. You work in their gardens for a firsthand experience with the Indians' organic agricultural methods. At night you sit with the villagers listening to stories of the tribe's oral history. Storytellers recount the creation and spiritual legends. The stories and parables contian practical living information representing generations of learned wisdom of how to be in the world. You dance and sing in their traditional ceremonies, which is like performing theology.

You visit to some of the tribe's sacred places, including hidden caves around Lake UU. On jungle hikes the Xavante show you medicinal herbs and how they are used in the tribe's healing system.

Slash-and-burn agricultural practices are often cited as the culprit in the deforestation of the Amazon. But between 1966 and 1975 large-scale cattle ranching caused 38 percent of the deforestation in the Brazilan Amazon; agriculture caused 31 percent; and highway construction caused 27 percent, according to Brazilian government figures. The government gave fiscal incentives to 90 percent of the ranchers. More than half of the clearing for agriculture was done under government-sponsored programs, points out Caufield.

Brazil has a foreign debt of $108 billion and must pay out a sizable portion of its gross national profit in interest payments. Converting the Amazon rain forest into quick cash through agribusiness, mining, and other export-oriented business is a national priority in order to reduce the huge debt.

Seventy percent of all plants having anticancer properties grow in the rain forests, according to the National Cancer Institute. Drugs used to treat childhood leukemia, Hodgkin's disease, hypertension, arthritis, and heart ailments come from rain forest plants. Much modern surgery depends on curare, a derivative of a South American tree bark used to relax skeletal muscles. Curare cannot be chemically synthesized in the laboratory. Fewer than one percent of tropical forest species have been examined for their possible chemical compounds, yet fifty million acres of rain forest—a chunk the size of England, Wales, and Scotland combined—are being destroyed annually, according to the National Academy of Science.

An estimated fifteen hundred square miles of Brazil's coastal rain forest is cleared every year for agriculture and development. Rain forest soils excel at supporting indigenous flora and fauna, but fail miserably as a base for cattle forage or imported crops. Four-fifths of the nutrients in the rain forests are in the vegetation. The soil is nutrient-poor and becomes eroded and unproductive within a few years after the rain forest is cleared.

After the Xavante visit, you fly to Mato Grosso and travel the rain forest by land and river. You stay at the Floresta Amazonia Hotel. For more information on the Mato Grosso, Pantanal and other sections of Brazil see COMFORTABLE WILDERNESS: South America/Brazil.

Tour operators:

Journeys International
Mountain Travel/Sobek
    Expeditions
REI Adventures

Safaricentre
Turtle Tours
Wildland Adventures

ECUADOR

Transportation: motor vehicle/dugout canoe/hiking
Accommodations: hotels/inns/lodges/tents
Land cost: $1,295-$2,990
Duration: 7 to 22 days
Seasons: year-round

Treks in Ecuador go through the country's three distinct regions: mountains, highland valleys, and lowland jungles.

You hike the Cordillera Occidental, one of two parallel mountain ranges of thirty volcanic peaks that run north and south for over two hundred miles. In the highland valleys, you walk from village to village in sight of snowcapped volcanoes. The hike ends in Oriente, with the green Amazon jungle rolling eastward away from the Andean slopes.

All tours start in Quito, the country's capital (elevation 9,000 feet). Treks from Quito go either north to the Mount Cayambe region or south along the Andes' backbone to the 19,347-foot Cotopaxi, the highest active volcano in the world. You can hike the mountains in segments north and south or do a loop that links Mount Cayambe and Cotopaxi. Separate trips go farther south to Mount Sangay in Sangay National Park.

Starting northward, the tours go to the Indian market town of Otavalo, famous for its weavings. A day or two in the region allows time for acclimatization before setting off on a three-hour hike in the Cotacachi-Caypas Ecological Reserve around Lake Cuicocha. The lake lies 10,500 feet up in the crater of an extinct volcano. From there you can see the glaciers on Mount Cayambe (19,100 feet) and the Antisana volcanoes, your next destination.

The real trek starts at the trailhead near the village of Papallacta. There you meet the camp staff and the Indian *arrieros* (wranglers) with their pack animals to carry the camping equipment, food, and your heavier personal gear. The rough trail goes up nearly five miles past a 4-mile-long lava field to your first campsite near Volcano Lake. For the next couple of days you hike the Antisana Plains. You walk down into valleys of terraced fields and then back up steadily climbing the foothills of the Sincho-lagua Volcano (16,055 feet).

Wildlife in these highlands consists mostly of birds: the Andean lapwing, short-eared owl, the rapturous carunculated caracara, and 126 species of hummingbirds. You have a good chance of spotting the world's largest flying bird, the Andean condor.

You climb through the paramo zone. This highly specialized ecological zone is found only in the tropical Americas from 10 degrees north latitude in Costa Rica to 10 degrees south in Peru. Here you see unusual plants: much of the vegetation grows close to the ground and has fuzzy hairs or succulent-type leaves.

You circle south around Sincholagua through a boggy area of marshes and long, spiky pajonal grass, home to the rare Andean pudu (one of the smallest deer species in the world). The Andean wolf, actually a member of the fox family, also lives here.

Near Sincholagua you ascend the trek's highest pass at 14,335 feet. The trail continues along a ridge before descending toward the Pita River and the plains of the Cotopaxi National Park, south of Quito.

You hike an average of 6 miles a day carrying only a light day-pack. Rain resulting in muddy and slippery trails is to be expected, even in the driest months, January and February. You sleep in tents or shelters of the local Quechua Indians.

A variation of the Mount Cayambe trek slips off the highlands and down into the Amazon jungle. The trek begins at the Quechua Indian mountain village of Cochapamba. You hike high Andean paramo along lakes and bogs to the 13,530-foot-high Cordillera Real pass. From there you see the snow-covered Mount Cayambe and the sweep of the Amazon Basin thousands of feet below.

You hike down to the village of Oyacachi through a cloud forest, referred to by the local people as the "eyebrow of the Amazon," to the Chalpi Chico River. Here you enter the heart of the Amazon region where the Spanish sought the legendary gold of El Dorado. Dense tropical jungle replaces the stark alpine mountain landscape.

You cross rivers on suspension bridges or, secured by a guide rope, wade across them as you hike farther down into the rain forest. You cross one river suspended by a harness on a cable high above the water. When you reach El Chaco, site of a pumping station for the Transequatorian oil pipeline, a vehicle takes you back over the Andes to Quito.

South of Quito trekking routes go around Chimborazo (20,000 feet), an extinct volcano laden with glaciers. You drive several hours from Quito through cultivated valleys. Every bit of land is put under the plow. Fields roll over the crests of steep hills like a seamless carpet. Villages of white-washed houses appear to be thumbtacked to the hillsides. The countryside's postcard neatness belies the subsistence living level endured by the rural population.

On a four-day circumnavigation of the volcano you cross between the twin volcanic cones of Carihuayrazo and Chimborazo, traverse canyons, pass beneath glaciers, and view vast alpine sand deserts. In the Abruspungo Valley, you walk between high glaciers and the low green fields of the Central Valley. The hike ends in the mountain town of Riobamba.

Some tours take you on a climb up one of Chimborazo's fourteen glaciers that creep down in all directions from the volcano's five summits. The glacier climb starts with a three-hour hike along a trail used by the local people to collect ice from the glacier. When you get close to the snowfields, at about 12,500 feet in elevation, camp is pitched.

In the morning you climb 1,500 feet past cairns bedecked with ribbons. The guide explains the ribbons are tributes left to the Chimborazo deity by the Indians. At the glacier, the guide, an experienced mountaineer, instructs you on how to use an ice ax. Then he kicks a toehold in the ice and starts climbing across the river of snow. You are expected to follow. You climb around on the ice for several hours before returning to camp.

The next day you take a leisurely four-hour hike among Andean lakes and streams surrounded by glaciers and volcanoes to the Hans Meyer Glacier. The trail passes through high meadows of Indian paintbrush, purple lupine, and yellow bread-and-butter flowers mixed among the wiry paramo grass.

Once off the mountain you drive southeast to Sangay National Park, the largest wild area in Ecuador. You hike this ecological reserve for six days. The park extends from the 17,000-foot summits of five volcanoes down to 3,000 feet in the Palora and Upano river valleys. Horses carry the gear up to the base camp at 11,800 feet. The hiking is moderate, although the altitude—varying between 9,000 feet and 13,000 feet—can make you short of breath.

The transition from highlands to jungle starts at Banos, a small town along the Pastaza River with hot springs renowned for their healing power. The hot water is contained in cement bins, like swimming pools. Most of the bathers are local people.

You drive down the Pastaza River Canyon to Cabanas Alihuani on one of the most spectacular mountain roadways in the world. Cabanas Alihuani is a rustic-but-comfortable lodge on a bluff overlooking the Napo River. After a night's rest, you continue by vehicle through dense jungle to Misahualli, a frontier town at the end of the road. You transfer to a dugout canoe and go several hours downstream to Coca, an oil boomtown.

Tours go down the Coca River to Las Selva Lodge. For details see COMFORTABLE WILDERNESS: South America/Ecuador. Or you make a short overland trip to the Aguarico River and really get into the jungle. You paddle through dense jungle, camp along rivers, and stay in Indian villages on the four-day journey.

Despite its appearance, the jungle is not empty land. Cofanes, Secoyas, and Sinaos ethnic groups live along the rivers. Each group has distinct cultural traits, but they come from the same Tucano lineage. They also share a common struggle to preserve their way of life from the intrusion of oil companies pushing drilling rigs farther and farther into their jungle home.

The tribes actively, and occasionally violently, resist the invasion of their land. They formed the Confederation of Indian Nations of the Ecuadorean Amazon and petitioned the government to halt the oil drilling. However, the government granted the oil concessions in order to generate cash to help pay off the national debt.

The Indians then issued a formal written warning: "Beginning June 20th, 1989, with the participation of all the Federations, we will cut the boundary lines and topographically mark the Huaorani territory. We will defend its integrity at all costs."

The threat was backed up with action. A band of Tagairi Waorani killed the bishop of Napo Province and a Capuchin nun who tried to mediate between the tribe and the consortium of oil companies. Armed Waorani raided oil companies' camps and stole equipment. The warriors were dubbed "eco-guerillas" by oil company workers.

On the river trip along the Coca, Cofane guides lead you to the mouth of the Cuyabeno River. The river marks the territory of the Secoyas and Sinaos tribes.

At the Cuyabeno River you are entrusted to a Sinaos guide who leads you upriver to Lago Grande. You pitch tents on the shore and explore the jungle for two days. Howler, squirrel, tamarin, and titi monkeys jump from tree to tree. Toucans, macaws, and a variety of parrots perch on branches.

You leave the jungle via the Tarapoa River, which emerges at the Tarapoa oil fields. You rejoin the Coca River and arrive back in Coca.

A different jungle river trip is offered by Turtle Tours, which specializes in trips to peoples who live in very remote places. On this trip, you stay with families of the Shuar and Achuar tribes who live deep in the Amazon Oriente. The Oriente is a rugged and isolated jungle region that covers over half of Ecuador's land area.

The Shuar are infamous for their ritualistic headshrinking rites. They used human heads until twenty-five years ago; now they shrink monkey heads.

The Achuar and the Shuar are traditional enemies who raid each other's villages. The Shuar live in completely closed stock-ade-type houses. The Achuar live in houses with no walls. The housing reflects the tribes raiding styles. The Shuar make it known they are about to hunt and kill a particular Achuar. The

Achuar keep their plans a secret, which is why the prudent Shuar sleep behind thick wooden walls.

The trip starts in the highlands of the Cajas National Park, near Cuenca, one of Ecuador's most important colonial cities in the southern Andes. You go on foot or horseback to the Mazon Woods, a subtropical valley at 13,000 feet. On the two-day horse-back excursion you go along mountain slopes covered with thick paramo grass and camp at alpine lakes. You meander across streams and broad open slopes where herds of wild horses graze.

You leave the cool mountains and drive through torid heat for seven hours to the jungle frontier town of Macas. Here you catch a medical supply plane to Miazal, a village located in the foothills of the Cutucu Mountain Ridge. From Miazal the Amazon Basin stretches east 3,000 miles to the Atlantic Ocean.

A twenty-minute dugout canoe ride from Miazal down the Mangosiza River takes you to a jungle lodge. A two-hour walk farther into the jungle takes you to the home of a Shuar family. As you approach their house, your Shuar guide explains the proper greeting etiquette so you are not mistaken for an Achuar. Part of being a good guest is to accept *chicha*, a drink made from masti-cated and fermented yucca.

Your host prepares lunch, the main dish being manioc (yucca), a staple the Shuar grow in small plots hacked out of the jungle. Some type of meat—monkey or tapir—is also usually served. The man of the house shows you how to use his *bodaqueira*, the tradi-tional blowgun that he used to kill the meat. After lunch he takes you on a short tour of his jungle, explaining how he makes a living. With luck you may see a rare hoatzin, a bird with hooks on its wings. The hoatzin is considered a direct descendant of archaeopteryx, a flying dinosaur of the Jurassic period.

You travel by river for two days visiting Shuar families. You sleep in their houses on a typical bed of banana leaves or palm tree bark, or in a tent.

When you arrive at Wicimi, an Achuar village, the Shuar guide turns you over to the Achuar village headman and departs safely for home.

You meet an important shaman during your two-day visit with the Achuar. He explains, through an interpreter, some of the Achuars' beliefs and customs. The men show you how to catch fish with a barbasco root. The root is pounded to release its sap which is thrown into the river. The sap contains a substance that temporarily removes all oxygen from the water in the immediate area. Soon suffocated fish float to the surface and are gathered for dinner.

Tour operators:

Exodus Adventure

Ibex Expeditions

Inca Floats

Innerasia Expeditions

Journeys International

Mountain Travel/Sobek
Expeditions

Safaricentre

Turtle Tours

Wilderness Travel

PERU

Transportation: motor vehicle/dugout canoe/hiking

Accommodations: hotels/lodges/tents

Land cost: $1,495-$2,590

Duration: 12 to 15 days

Seasons: year-round

In the selva, the Amazon lowland basin three-fourths the size of the United States, live over 400 species of birds, 4,000 species of butterflies, 20,000 species of moths, over 2,000 kinds of fish, 60 species of reptiles, and 15,000 species of identified plants. In that type of crowd almost anything can happen.

Peru hiking and camping trips go to the Manu National Park/ UNESCO biosphere reserve in southeastern Peru. The park is 4.5 million acres of pristine cloud and rain forests along the Andes' eastern watershed. Manu shelters more life forms than any place on earth, with many of the plants and animals found nowhere else. Two tribes of uncontacted natives live within an area of the park closed to all visitors.

Manu represents the wildest, least disturbed section of the South American east slope cloud forest. This type of rain forest is found in a narrow band along the Andes running south from Colombia through Ecuador to Peru. Unfortunately, this uniquely species-rich belt is the first to be destroyed when people move into the highlands.

You reach Manu by two routes: a riverboat up from Iquitos, Peru's largest jungle city, or by crossing the Andes from Cuzco and traveling by dugout canoe down rivers to the national park.

On the Andes route, a four-wheel-drive vehicle takes you through high-altitude puna grasslands and over a 13,000-foot pass. The dirt road descends through a lush temperate cloud forest of cascading streams where the trees drip with mosses, bromeliads, and orchids. Spectacled bears, umbrella birds, quetzals, woolly monkeys, capybara, horned screamers, macaws, and caimans live here.

At the Alto Madre de Dios River, a tributary of the Amazon, you board a motorized canoe for a two-day trip down the Manu River. Along the way you see Machiguenga and Piro Indian villages on the banks of the river.

You pitch camp on sand beaches. The walk-in tents have zipped-in screens and folding tables and chairs. You sleep on mattresses that double as cushions in the canoes. Where the dark green Alto Madre de Dios River meets the cafe au lait-colored Manu River you start upriver into the Manu park.

Surprisingly, there are several choices of accommodations. Tours stay at the Amazonia Lodge or Blanquillo Lodge. The Blanquillo Lodge is near a "colpa," (macaw lick) where each morning hundreds of colorful, and noisy, birds gather to "lick" the clay found in the riverbanks. Minerals in the clay aid the birds' digestion and perhaps neutralizes toxins found in the seeds they eat.

Another type of accommodation found on the river journey is at Cocha Salvador. Floating platforms with a sleeping structure serve as your base camp for explorations on foot and by dugout canoe into the jungle. You go into riverine habitats, high forests, inundated woodlands, oxbow lakes, cane thickets, and groves of 21-foot-tall bamboo. Using ascenders to climb trees or hoisted up by pulleys, you "walk" the jungle canopy 60 feet above the ground. Most of the jungle wildlife lives in the canopy.

You paddle up to Cocha Ororango, a small oxbow lake, looking for hoatzins (prehistoric birds), giant river otters, the emperor tamarin, and howler monkeys. At night you take jungle walks in hopes of seeing nocturnal animals, such as the jaguar.

After three days in the deep jungle you backtrack up the Alto Madre de Dios River and emerge from the green ocean of jungle.

For more details on Manu and the Peruvian Amazon, see COMFORTABLE WILDERNESS: South America/Peru.

Another way to see the Amazon is by spending fourteen days floating on a log raft 700 nautical miles down the river. The raft is built of topa balsa, a very lightweight, strong, water-resistant wood similar to cork that is found in the forest of the upper Amazon. Eighty logs are needed to construct a 39-by-90-foot raft capable of carrying fifteen people. Forty logs form the first layer of the raft that rides on the water. Forty more logs are lashed horizontally on top with tambishi (a vine used as rope) and heavy wire. A floor of close-fitting, smooth, thick wooden planks is nailed across the second layer of logs.

The walls of the sleeping quarters are made of cana brava cane. A hallway leads to the kitchen area on the stern. Mud under the hand-made cookstove prevents the fire from burning the logs.

The washing area and men's and women's bathrooms hanging off the stern boast a real toilet seat and ample American toilet paper. A tablecloth serves as a door. A thatched roof of dried yarina palm fronds covers the raft, except for the 12-foot observation tower. Fifteen-foot oars of renaco wood propel and steer the raft.

When the trip is over, the raft is sold cheaply to local people for building material.

The raft is always called "Yuca Mama" after the legendary "Sea Monster Queen of the Amazon," an Amazonian monster said to abduct people and keep them in its watery lair.

The river trip starts with a small plane ride from Iquitos to

Tarapoto. Then you take a minibus over dirt road, or mud road depending on the day, to Chasuta on the Upper Amazon. During the float trip you stop at Bora, Huitoto, and Ticuan Indian villages. Jungle hikes with local guides and camping a couple of nights breaks the river journey. You drift into Brazil and eventually dock at Tefe for a return flight to Iquitos and on to Lima.

Writer and humorist Roy Blount Jr. took this trip and wrote a lively account of it in *Paths Less Traveled* (Atheneum, 1988).

Tour operators:

Amazonia Expeditions
American Wilderness
   Experience
Ecosummer Expeditions
Exodus Adventure
International Expeditions
Mountain Travel/Sobek
   Expeditions

Oceanic Society Expeditions
Outer Edge Expeditions
Safaricentre
Wilderness Travel
Wildland Adventures

VENEZUELA

Transportation: motor vehicle/dugout canoe/hiking/riverboat

Accommodations: hotel/lodges/tents

Land cost: $2,090-$2,690

Duration: 8 to 17 days

Seasons: year-round; December to April is best time; rainy season is June to October

The Gran Sabana is a land of savanna, marshland, and rain forest, and the home of Angel Falls (fifteen times higher than Niagara Falls) and *tepuis*. (*Tepui* is the Pemon Indian word for mountain.)

Tepuis are gigantic sandstone plateaus, former seabeds, towering 8,500 feet above the jungle. The flora and fauna on top of the tepuis are evolutionary throwbacks, or, more accurately, they never evolved—for example, a toad that cannot swim or hop. More than a hundred tepuis are scattered over 200,000 square miles of Venezuela. Nearly all have been visited, but less than half have been extensively explored.

The Gran Sabana, located in southeast Venezuela next to the Brazilian-Guyanan border, forms part of the world's third largest national park. On tours into the region you hike up tepui escarpments, go on river trips to the base of Angel Falls, and explore the Amazon abroad a thatched-roof riverboat.

A favorite tepui for hiking is Auyan-tepui (9,688 feet), from which Angel Falls tumbles 3,212 feet to the jungle. A ninety-minute flight in a light plane takes you from Ciudad Bolivar, on the banks of the Orinoco River, to the tiny Kamarata mission. Kavac Indian guides lead you on a several hour hike to their village near the Kavac Canyon, where you camp for the night. The next day you hike two and a half hours over rolling savanna and wade across rivers to Auyan-tepui's sheer 3,000-foot walls. You camp near the Indian settlement of Uruyen.

Three days are needed to climb to the summit of the Auyan-tepui. You hike four to five hours a day through swampy areas and up the escarpment. Steep, muddy trails lead through the steaming hot virgin jungle. Indian porters carry the heavier camping equipment and food. You carry a daypack with water. Being in good physical condition is essential to successfully complete the trek.

On the climb you see carnivorous plants, orchids, giant ferns, and balancing rock formations sculpted by wind and rain. You hike across an orchid-filled plain and camp in a huge cave.

Mount Roraima, called a land-locked Galapagos Island, is another tepui climb offered by some tours. You set out by jeep from Cuidad Bolivar through the Imataca Tropical Forest Preserve. The road goes through the Las Claritas gold and diamond mining area. On the second day you arrive at Paraitepui, a Tauepan Indian village, and start walking. You spend the next three days hiking to Mount Roraima's summit. You set up a base camp and explore for two days the Valley of Crystals, dwarf forests, and the Daliesque rock formations.

Hiking back to Kamarata, you load your gear into a 30-foot-long motorized "bongo," a dugout canoe, and travel by boat down the Akanan River to the Aiwana Meru River. Here you camp at the base of a waterfall. You ride the river for two days, passing occasional Indian settlements in the dense jungle. If the river is low, you help the guides pull the dugouts over Mayupa Rapids or portage the gear on a twenty-minute walk around the rapids. Macaws, toucans, otters, kingfishers, water snakes, and jaguar live along the banks of the river.

You pull ashore at Rantoncito Island on the Churun Meru River just below Angel Falls. A two-hour hike to Mirador, a small hill facing the falls, takes you to your next campsite. A day is spent exploring the jungle around the falls. Then you travel downstream in dugouts to Canaima and fly back to Cuidad Bolivar.

For more information on this region see COMFORTABLE WILDERNESS: South America/Venezuela.

On the western edge of the Gran Sabana, in the heart of the Venezuelan Amazon, stands the most remarkable tepui, Cerro Autana. The tepui looks like a giant tree trunk towering above the jungle. In local Piarao mythology the tepui is the ancestoral stump of all the fruit-bearing trees in the surrounding jungle.

Once up the tepui's steep 2,800-foot escarpment, you discover another 1,000 feet of jungle rising to the summit. A labyrinth of caves connected by interlocking galleries and enormous cathedral-like caverns of red quartz lies within the tepui.

Cerro Autana is 130 miles southeast of Puerto Ayacucho, capital of the Amazon Territory. The town is the departure point for an expedition through the Amazonas region along the Venezuela, Brazil, Colombia border to the south. You fly to San Carlos de Rio Negro and board the *Alexander von Humboldt*, a rustic thatched-roof riverboat. The 66-foot-long and 15-foot-wide vessel is named after the German scientist and explorer who, in 1800, discovered the link between the Orinoco River and the Rio Negro, the largest of the Amazon River's northern tributaries.

The boat is equipped with a shower, a toilet, and a kitchen. You sleep in hammocks slung on the open deck. You cruise the Rio Negro for three days. Small dugout canoes manned by the ship's Indian crew takes you on excursions close to shore for a detailed look at the river plants and animals. You stop at the small Indian settlement of Saint Lucia, near the Brazilian border, before arriving at Cocuy, a Brazilian garrison town.

At Cocuy, a guide takes you on a day hike to Cocuy Rock. The hike goes through a rain forest where parrots, macaws, and monkeys watch you from the canopy. You crawl through caves and use roots and vines to pull yourself up steep rock walls. The hot, sweaty, exhausting effort is well-rewarded by the commanding view of the surrounding jungle from the top.

You return to Puerto Ayacucho in a light plane.

Tour operators:

Exodus Adventure

Explore Worldwide

Journeys International

Lost World Adventures

Mountain Travel/Sobek
    Expeditions

Safaricentre

Wilderness Travel

Wildland Adventures

World Expeditions

PART II

Comfortable Wilderness

The organized tours in this section are designed for comfort, even luxury, while taking you into the wilderness. You do not carry gear, set up camps, prepare meals, or sleep on the ground. Physical demands are moderate. You may take a day hike carrying only a camera, spend a day in a four-wheel-drive vehicle bouncing across an African savanna, or paddle a canoe down a gentle jungle river.

This category includes safaris in Africa, cruises in Alaska, wildlife tours in Central and South America, and hikes and canoe trips in the United States.

Africa

BOTSWANA

Transportation: motor vehicle/canoe
Accommodations: hotels/lodges/luxury camping
Land cost: $2,400-$6,000
Duration: 14 to 21 days
Seasons: year-round

Botswana's smart. The country has two treasures: diamond mines and the land with its wildlife. The government said, "The mines are only going to be holes in the ground some day. But our father's-father's-land is a precious resource we can protect." So the national game park fees were increased by 1700 percent to help preserve the land and its inhabitants by keeping the tourist traffic down.

Botswana's wildlife is perhaps the richest in Africa. Leopards, elephants, lions, cheetahs, zebras, buffalo, hippos, giraffe, kudu, lechwe (swamp-dwelling antelope), and the sassaby (the swiftest of all antelope) are part of the country's wealth. All of these animals plus giant kingfishers, egrets, bee eaters, pygmy geese, saddle-billed storks, African fish eagles, and the rare Pel's fishing owl live in the Okavango Delta and the game parks.

However, it is unlikely that you will spot all of these animals. Sightings of the nocturnal leopard are very uncommon. Likewise, Pel's fishing owl, which lives in remote ebony groves in the heart of the delta, is considered rare, in part because it is rarely seen. The equally rare pangolin, an anteater whose small head is covered with large brown hairy scales, probably won't be spotted either. The local Africans believe the scales bring good luck in love. The pangolin has learned to be elusive.

But the large vertebrates—elephants, giraffe, buffalo—are easily observed, and the swamp-dwelling lechwe is often seen bounding through the water.

Most tours in Botswana follow the same route and include the Okavango Delta, the Moremi Wildlife Reserve, the Chobe National Park, and the Central Kalahari Game Reserve. The itinerary usually also includes a day fly-in to the Tsodilo Hills.

The Okavango River, which starts in the Angolan Highlands 650 miles to the northwest, creates the delta's thousands of islands, meandering oxbows, and lagoons. In its descent, the river swells to become one of the mightiest waterways in Africa, with a 100-yard-wide channel. One hundred and eighty miles from the mountains, the river turns away from the Atlantic Ocean and strikes out in the opposite direction across the Kalahari Desert toward the Indian Ocean 1,400 miles away. The river disappears in the desert.

During the annual July to August flood, the delta, which is surrounded by the Kalahari, encompasses more than 7,000 square miles. Even in the dry season (November to April) water covers the delta, although only a foot deep in places. Grass sticking above the water creates the illusion of boating across a meadow.

Tsodilo Hills, located west of the Okavango Delta, is one of the last places in Botswana where Bushmen are readily accessible. Bushmen have lived in the region for perhaps thirty thousand years, according to archaeological evidence. They explain to visitors the rock paintings, most over two thousand years old, that depict their people's history.

One thing the Bushmen do not sell is something to drink. Water is scarce, especially in East Africa, which suffers severe droughts. The Secretary-General of the United Nations warns that drought and its rippling consequences can pose an imminent threat of wide-scale starvation for people and wildlife.

All tours start in Maun on Botswana's northern border. You reach this very African town by small plane. A single asphalt strip along the river serves as the runway. A collection of round mud houses and a few stores along the one paved road make up the town.

From Maun, the tours head to the various base camps scattered in the delta. For the most part, all tour operators use the same established, very comfortable camps. Main camps, such as Tsaro Lodge and Xugana Lodge, are thatched chalets featuring bedrooms with twin beds, a sitting room, a private bathroom, and a private patio. The camps, situated on lagoons where animals congregate, are not fenced. Animals can, and do, come visit.

You tour the delta and the nearby game parks on foot and by open Land Rovers, *mokoros* (traditional hardwood dugout canoes), and motorized boats.

Chief Island, geographically larger than New York City, Shinde Island, and the Moremi Wildlife Reserve are the delta's main attractions. Shinde Island, buried in papyrus beds, is a perfect microcosm of Okavango, complete with its own plains, swamps, and groves.

The Moremi reserve, which encompasses 1,200 square miles, lies in the northeastern part of the delta and is bounded by the Khwai and Boro rivers. You cross a rickety wooden bridge to enter the reserve, the largest private game park in the world. The owners of the reserve, the Tawana tribe, established it in the 1960s when they realized hunters were wiping out the wildlife. Moremi is known for elephant-watching. When you go to places where elephants like to feed, you can approach within thirty feet and watch them wallow in the swamps.

From the base camps, excursions are made to smaller bush camps such as Machaba (which takes its name from the machaba tree, a sycamore fig) on the edge of the Khwai River and Jedibe, in the northern delta area. These camps have none of the discomforts associated with wilderness camping. The walk-in tents, which zip tightly to keep bugs out, have proper twin beds with sleeping bags, and adjoining bathrooms with hot showers and flush toilets. Meals, prepared by the cooks, are taken in the main dining tent or around the campfire. Some tour operators even provide fine china and a traditional English afternoon tea.

These smaller camps, often accessible only by boat or walking, conjure up the illusion of pre-colonial Africa, before the wilderness was neatly packaged. A reminder that there are forces greater than our own is perhaps the most important reason to visit the delta.

The field guides, often local men, are well-versed in interpreting the delta's various ecosystems, their interplay, and the intimate details of the animals' lives. They explain to visitors the natural mechanics of the place—how the ecological balance is maintained and how it is threatened.

The Okavango Delta, considered one of the most important wetlands in Africa, is at serious risk due to years of chemical spraying in an attempt to eliminate the destructive tsetse fly.

In general, however, overgrazing is Botswana's biggest environmental problem. Many conservationists blame the World Bank for this situation. The bank's policies strongly encourage exporting cattle for cash to pay off the country's debts. This strategy, according to critics, has resulted in environmentally unsound growth in the livestock industry.

The plan to dredge 25 miles of the Boro River, one of the delta's main channels, poses another ecological threat. The government wants to increase the water supply to Maun and to a diamond mine in Orapa, 160 miles away. The project would increase water outflow from the delta by fifty million cubic meters per year. Local people oppose the project because a similar effort years ago resulted in serious silting of the Boro River. Conservationists sounded an international alarm about the plan, so it is currently on hold while the World Conservation Union completes an evaluation.

The government of Botswana did not sign the 1970 Ramsar Convention, one of the first international agreements dealing with environmental problems in wetlands such as the Okavango Delta. More than fifty countries signed the convention, which covers 470 wetlands worldwide. That number, however, is only 3 percent of the world's wetlands. The World Wildlife Fund estimates that least twenty of the sites not covered by the convention are endangered.

To protect the delta, environmentalists in Botswana started the Tshomolero Okavango Conservation Fund to educate people about the importance of protecting the local wild animals and conserving their habitats.

The Chobe National Park and the Central Kalahari Game Reserve are other major tour stops.

The Chobe National Park, in northeast Botswana near the Zimbabwe, Namibia, and Zambia borders, has four main divisions. Two of these sections, Serondela in the northeast and Savuti in the southwest, are included in nearly all tours to the region. The Serondela region is renowned for large elephant herds. Approximately 67,000 elephants roam freely, the largest concentration in Africa. A great elephant-watching site is the Chobe River, either from the banks or by canoe. The park is also a sanctuary for lions, leopards, cheetahs, jackals, and bird life.

Botswanan elephants are bigger than most other African elephants. Bulls carry tusks weighing perhaps seventy pounds each. Botswana is the last true sanctuary of the African elephant, because they are not hunted, poached, or culled.

The African elephant is a fading species. Two million elephants roamed the continent twenty years ago; today about

600,000 remain. Decreasing habitat and poaching account for much of this drastic decline. Most countries have banned the import of ivory from elephant tusks, but, unfortunately, the trade continues.

Although Botswana protects its elephants, it has not, along with Zimbabwe, Zambia, Malawi, and Namibia, agreed to the ivory ban. The only other countries opposing the ban have elephant overpopulation problems that have serious economic ramifications for agriculture since elephants destroy crops. These countries formed the Southern African Centre for Ivory Marketing to allow sales of ivory in a monitored way.

The Savuti region is known for lions. They prey on herds of giraffe, zebra, buffalo, and roan antelope. Leopards, cheetahs, spotted hyenas, and black-backed jackals are also seen hunting across the arid, sandy landscape of mopane forests, acacia savanna, and rocky outcrops.

April to October, the dry season, is the best time for game viewing because the animals stay close to their water supply. Another prime time is from March to May, when Burchell's zebra migrate back into the region.

In the 21,000-square-mile Central Kalahari Game Reserve, Deception Valley, an ancient riverbed that still carries water, is one possible campsite for your group. The riverbed ecosystem supports a wide diversity of flora and fauna, including lions, leopards, brown hyenas, giraffe, wildebeest, bat-eared foxes, and eagles. Springbok and gemsbok graze on the low-slung acacia trees dotting the dunes. The delicate balance maintained in the desert environment is more impressive than the quantity of the wildlife. The rainy season, from December to April, is the best time to view game. May and June are also good months.

The Botswanan safaris, limited to eight to sixteen people, require no physical preparation or special gear. Binoculars, insect repellent, and a warm jacket or sweater for the chilly mornings and evenings are recommended. As health precautions, antimalarial tablets and yellow fever vaccinations are recommended before departure.

Tour operators:

Abercrombie & Kent
   International
Africa Adventure Company
Africatours
Cheesemans' Ecology Safaris
Exodus Adventure
Explore Worldwide
Forum
Geo Expeditions
Guerba Tours and Safaris
Hemingway Safaris
Journeys International
Ker & Downey Safaris
Mountain Travel/Sobek
   Expeditions
Nature Expeditions
   International

Overseas Adventure Travel
Questers Worldwide Nature
   Tours
Safaricentre
Special Interest Tours & Travel
Sue's Safaris
Tamu Safaris
Trek Africa
Voyagers International
Wanderlust Adventures
Wilderness Safaris
Wilderness Travel
Wildland Adventures
World Wildlife Fund
   Explorations
Zegrahm Expeditions

KENYA/TANZANIA

Transportation: motor vehicle
Accommodations: hotels/lodges/luxury camping
Land cost: $3,200-$4,800
Duration: 14 to 21 days
Seasons: year-round

On a circuit that loops through Kenya and Tanzania, tour operators string together the crown jewels of the East African game parks—Masai Mara, Serengeti, Ngorongoro, Tsavo, and Amboseli. Several smaller parks and private game reserves, such as Kenya's Samburu Game Reserve and the Ol Pejeta Ranch, also may be on the itinerary.

All tours start in Nairobi (originally N'erobi, a Masai word for "place of cold waters"). The Nairobi National Park, only minutes from the city's center, can give visitors a wonderful introduction to the wild animals of East Africa. However, many tour operators often overlook the park in the rush to embark on a grand safari.

From Nairobi tours head south across Kenya's highlands and then drop down the east face of the Rift Valley, a 3,500-mile cleft in the earth's crust stretching from the Red Sea south to Mozambique. The first stop on the tours is often the 1,235-square-mile Amboseli National Park, including the surrounding game reserve, near the Tanzanian border.

Amboseli is dry and dusty most of the year, which makes bouncing across the rolling brown plains in a Land Rover hot-and-dirty fun. The safari takes you to the water holes where wildlife congregate. Most of East Africa's birds and large mammals, especially rhinoceros and elephants, can be easily observed in Amboseli.

People and animals crowd into the 146-square-mile park proper, a popular day-trip destination for tours flying in from Mombasa on the Indian Ocean coast. In between breaks at one of the park's three lodges, the day-trippers rush about searching for animals. Good tour operators take you away from the crowd. But even good tours do not penetrate the park's inhospitable far reaches, where nomadic tribes live as their ancestors did.

In the center of the park, springs and swamps, fed by underground runoff from Mount Kilimanjaro 30 miles away, create an oasis of grasslands and acacia woodlands. At the Enkongo Narok Swamp striking photos of elephants can be taken with Kilimanjaro providing a dramatic backdrop.

In Kenya's southeast corner near the Tanzanian border, huge bull elephants roam the 8,000-square-mile Tsavo National Park. A 14-foot-high elephant standing along the road spraying itself with red dust is not an unusual sight.

A two-lane asphalt road connecting Mombasa to Nairobi divides the park into East and West Tsavo. Tours largely ignore East Tsavo since not many animals live there. In West Tsavo a favorite attraction is Mzima Springs, where crocodiles and hippos can be watched in their natural environment from an underwater observation tank. It is a bit like a zoo exhibit perhaps, but preferable to sitting on the bottom of a river at risk of being eaten or trampled.

Kenya's most famous game park, the Masai Mara National Reserve, is a few hours' drive west of Tsavo in Masailand, home range of the Masai tribe. The local Masai council, which controls the reserve, collects fees from tourists to distribute to local tribespeople. Being able to directly contribute to local economies is a big selling point of eco-tourism.

The tall and stately Masai consider themselves the nobles of the plains. These nomadic herdsmen count their wealth in heads of cattle, a readily available food source. They shun agricultural work as being below their status.

Masai tribesmen often visit tourist campsites at the edge of the reserve. They may perform traditional dances or come by just to meet foreigners. Some tours stop at Masai villages, which are made up of houses constructed with mud and cow dung over wooden frames, technologically and environmentally appropriate building materials.

Against the southern edge of Masai Mara lies Tanzania's 5,700-square-mile Serengeti National Park, Africa's finest natural animal sanctuary. The park is well regarded for its abundance of lions, cheetahs, and leopards. Representatives of virtually all of East Africa's main animal species live on the rolling grasslands and in the woodlands of the park, which is larger than the state of Connecticut.

You spend days driving across the plains photographing herds of wildebeest, elands, and Thompson and Grant gazelle. Grazing zebra take little notice of you, but lions grab their attention.

Zebra' stripes are their best defense against a lion attack. When a lion rushes a herd, the zebra frantically dash in all directions. The herd becomes a confusing blur of black and white, making it difficult for the lion to target one zebra against the constantly moving backdrop.

The Serengeti (which means "endless plains" in Masai) offers two distinct game-viewing experiences. Large herds of grazing animals with nowhere to hide speckle the vast, open plain of the southern Serengeti. Viewing them is not unlike being in a huge drive-in theater. In the northern woodlands, you bushwack through scrub and jostle in and out of gullies trying to spot the elephants and buffalo hiding among the trees.

The mass migration of millions of wildebeest north to Masai Mara is the Serengeti's grandest spectacle. The herds start moving after the May/June rains and reach Masai Mara by the end of July. In December the wildebeest migrate back to the Serengeti.

South of the Serengeti lies the Ngorongoro Crater, a caldera of wildlife. The crater's floor, a 10-mile-wide grassland 2,000 feet below the rim, is a natural amphitheater where lions, rhino, giraffe, buffalo, cheetahs, zebra, and the occasional leopard roam freely, yet are contained. Nearly every large vertebrate in East Africa and the lesser ones—gazelle, antelope, wildebeest, and warthogs—live in the Ngorongoro. A soda lake attracts a wide variety of bird life, including flamingos, crested cranes, and ostriches.

A thick canopy of lichen-draped tropical forest covers the crater's often mist-shrouded rim. The plants and animals found on the rim differ from those found 7,600 feet below on the crater floor.

The Olduvai Gorge (the Masai name for "bayonet aloe" or "bowstring hemp") lies between the Ngorongoro and the Serengeti. It was in the gorge that in 1959 anthropologists Mary and Louis Leakey discovered skull shards of the 1.75-million-year-old "Nutcracker Man." In the early Pleistocene era, perhaps three million years ago, this species emerged from the central Africa forest and began to hunt on the plains. East of Olduvai stands the largest complex of volcanic craters in the world, extinct for eight million years.

In the hot, semidesert of the Samburu Game Reserve, located in Kenya's Northern Frontier District, animals stay close to the ribbon of green vegetation that grows along the muddy, crocodile-infested Ewaso N'giro River. Doum palms, acacia trees, conical hills, and stark rock outcroppings create a dramatic setting. The great rock mountains "ol donyo Sabaachi" and "Wharguess" shimmer in the blue haze. Snowcapped Mount Kenya looms in the distance.

Somali ostriches, red-billed buffalo weavers, and Abyssinian rollers add flashes of color to the 40-square-mile reserve, which is well known for its large population of birds. Kingfishers spear dinner in the river. Brightly colored weavers and starlings perch in the acacia trees. Spurfowl and francolin forage in the underbrush. Eagles, kites, and vultures wheel high overhead.

Distinctly northern animal species not found in the southern game parks live in Samburu: reticulated giraffe, Grevy's zebra, long-necked gerenuk antelope, dik-diks, and Beisa oryx.

The tours also go to game parks centered around lakes. Lake Baringo, in the northern end of the Rift Valley, is home to over three hundred bird species. Migrating pink flamingos make the lake a rest stop. The hot and dusty region, inhabited by the Samburu, Rendille, Turnkana, and Kalenjin nomadic tribes, is off the more populous tourist track.

Kenya's Lake Nakuru National Park is famous for its huge flocks, up to two million, of pink flamingos. Pelicans and hundreds of other bird species nest here. Big game, such as the Rothschild giraffe, use the lake as a watering hole.

Birds and crocodiles are the big attraction at Kenya's Lake Naivasha near the Ethiopian border. The huge lake, half the size of England, is the most highly concentrated crocodile breeding ground in Africa. You can rent a boat and row out to Crescent Island, home to the Goliath heron, the grey heron, and more than three hundred other species of birds. Hippos live in the lake. In the evenings, antelope and monkeys come to the shore for a drink.

One of Africa's most beautiful little parks is Tanzania's Lake Manyara National Park. Consisting of a thin strip of land sandwiched between the lakeshore and the Rift Valley's wooded west escarpment, the park has thick forest, marshes, and rough scrub. Each habitat provides shelter for many different types of animals:

tree-climbing lions, elephants, buffalo, kudu, and aquatic bird species, all easily spotted.

Tour accommodations include top-flight lodges—such as the Mount Kenya Safari Club. Many of the lodges feature a swimming pool. Some lodges, such as Treetops and the Mountain Lodge, have wooden platforms overlooking floodlit water holes for night viewing of animals.

Bush camps, set up by the tours' staff after a hot day of game watching, consist of spacious walk-in tents with mattresses on the twin camping beds, private showers, and toilets. Sewn-in ground-sheets and mosquito netting make the tents water- and insect-proof. Some tours even offer free laundry service in their bush camps.

Meals at the lodges equal those found at fine hotels. In the bush camps, cooks prepare a variety of meals ranging from a traditional English breakfast to four-course dinners served with chilled drinks.

Minibuses or four-wheel-drive Land Rovers with photography hatches ferry you around the parks. Only six passengers per vehicle guarantees everyone gets a window seat.

According to David Western, a Tanzanian-born conservationist, one of the biggest threats to Kenya's wildlife concerns "the future of the land around the national parks."

Quoted in an article by Graham Boynton in *Conde Nast Traveller* (August, 1991), Western says, "My concern is that unless the right thing is done to convince landowners to keep their lands open to wildlife, the parks will become a very small part of the ecosystem that the animals need to survive. The amount and variety of land will decline precipitously, the parks will become mega-zoos, and the tourist industry will collapse because the parks will have lost their appeal as unspoiled wilderness."

Overpopulation of some species in an area, caused by encroaching agricultural development that limits their range, is also a serious concern. The elephants in Amboseli National Park have nearly stripped the place of trees. Elephants venturing into neighboring farmland cause serious damage, one reason farmers resist Western's call for more open land.

Tourists are also becoming a problem for the wild animals in the game parks. There is concern that the sheer number of safari vehicles intruding on the animals' space is affecting their hunting ability and causing stress. Lions, a favorite photo subject, are incessantly harassed. Camera-toting tourists trail after cheetahs because the cat's daytime hunts provide live-action drama. But the presence of the tourists limits the cheetahs' ability to hunt effectively and to teach hunting skills to their young. Practicing good eco-tourism would alleviate much of the stress on animals caused by humans. Observe the animals from twenty or thirty feet away so they do not feel crowded. If other safari groups arrive, be the first to leave. You will have plenty of opportunities to see animals going about their business in the wild.

Tour operators:

Abercrombie & Kent International
Africa Adventure Company
Africatours
Explore Worldwide
Forum
Foxglove Safaris
Geo Expeditions
Guerba Tours and Safaris
Himalayan Travel
International Expeditions
Joseph Van Os Nature Tours
Journeys International
Ker & Downey Safaris
Kimbla
Luxury Adventure Safari
Nature Expeditions International
Overseas Adventure Travel

Questers Worldwide Nature Tours
Safaricentre
Sierra Club Outings
Siria Tented Safaris
Special Interest Tours & Travel
Sue's Safaris
Trek Africa
Tusker Trail & Safari
Voyagers International
Wanderlust Adventures
Wilderness Safaris
Wilderness Travel
Wildland Adventures
WomanTrek (women only)
World Expeditions
World Wildlife Fund Explorations

NAMIBIA

Transportation: motor vehicle
Accommodations: hotels/lodges/luxury camping
Land cost: $1,700-$4,000
Duration: 12 to 21 days
Seasons: year-round

Namibia, located between the Kalahari Desert and the Namib Desert, has a population of little more than one million in an area four times the size of the United Kingdom. Wild animals nearly outnumber the people.

Tours start in the capital, Windhoek ("windy corner"), the location of the country's only international airport. The Etosha National Park, in northern Namibia, is usually the first tour stop. The huge Etosha Pan, the bottom of a shallow lake that dried and left a white, alkaline residue, covers nearly a quarter of the 8,600-square-mile park. Etosha literally means "huge white area." Grassland, shrub, mopane savanna, and dry woodland surround the pan.

The park's centerpiece is the 60-mile-wide Etosha Pan. Many animals "winter" around the slowly evaporating water holes and artesian springs. The first impression one gets of the pan is that it is a desolate, threadbare place, where the Earth's bones show through its dry, thin skin. But with time you will appreciate the pan's stark beauty and marvel at how many creatures live there.

Only the pan's southern edge is open to tourists. The remainder of the park is set aside as a conservation area. But the limited open area offers plenty to see. The diversity of mammalian species is equal to anywhere else on earth. Etosha boasts 325 animal species, including the endangered "black-faced" impala, black rhino, lions, leopards, cheetahs, and the greater kudu—antelope with large, corkscrew horns. Large elephant herds spend the dry season (our winter) in the central part of the park.

August and September are the best months to view elephants. When the rains come in October and November the herds migrate north to Angola and west to Kaokoland. They return to Etosha in March.

The Okaukuejo area, near the southwestern corner of the pan, attracts a typical variety of wildlife: red hartebeest, greater kudu, silver-back jackals, elephants, rhino, honey badgers, spotted hyena, and the gray duiker. Large herds of blue wildebeest, zebra, springbok, and gemsbok graze in the area from March to May.

Birds in the Halai region, on the southeast side of the Etosha Pan, include kori bustard, black korhaan (bustard), secretary bird, blue crane, double-banded courser, and swallow-tailed bee eater. Over three hundred species of birds stay on the Etosha Pan during the mid-January to March rainy season, including pelicans, flamingos, and marabou storks.

Etosha National Park receives less than sixteen inches of rainfall annually due to prevailing easterly continental winds and the cold Benguela current from Antarctica. However, the park is not entirely desert; extensive woodlands cover the eastern section. Greater kudu, giraffe, warthogs, "black-faced" impala, and Damara dik-diks, Africa's smallest antelope, are often found in the woodlands of the park's Namutoni region. The western section of Etosha contains arid grassy plains interspersed with acacia scrub.

Tours next stop at the 19,215-square-mile Namib-Naukluft National Park, one of the world's largest, on Namibia's South Atlantic coast. The park encompasses part of the world's oldest desert, the Namib (the Hottentot word for "Great Plains"). The park's widely diverse ecology includes granite mountains, an estuarine lagoon, quartz plains, desert, savanna, a river, a canyon, and huge drifting sand dunes.

Within the park is the Mountain Zebra Park, where the rare Hartmann's mountain zebra roams the hilly terrain. Mountain zebra are found also in the Hobatere Game Park, on the northwestern edge of Etosha National Park.

The rugged mountains of Damaraland harbor mountain zebra and black rhino. This infrequently traveled region has fascinating geological formations, such as a petrified forest dating back two hundred million years B.C. Thousands of ancient Hottentot petro-glyphs are well-preserved on the 8,400-foot-tall Brandberg Mountain, which covers an area 19 by 14 miles. The Ovahimba people, who make this isolated region their home, occasionally appear to look over the tourists. From May to December is the most comfortable time weather-wise to visit the region.

The Namib-Naukluft park borders the Skeleton Coast National Park. The Skeleton Coast was notorious for shipwrecks in the days of sailing vessels. In June and July a cold, rainy fog bank, which extends 60 miles inland, obscures the coast. The best time for sun is from December to February, but even then expect fog in the morning.

On the water's edge winds form the world's largest sand dune complex, with some dunes reaching one thousand feet in height. A variety of birds live their entire lives in the narrow band of beach and intertidal habitat. Approximately one hundred thousand Cape fur seals use this beach as a pupping area and seasonal haul-out location. The northern part of the coast is only accessible by plane. Another large seal colony lives to the north at Cape Frio.

You may occasionally see lions hunting seals, but large animals are sparse in this area of the park. Black rhino, desert elephants, baboons, and leopards do live in the park, but not in large numbers.

Animals are not the only interesting life in the Namib Desert. Plants have made remarkable adaptations to the harsh climate. The *Welwitschia mirabilis*, a modified tree named after its discov-erer, Austrian naturalist Fredrick Welwitsch, has a turnip-like stem that can be three feet thick but is only four feet high. On either side of the stem, two leaves, about the same width as the stem, split lengthwise, fraying into long ribbons. Some Wel-witschia plants are fifteen hundred years old.

One enjoyable aspect of touring Namibia's parks is not meet-ing many other tourists. It is not that tourists are scared off by arduous travel conditions in Namibia. The days searching for wildlife in Land Rovers are hot, often long, and usually dusty and tiring, but they are not overly demanding. The nights are spent in hotels and well-appointed lodges with comfortable beds, hot showers, and private bathrooms. The food is often cooking like you would find at home. Rather, unlike other popular tour destinations in Africa, Namibia simply has not yet been fully discovered.

It might not ever have been discovered but for the efforts of the South African conservationist Garth Owen-Smith. Namibian wildlife, the engine of the country's tourist industry, was nearly wiped out under the policies of the South African government, which governed the territory, then known as South West Africa, from 1945 until Namibia's independence in 1990. The guerilla war for independence further devastated the wildlife.

During its rule, the South African government designated the northwest region of Kaokoland, bordered on the west by the Skeleton Coast National Park, as a "homeland" for about eighteen thousand black people. This sudden population influx severely taxed the desert region's resources, so people resorted to killing the wild game for food.

The rhino and elephant populations were further reduced by illegal hunting to meet commercial demands for horn and ivory.

In 1982, Owen-Smith created a sustainable conservation program. The South African-based Endangered Wildlife Trust and the Save the African Endangered Wildlife Fund, based in the United States, gave assistance. Due to these conservation efforts, wildlife made a comeback and tourists began to trickle into the country. They brought in much-needed hard cash and took home a sensibility for a land of stark beauty that, somewhat surprisingly, has developed into one of Africa's premier game-viewing regions.

Tour operators:

Explore Worldwide

Forum

Guerba Tours and Safaris

Joseph Van Os Nature Tours

Journeys International

Mountain Travel/Sobek Expeditions

Overseas Adventure Travel

Questers Worldwide Nature Tours

Safaricentre   Tusker Trail & Safari
Special Interest Tours & Travel   Voyagers International
Sue's Safaris   Wilderness Safaris
Trek Africa   Wilderness Travel

ZAMBIA

Transportation: motor vehicle/raft/walking
Accommodations: hotels/lodges/luxury camping
Land cost: $1,200-$3,400
Duration: 10 to 17 days
Seasons: year-round

In Zambia, tourists in search of wildlife are encouraged to hike game trails through grasslands, woodlands, water meadows, and around lagoons in the 3,500-square-mile South Luangwa National Park. The highest concentration of wild animals outside the Serengeti Plain reputedly lives within this park, where elephants, leopards, rhino, giraffe, lions, impala, and four hundred bird species have their own favored habitats.

The sensation of being on foot in the open with wild animals is much different than approaching them in a vehicle. You are naked. You cannot outrun any of the animals. You cannot hide anywhere they will not find you. You are just another vulnerable animal. Suddenly, goodwill and a practicing belief in the live-and-let-live philosophy make a great deal of sense.

Armed guards and a naturalist accompany the walking tours, which take place from June to October when the foliage is thin enough to see animals lurking in the bush. The guards are chiefly for psychological support; the naturalist interprets the environment. The leisurely paced hikes allow ample time to observe the wildlife and to appreciate where you are.

Most tours follow the tree-lined Luangwa River and its tributaries, although individual tour operators have their own favorite routes. Life along the river is busy. A wide variety of bird life thrives, including the impressive crested crane, saddle- and yellow-billed storks, egrets, and vultures. Hippos sink in the river's lagoons, as if playing peekaboo.

The hikes cross the wide, flat plateau of the Luangwa Valley, an open woodland covered with coarse grasses, scrub, and herds of elephants, Cookson's wildebeest, zebra, and antelope.

Nights are spent in bush camps with thatched huts, beds, and hot showers. Laundry service is available. Meals are prepared by the staff. The camps serve as bases for morning and afternoon walks and are located near water holes for optimal game viewing. When walking from camp to camp your luggage is transported for you.

The tours usually include a canoe trip on the Zambezi River, to which elephants, hippos, and crocodiles lay rightful claim—they appear frequently to remind you of their rights. Herds of kudu, zebra, and eland sable graze on the floodplains bordering the river. Fish eagles, herons, and kingfishers are also common sights.

The raft trips are on the river below Victoria Falls, the usual beginning and ending point of the tours. You float down deep basalt gorges carved through ancient lava flows. A series of class five rapids—the biggest and baddest run-able white water—makes the river a thrill ride. One-day trips go from March to April and from mid-June to December. Longer trips, which entail camping on sandbars, run from July to December.

Water is a common theme for Zambian tours. At Lake Bangweulu you stay at the Shoebill Island Camp. The rare shoebill stork and fifteen thousand lechwe, semi-aquatic antelope, call this swampy area home. Resident biologists give guided walking tours through the Bangweulu Swamp for a firsthand look at the ecosystem.

The Kasanka National Park is a sanctuary for the endangered wattle crane, the martial eagle, and the sacred ibis, thanks to the efforts of David Lloyd, proprietor of the only national park in Zambia. His conservation efforts show just how much one individual can do to preserve and support wildlife.

Tour operators:

Abercrombie & Kent
    International
Africa Adventure Company
Forum
Guerba Tours and Safaris
Journeys International
Mountain Travel/Sobek
    Expeditions

Nature Expeditions
    International
Overseas Adventure Travel
Safaricentre
Trek Africa
Tusker Trail & Safari
Wilderness Travel

ZIMBABWE

Transportation: motor vehicle/canoe/raft
Accommodations: hotels/lodges/luxury camping
Land cost: $1,200-$3,300
Duration: 10 to 17 days
Seasons: year-round

Tours start at the mile-wide Mosi-oa-Tunya ("The Smoke that Thunders"), better known as Victoria Falls. From a wooden boardwalk meandering through the mist-drenched rain forest you get great views of the Zambezi River as it cascades 350 feet over the five cataracts of the horseshoe-shaped falls. The area around the falls, discovered for the outside world by David Livingstone in 1855, is spared from commercial blight.

You also take canoe and raft trips on the river. Several days are spent paddling through the Lower Zambezi National Park. One-day trips run in March and April and from mid-June to December. Longer trips, up to a week, are offered from July to December, when the water level is the highest and the rafting the most exciting. During June, July, and August be prepared for chilly weather. No experience is required to run the river; seasoned river guides do all the hard work. You need only to hang on tight and enjoy getting soaked while your heart is in your throat.

In the Kariba Gorge the current is calm, so you have ample

time to photograph the abundant wildlife, especially birds, along the shores.

The river carries you to the 956-square-mile Mana Pools National Park in the Middle Zambezi River valley. The park is considered one of Zimbabwe's finest for its abundance of wildlife and birds. The Mana Pools are lakes seasonally filled by overspill from the flood-swollen Zambezi. Hippos love the lakes, and elephants occasionally go for a swim. Extensive stands of large acacia albida trees and mixed woodlands harbor a varied bird life. The large floodplains along the river are pasturelands for 12,000 elephants, 16,000 buffalo, and herds of kudu, zebra, bushbucks, impala, lions, and leopards. The park is open from April to November.

The Hwange National Park, the country's premier game reserve, is an elephant refuge slightly larger than the state of Connecticut. Rhino are also abundant, so this is your best chance to spot the rare white rhino. The Deka River, a permanent water source, is the prime game-viewing spot. Four-wheel-drive vehicles take you across the open grasslands and through woodlands in search of kudu, zebra, eland, tassessebe, impala, warthogs, baboons, jackals and several species of monkey. Leopards and cheetahs are also found there, though these nocturnal cats are rarely seen.

The Mazuir Rhino Sanctuary is reputedly the best place in Africa to observe the black rhino. The Lowe family, owners of the 12,000-acre ranch, dedicated the land to saving this endangered animal. Approximately thirty black rhino live there.

At the sanctuary, naturalists accompany you on walks, or horseback rides, through the bush looking for wild animals. Special blinds at choice game-viewing sites nearly guarantee you will bring back impressive photos.

The 600-square-mile Matusadona National Park, on the shores of Lake Kariba, boasts a high concentration of rhino. Elephants and buffalo use the man-made lake as a watering hole. Drifting around the lake in a canoe through the tops of drowned trees is the best way to observe Goliath herons, fish eagles, and other bird life.

The Chizarira National Park, near Lake Kariba, is Zimbabwe's newest (opened in 1981) and most remote park. Not easily accessible, the park is sparingly visited, which is perhaps its greatest charm. Guided foot-safaris take you in close proximity of black rhino, elephants, buffalo, and lions.

Tour operators:

Abercrombie & Kent
    International
Africa Adventure Company
Africatours
Cheesemans' Ecology Safaris
Explore Worldwide
Forum
Great Expeditions
Guerba Tours and Safaris
International Expeditions
Joseph Van Os Nature Tours
Journeys International

Mountain Travel/Sobek
    Expeditions
Questers Worldwide Nature
    Tours
Safaricentre
Special Interest Tours & Travel
Trek Africa
Tusker Trail & Safari
Wanderlust Adventures
Wilderness Safaris
World Wildlife Fund
    Explorations

Asia

INDIA/NEPAL

Transportation: motor vehicle/train/canoe/elephant
Accommodations: hotels/lodges
Land cost: $1,400-$4,000
Duration: 10 to 17 days
Seasons: year-round, but best time is from mid-October to March

Tours to India and Nepal generally intertwine the cultural highlights and game parks of both countries. The India tours include Delhi; the Taj Mahal; Jaipur, the "Pink City of Rajasthan"; and several wild game parks and reserves. The Nepal tours, embarking from Kathmandu, start with visits to several holy temples and monasteries and then head into the mountains for a good look at

Mount Everest and Annapurna. The final leg of the trip goes down the Pokhara Valley to Nepal's Royal Chitwan Wildlife Reserve on India's border.

The Ranthambhore National Park and Tiger Reserve is India's most bounteous game park. There you look for tigers, leopards, sloth bears, chinkaras, and wild boars on a jeep ride through deciduous savanna forest in the Aravalli and Vindhyan hills, a four-hour drive from Jaipur. Pavilions and lakes dot the park, which is dominated by the hilltop Ranthambhore Fort. The number of tigers in the park has increased from fourteen to forty in the past twenty years as a result of strict preservation efforts. The tigers, accustomed to the presence of humans, are active during the day, and you will have excellent opportunities to view and photograph them.

Sariska Tiger Reserve and Wildlife Sanctuary, between Delhi and Jaipur, is a forest pocket in the Aravalli Mountain Range. Besides tigers, the reserve is noted for plains animals, especially the nilgai, the great sambar, chital, and wild boar. The Egyptian vulture and the crested serpent eagle nest in the cliffs. Overnight accommodations are provided at a hunting lodge constructed by the Maharaja of Alwar.

The total number of tigers, exclusively an Asian animal, has steadily declined from one hundred thousand at the turn of the century to perhaps no more than five thousand today. Loss of habitat and widespread hunting are the main reasons tigers are a disappearing species.

Wildlife expert Arjan Singh has been a one-man band working to save the tigers. He was instrumental in the creation of the Dudhwa National Park, another big cat haven.

The Dudhwa park is famous for its large herds of blue bull, India's largest antelope, as well as several varieties of deer and wild pigs. Rhino have been reintroduced to the park. Crocodiles, otters, pythons, and monitor lizards are plentiful in a river running through the park. The park's lakes attract over two hundred species of birds, including the swamp partridge and the Bengal florican.

Tigers are also found in the moist, deciduous forests of the Kanha National Park. However, the massive gaur, or Indian bison, is the park's most famous resident. This timid creature spends most of its days hidden in dense foliage. At dawn and dusk the gaur come out to feed in grassy meadows. The park's other notable animals are the blackbuck (an antelope with long, spiraled horns), the elusive dhole (a wild dog), the barasingha, and the sambar (a large deer sporting a mane and three-pointed antlers).

Keolodeo Ghana National Park and Bird Sanctuary, at Bharatpur, is considered the most beautiful freshwater marsh in India. Originally created as a duck-shooting preserve for the Maharaja of Bharatpur, the sanctuary has the largest concentration and variety of bird life in Asia.

You can walk along tree-lined levees and find nests of as many as ten different species in a single tree. Floating in the water are nests of jacanas and island nests of the sarus crane, India's tallest bird. Herons, storks, and the rare Siberian crane, only two hundred of which are believed to exist, also live in the park.

In Kaziranga National Park, a classic example of wetland savanna, you ride elephants through the morning mist searching for the one-horned Indian rhinoceros. Once close to extinction, one thousand of these prehistoric looking creatures with sculptured plate-like armor live in Kaziranga. The park's streams and marshes are home to gharials, smooth Indian otters, and river dolphins. Bird life includes thousands of blossom-headed parakeets and emerald-winged doves.

Corbett National Park and Tiger Reserve, near the Himalayan foothills, is usually the last stop before Nepal. The reserve hosts a healthy population of tigers and leopards. Marsh crocodile and gharial live along the river flowing through the park. Most tours stay in the famed Tree Tops Corbett Lodge.

The best time to visit northern India is from mid-October, when the monsoon season ends, until March. The high country gets cold in November. In February, when daytime temperatures warm up, many trips start before dawn to escape the full heat of day.

Nepal's 360-square-mile Royal Chitwan Wildlife Reserve is one of Asia's premier game parks. You ride elephants through tall grass looking for Bengal tigers and one-horned rhino. Although it is unlikely that a tiger will leap on you, the prospect adds an extra excitement to the adventure. The rhino will also avoid confrontation, unless they feel their young are in danger. If one does charge, watch its eyes. Rhino have extremely poor eyesight, but an excellent sense of smell. If the rhino is looking up as its snout nearly drags the ground, relax and get some great pictures. If the rhino is looking straight down at the ground, following its nose, then hope your elephant has the good sense to get out of its way.

Canoeing or rafting on the Rapti River in the reserve requires no experience and gives you an opportunity to see sloth bears, leopards, barking deer, wild boar, marsh mugger crocodiles, and over three hundred species of birds.

Tours to the Royal Chitwan National Park usually stay at the very comfortable Tiger Tops Jungle Lodge or the Tiger Tree Tops Tented Camp. Accommodations at the lodge are bedroom suites elevated well above the jungle floor with private bathrooms and solar-heated showers. The camp, in a clearing above the small Surung Khola (river) features twin beds in African-style safari tents with separate showers and toilets.

Tour operators:

Abercrombie & Kent
    International
Cheesemans' Ecology Safaris
Exodus Adventure
Explore Worldwide
Himalayan Travel
Innerasia Expeditions
International Expeditions
Mountain Travel/Sobek
    Expeditions

Overseas Adventure Travel
Questers Worldwide Nature
    Tours
Sierra Club Outings
Voyagers International
Wilderness Journeys
World Wildlife Fund
    Explorations

Central America

BELIZE

Transportation: motor vehicle/hiking/boat
Accommodations: hotels/guest houses/lodges
Land cost: $1,600-$2,200
Duration: 7 to 14 days
Seasons: year-round

Belize, the Mayan word for "muddy," is not brown but green. Forests cover 70 percent of the country, which is roughly the size of New Hampshire and has a population of less than two hundred thousand. Ninety percent of the 8,000-square-mile country has not been developed or planted, or even weeded. A largely unspoiled barrier reef—the second longest in the world after Australia's Great Barrier Reef—hugs the coast. Not surprisingly, Belize has become a popular destination for eco-tourists.

Belize's natural resources have been largely unexploited since pre-Columbian times. A thousand years ago, the land was heavily cultivated to support a population of one million Mayan, aboriginal Garafuna, and other indigenous peoples. Today, only stone ruins mark the former cities like tombstones. The land reverted back to a wild garden that is now carefully tended by the government and the people of Belize. In Belize, you can find animals that were once common throughout the southern United States, Mexico, and Central America.

Tour operators follow a somewhat set route, partly because there are few roads into the countryside. All tours include the Cockscomb Basin Wildlife Sanctuary, the world's only jaguar reserve. A few years ago, jaguars were considered big game trophy, and uncontrolled hunting rendered them extinct in most of the Americas. The jaguar is now a protected species. A true jungle cat, the jaguar likes to swim and catch fish.

The Mayans—captivated by its green eyes and tawny, sensuous body—revered the jaguar. They often depicted it in a peaceful pose, rather than as a fierce predator.

Ocelots, margay, the reclusive tapir, peccary, monkeys, coatimundi, kinkajou, and jaguarundi also live in the reserve. On walking tours a naturalist guide reveals hidden and easily overlooked wildlife in this tropical rain forest basin, bounded on three sides by ridges of the Maya Mountains. To an untrained eye, the dense vegetation could seem as devoid of animal life as a desert. But the rain forest teems with perfectly logical, amazingly interlocking, intricacies of life.

Next, tours stop at the Crooked Tree Bird Sanctuary. You can tour the sanctuary via a road north from Belize City, or you can spend a day paddling a canoe through the sanctuary's languid waterways. Orioles, warblers, and other songbirds transform the swamp into a music box. You may see the endangered jabiru stork, an arresting bird standing five and a half feet tall with pure white plumage, black head, black beak, red collar, and a 12-foot wingspan. Only an estimated one hundred jabiru nests remain in all of Central America.

The sanctuary borders the one-shop village of Crooked Tree, a complacent collection of wooden houses given a gray sheen by rain and wind. The shop owner rents the boats and supplies the guides necessary to tour the sanctuary. The local people are strong supporters of the natural world around them: It supports an economy based on nature tourism.

Nearly all tours in Belize start in Crooked Tree with a boat trip on the Northern Lagoon of the bird sanctuary, a grassy expanse dotted with cashew and mango trees. The lagoon, which is actually a group of eight individual lagoons, is a critical habitat for water birds and an important ecosystem for fish populations. Unlike the wetlands in the nearby seasonally dry Yucatan Peninsula, the 6,400-hectare sanctuary has open water year-round.

Here, too, you find the rare black howler monkey and troops of the more common howler monkey. The howler enjoys a special place in Belizeans' hearts for its human-like facial expressions, its winsome personality, and the tender care showered on its young. To insure the survival of the species, over seventy landowners downstream from the bird sanctuary have, with guidance from zoologist Robert Horwich and monies from the World Wildlife Fund, established the Community Baboon Sanctuary. They pledge to maintain a 70-foot-wide corridor of forest along the river banks through their fields as habitat for the monkeys.

Many tours include a 12-mile trip up the New River to visit. Lamanai, a 2,500-year-old Mayan ruin. This is real backcountry traveling by skiff through dense rain forest. The ruin's 2-mile-square center is largely uncleared. You can climb three temple pyramids via stone stairways up the steep sides. More than seven hundred buildings have been identified on the site, but only rough approach trails cut by archaeologists go to the outlying areas.

Another ancient Mayan ruin on the tour route is Chan Chich (Mayan for "little bird"), a private nature reserve. You can tour the 125,000 acres on horseback, by canoe, or on foot looking for howler monkeys, parrots, spider monkeys, deer, fox, and a variety of birds. You may even find jaguar pug marks (footprints).

Most tours travel up Mountain Pine Ridge to explore the Rio On, the 1,000-foot Hidden Valley Falls, and the Rio Frio Caves. On hikes through the densely forested low mountains, guides take you on the old Panti Maya Medicine Trail and explain the use of the native medicinal plants found there.

The tours also take a side trip to Tikal in nearby Guatemala. Once a Mayan city covering 25 square miles with about one million inhabitants, Tikal is one of the best examples of Mayan urban civilization in Central America.

Belize's natural resources, especially the valuable mahogany trees and the rain forest, are not beyond peril. Because of the country's relatively pristine condition and the availability of land, developers want to build large resorts. In this poor country the economic pressures to turn forests into farmland and to "harvest" trees for export to earn hard cash are real. Nature tourism offers an economically viable alternative to environmental degradation.

Tour operators:

Canada Canoe Adventures

Explore Worldwide

International Zoological
   Expeditions

Journeys International

Safaricentre

Sierra Club Outings

Wilderness Southeast

Wildland Adventures

World Wildlife Fund
   Explorations

COSTA RICA

Transportation: motor vehicle/hiking/boat
Accommodations: hotels/lodges
Land cost: $1,000-$2,600
Duration: 9 to 14 days
Seasons: year-round

In Costa Rica national parks, wildlife refuges, and biological reserves occupy 12 percent of the country, which is less than half the size of Ohio. In the United States, only 3.5 percent of the natural land is so protected.

Costa Rica's cloud forests, rain forests, active volcanoes, marshlands, rivers, and sea water estuaries are linked by wildland corridors and are home to over 850 species of wild birds, 100 species of mammals, 218 species of reptiles, 160 species of amphibians, and 490 species of butterflies, 10 percent of the total butterfly species on earth.

Costa Rica's tropical rain forest has 8,000 species of trees and plants, including 1,200 species of orchids. Patches of forest isolated by farmland are increasingly being linked to allow animals to move from area to area as their needs demand.

If you like cool weather, from November to February is the best time to visit Costa Rica. In March, the weather turns warm in the highlands and hot in the lowlands.

Tour operators provide a sample of the country's diversity. One of the first stops on most tours is Poas Volcano National Park, an hour's drive from the capital of San Jose. The volcano last erupted in 1989, and wisps of smoke continue to rise from the interior. Dwarf vegetation and red and green bromeliads abound near the steaming crater. A half-mile above the active crater lies a dormant crater rimmed with a highland forest. Coati, tapir, brilliantly colored trogons, emerald toucans, and wild hummingbirds live in the 8,800-foot-high cloud forest. A rain-fed lake fills the bottom of the crater.

A four-hour drive north of San Jose is the Monteverde Cloud Forest Reserve. The last 22 miles of road in the 113-mile trip resemble a vine twisting and looping 4,600 feet up a vertiginous mountain. Two hours of negotiating the holes and bumps make the ride a physical test.

Immigrant Quaker families from the United States established the 10,000-acre private reserve in the early 1950s. Straddling the Continental Divide on the upper slopes of the Cordillera de Tilaran, the Monteverde Cloud Forest Reserve contains the most complex tropical cloud forest in the Northern Hemisphere. Within the reserve are six different ecological zones, each with its own separate, yet intertwining, plant and animal life. More than two thousand plant species, including wild orchids, are native to the area.

The reserve is one of the last remaining nesting sites of the quetzal, which many naturalists consider to be the most beautiful and spectacular bird in the world. The early Mayans and Aztecs prized the quetzal; only their emperors were worthy of the bird. They created a god, Quetzalcoatl, the Feathered Serpent, who wore a headdress of quetzal plumes taken from the bird's 2-foot-long emerald-colored tail.

Hours spent tracking the quetzal's plaintive cry, "no-no," are worth the effort. Other birds among the reserve's four hundred species are the three-wattled bellbird, the buffy tufted-cheek, the prong-billed arbet, and the keel-billed toucan.

Resident mammals include black howler monkeys, brocket deer, and a hundred other species. The world's entire population of the extremely rare and endangered golden toad lives in the reserve's woodland of moss- and fern-covered trees. The two-inch toad is not technically golden in color; the males are orange, and the females are yellow and black with patches of scarlet. In the past, the best time to see the toads was from the end of April to the first of June, but none have been seen in the past two years, rising the specter that yet another species may have disappeared.

The 6 miles of trails through the reserve range from gentle to fairly steep. They can also be crowded. On one busy day, 275 people were recorded jostling along looking for quetzals. Recent regulations allow only 100 people on the trails at the same time. Priority is given to tours on natural history walks. Come prepared for mud; rain storms are frequent.

Naturalists lead tours through the forest, explaining the unusual combination of wet and dry forests and the ecosystems they support. You may be fortunate to hook up with a visiting scientist; many come here from around the world to study the flora and fauna.

Tours also stop at the Carara Biological Reserve, a thirty-minute drive from San Jose. This transition zone between dry and wet tropical forests harbors many birds endemic to Costa Rica, as well as one of the few remaining populations of Mesoamerican scarlet macaw. The lush primary forest of the 11,614-acre reserve is home to monkeys, coati (similar to raccoons), agouti (rodents about the size of a rabbit), boat-billed herons, and crocodiles.

Trails through the reserve go into deep canyons with sheer vertical walls that enclose wet tropical, wet premontane, and cloud forests. White-faced, spider, and howler monkeys and a wide variety of birds live there.

The tours next go to La Selva Biological Station in the 3,700-acre La Selva lowland rain forest in the northeastern region of the country. This vast puma and jaguar habitat stretches nearly to the Nicaraguan border. Trails meander through virgin tropical wet forest, swamps, secondary forest, and across the Puerto Viejo River on a long, swaying suspension bridge. The usual tropical forest animals live here—jaguar, tapir, agouti, coati, sloth, keel-billed toucan, crest owl, the purple-throated fruitcrow, and howler, spider, and white-faced monkeys. Do look out for the inch-long bala (bullet) ant; it packs a painful sting. Resist trying to catch the brightly colored frog you see along the trails. It is the poison dart frog. Colombian Indians use the toxin in the frog's skin glands to make their lethal blowgun darts.

The biological station began as an experimental farm in the 1950s and was sold to the Organization for Tropical Studies Center in 1960, a local organization headquartered in San Jose. The station is dedicated to biological research and education, primarily to discover how this rain forest can be made useful to humans without destroying it.

Visitors are welcome to stay overnight if space is available. The rooms—four beds per room with a shared bath (hot water)— are mainly for visiting scientists. Meals are taken cafeteria style in a modern dining room.

Most tours stay at the rustic-but-comfortable Selva Verde Lodge. The lodge has its own 500-acre private nature reserve of tropical lowland rain forest adjacent to the Braulio Carrillo National Park. A resident naturalist guides you along eight well-marked trails, ranging in difficulty from easy to steep. You can also float through the rain forest on the Sarapiqui River.

A protected zone connects the Braulio Carrillo with La Selva rain forest. The zone also protects the rich flora and fauna of the Caribbean slope, currently threatened by rapid deforestation. In the lowlands, well-maintained trails traverse the rain forest, which shelters over 400 species of birds, 63 species of bats, 122 kinds of amphibians and reptiles, and 2,000 plant species.

The Rara Avis Waterfall Lodge is another jungle hideaway included on most tours. The rough-hewn lodge, set in a clearing atop a steep hill in the midst of deep jungle, has eight spacious rooms each with beds, a private bath with shower and bathtub, and a hammock on a wraparound balcony. A 180-foot double waterfall is a two-minute walk away.

However, getting to the lodge is an ordeal. First you drive on mostly dirt roads to Las Horquetas, about an hour from San Jose. Next you rent horses for a four-hour ride, up a twisting mountain track that fords streams, to El Plastico. At this former jungle prison colony the horses are replaced by a large open trailer hitched to a four-wheel tractor for two more hours up a slippery, steep track. Some tour operators improvise on the transportation, but there is not much room for inventiveness. An effort is afoot to raise $100,000 for road improvement.

Lodge owner Amos Bien wants to make the rain forest produce cash revenue without destroying it. Instead of clearing the forest for farmland, a real need in Costa Rica, Bien raises commercial plants on his 3,000-acre jungle patch. The ornamental dappled palm, harvested to extinction in Panama, is one promising crop. Hardwoods, ferns, flowers, and medicinal plants are other possible money-makers.

Income from people staying at the lodge helps keep Bien's project afloat. Visitors usually stay one or two nights. Days are spent hiking trails with a resident naturalist discovering the not-so-obvious in very obvious places. On one trail you ride in a motorized cable car designed to move horizontally and vertically through the upper forest canopy forty feet to sixty feet above the ground. Most of the time the trail is used by scientists, but when it is not being used tourists can take it up to where most of the wildlife spend their time.

The Manuel Antonio National Park on the Pacific coast is a favorite tour stop as much for its beaches as for the wildlife. The peace of an early morning beach stroll along one of the four coral sand beaches can be disturbed by bands of capuchin and squirrel monkeys noisily scampering through the jungle to feed inland. The park is one of the few remaining Central American habitats of the shier squirrel monkey. In the evening, the monkeys return home to Cathedral Point, a conical hill that separates South Espadilla and Manuel Antonio beaches. If you stand in the right spot at the right time, the monkeys stream around you like commuters emerging from a subway.

The 1,687-acre park has a limited trail system through the jumble of palms, vines, wild orchids, ceiba, and cecropia trees. Sharp eyes scanning the trees can spot blackhooded antshrike, white-crowned parrot, blue-crowned manakin, and rufous-backed ant-wren. Three-toed sloths, which, at top speed, take 4.5 hours to go one mile, and scarlet-rumped tanagers hang from the branches.

The Tortuguero National Park ("place of the turtle") is another major tour stop. It is Costa Rica's wildest and most isolated park. The park is reached by a 50-mile, four-hour boat ride upriver from Limon or nearby Moin, or a thirty-minute flight in a small plane.

Located on the northeastern Caribbean coast, the park is a major nesting beach for Atlantic green, leatherback, hawksbill, and occasionally loggerhead turtles. From June to September, thousands of green sea turtles come onto the beaches at night to lay their eggs. Hawksbill turtles lay their eggs from July to October and leatherbacks from February to July. Tortuguero is also home to parrots, monkeys, and the endangered West Indian manatee.

Establishing the park to protect the turtles eliminated a major source of employment for the local people—hunting turtles and gathering their eggs. Tensions grew between the newly unemployed and the park rangers and scientists. The situation improved when the former hunters were hired as guides to take visitors to the nesting sites.

One of Central America's last great stands of tropical virgin rain forest lies within Tortuguero's 21,000 hectares. Such large tracts of wilderness are necessary for species survival. Despite Costa Rica's excellent environmental record, almost all the land outside the protected areas has been deforested.

Within the 260-acre Santa Rosa National Park, near the Pacific Ocean, in the northwest region of the country, are beaches, mangroves, wooded savannas, and six other different habitats. One of Central America's few remaining primary dry tropical forests lies within the park, which can be seen by horseback. Scientists study the forest's seasonal patterns and interlocking ecosystems to ascertain the size of habitats necessary to sustain a species and its food chain.

The northwestern Guanacaste Province—where Santa Rosa, the

Orosi Volcano, and Guanacaste National Park are located—was once covered with deciduous, semideciduous, and evergreen forests. The forests have since been converted into pastureland. Now the province bears the economic burden of drought and infertile soil. The 80,337-acre Guanacaste National Park was created to preserve and restore one of the last remaining dry forests, which once stretched from central Mexico to Panama.

Even Costa Rica's protected lands are not necessarily safe from environmental degradation. Tortuguero's turtles are threatened by poachers; Manuel Antonio National Park is being squeezed by oil-palm plantations; and fires set by ranchers scorch the borders of the Santa Rosa National Park.

Eight percent of the earth's land is still covered by rain forest, an area about the size of the United States. But each year ranchers, loggers, and farmers, many employed by international corporations, cut down or burn a California-size chunk. As goes the rain forest, so goes its wildlife and ecological diversity. Scientists estimate that by the end of this century, about one million flora and fauna species will vanish without ever having been identified.

Tour operators:

Cheesemans' Ecology Safaris

Exodus Adventure

Forum

Great Expeditions

International Expeditions

Journeys International

Lost World Adventures

Mariah Wilderness Expeditions

Pioneer Tours

Questers Worldwide Nature Tours

Rainbow Adventures (women only)

REI Adventures

Safaricentre

Sierra Club Outings

Voyagers International

Wilderness Southeast

Wildland Adventures

Woodswomen Adventure Travel (women and children only)

World Expeditions

World Wildlife Fund Explorations

North America

UNITED STATES—WEST

ALASKA

Pribilof and Aleutian Islands, Glacier Bay, Inside Passage

Transportation: cruise ship/yacht

Accommodations: on-board

Land cost: $1,000-$7,000 (prices vary depending on type of on-board accommodations)

Duration: 11 to 14 days

Seasons: summer

Cruising the Alaskan coast is the epitome of a cushy wilderness tour. All your creature comforts are catered to, and your mind feeds on environmental-issue and animal-behavior lectures as the real stuff glides past. Occasionally, you leave the ship for hikes conducted by naturalists. More than occasionally, you reach places accessible only by sea.

The Pribilof Islands are one such place. The four remote volcanic peaks in the Bering Sea harbor one of the world's largest concentrations of seals, walrus, and sea otters. More than one million fur seals return to the islands each year to mate and give birth. Harbor seals, Stellar sea lions, and long-tusked walrus bask on the rocky shores. In addition, over one hundred and ninety different bird species nest here.

Unfortunately, not many Stellar sea lions will be seen. Their population has declined by 80 percent in the Bering Sea and along Alaska's coast. They die in fishermen's nets and are occasionally shot by fishermen who do not like the competition for the pollock, Pacific cod, and other fish the Stellar sea lions feed on. According to Greenpeace International, which has launched a campaign to aid the sea lion, the National Marine Fisheries Service designated the Stellar as "threatened" under the Endangered Species Act but has enacted no measures to help the Stellar population recover.

The Semidi Islands, a group of small, rugged islands on the south side of the North Aleutian Peninsula, are nature's own rookeries for horned and tufted puffins, murres, sea parakeets, auklets, and northern phalaropes, small swimming and wading birds that resemble the sandpiper. Inflatable Zodiac boats launched from the main ship take you to nesting grounds on Aghiyuk, Chowiet, and Alikesmir Islands, which are inaccessible by land.

On Kodiak Island you go ashore to visit the Fort Abercrombie State Park. Puffins, bald eagles, sea otters, and sea lions call the park's forest and beaches home. The port of call is the town of Kodiak, the first Russian settlement in Alaska, established in 1784.

The island is the site of the Kodiak Island National Wildlife Refuge, home of the Kodiak bear. The bear's habitat is threatened by the desire of the island's native population to develop their land within the refuge. Under the Alaska Native Claims Settlement Act, the residents of the Akhiok and Kaguyak villages own 138,000 acres on the island, nearly all of it in wildlife refuge. They want to construct an airstrip and tourist facilities within the refuge to increase the land's profitability. The additional income is sorely needed in this area, which has the highest unemployment in the country.

Tour ships nose into the extensive network of fjords of the Kenai National Park. Primeval forests cover the fjords' steep sides. Sea lions, sea otters, and whales are abundant in the waters, and kittiwakes nest in the cliff faces. The two-million-acre Kenai National Wildlife Refuge, adjacent to the fjords, is the range for moose, Dall sheep, and black bears.

In Prince William Sound, site of the infamous *Exxon Valdez* oil spill in 1989, on-board naturalists explain the spill's impact on the environment and the local economy. The centerpiece of Prince William Sound is the 300-foot face of the 4-mile-long Columbia Glacier. North America's most active glacier, it covers 400 square miles. The birthplace of icebergs, chunks of its ice often fall into the water with resounding booms and accompanying splashes.

The cruises also stop at Yakutat, an isolated Tlingit Indian village. Above the village looms the 9-mile-long, 6-mile-wide Hubbard Glacier, the longest and fastest-growing glacier in North America. This region is home to Aleutian terns, bald eagles, trumpeter swans, snow geese, and the rare blue bear. Motorized raft excursions provide close-up views of the Hubbard and Mabaspine glaciers.

Glacier Bay National Park, at the entrance to the Inside Passage, is home to humpback whales, harbor seals, porpoise, eagles, numerous varieties of seabirds—and icebergs. Tiny murrelets dive into the water for food and then rocket back into the air. More Kittlitz's murrelets can be seen here than anywhere else in their restricted Pacific range. Mountain goats feed on the craggy slopes around the bay. A United States Park Service ranger or another on-board naturalist gives a running commentary as the ship slowly trolls the shoreline.

The Inside Passage, which winds through a maze of offshore islands, is one of the richest marine and avian habitats in the world. Whales, seals, and sea otters share the water with icebergs. Greater yellowlegs, eagles, northern shrikes, and squaw ducks are a small sampling of the bird life. The hundreds of islands in the area are covered with old growth spruce and hemlock.

An onshore visit to Admiralty Island, one of only three islands in southeast Alaska the grizzly bear calls home, is part of many tours. The island is also a nesting site for many bald eagles. Unfortunately, clearing of the forest on the southeastern end of the island raises concern for the future of their habitat.

Alaskan Safari

Transportation: motor vehicle/raft/train/hiking
Accommodations: cabins/lodges/hotels
Land cost: $2,000-$2,800
Duration: 10 to 20 days
Seasons: June to September

Safari tours give you a sampling of Alaska, from a raft float down the Kenai River or a yacht tour of the Kenai fjords to easy hikes through a forest. Many of the safaris are geared toward the senior traveler. Chugach State Park, Kenai National Park, Seward Peninsula, and the Denali National Park are part of the itinerary.

Denali is one of the premier places in northwestern North America to view wildlife. Grizzly, black bear, caribou, moose, fox, and myriad birds and small mammals—nearly the whole encyclopedia of animals native to the region—live in the 6,028,091-acre park located in southcentral Alaska. The park's crowning jewel is 20,300-foot-high Mount McKinley.

Buses, either the tour operators' or the Park Service's, are the only vehicles allowed in the park. You can be dropped off along the buses' route at Wonder Lake to watch moose, caribou, an occasional bear, or perhaps wolves. Approximately one hundred and ten wolves live in the park.

The strictly controlled vehicle traffic helps preserve the air quality and the general sense of wilderness in the park, but there is a large development of tourist facilities, mostly high-priced hotels, along the southern edge of the park.

The Seward Peninsula is subtle rather than spectacular Alaska. The tundra's soggy permafrost rises in hillocks rather than in the towering peaks often associated with the state. Miniature plants hug the ground for better protection from the biting Arctic wind. They burst into color during the short summer, each species trying its fragrant best to attract the few pollinators, orange/black Arctic bumblebees and butterflies.

The long-tailed jaeger, the quickchange artist of the Arctic, summers on the Seward Peninsula. A pelagic seabird, the jaeger winters in Chilean waters, feeding on fish and krill in the Humboldt Current. It then migrates north and transforms into a hawk-like predator of small birds and mammals.

Few people travel the peninsula, which is a hunting and fishing ground for the indigenous people.

In the Katmai National Park and Preserve the tours may take

you to the river to watch the Alaskan brown bear, better known as the grizzly, catch salmon. Keep a discreet distance. The grizzly, which commonly tips the scales at 800 pounds, is the largest and fastest land predator. The park is one of their last refuges.

Tour operators:

Alaska Wildland Adventures
International Expeditions
Mountain Travel/Sobek
   Expeditions
National Audubon Society
Nature Expeditions
   International
Overseas Adventure Travel

Questers Worldwide Nature
   Tours
REI Adventures
Sierra Club Outings
Wildland Adventures
World Wildlife Fund
   Explorations

CALIFORNIA

Sierra National Forest

Transportation: boat/hiking
Accommodations: lodges
Price: $1,135-$2,150
Duration: 8 days
Seasons: July

The John Muir Wilderness in the Sierra and Inyo National Forests is a land of lakes, streams, meadows, and snowcapped mountains. Paiute Indians once passed through this region on their way from the Eastern Sierras to Auberry Valley to trade obsidian, basalt, and arrowheads for acorns and meal. They stopped at the same hot springs where you will soak away trail weariness.

The Muir Trail Ranch, in the upper Blaney Meadow, serves as base camp for trips into the wilderness. The ranch, reached by boat and a 4-mile hike (without backpacks), is on 200 acres in the Sierra National Forest in central California, 90 miles northeast of Fresno. Accommodations are log cabins with bathrooms or tent cabins, both with beds and electricity, fronted by the San Joaquin River. Comfortable mattresses and pillows are furnished, but you must bring your own sleeping bag. Meals are taken at an outdoor barbecue area or in a log cabin. Lending a hand at cooking, cleaning, or other camp chores is part of the experience.

Seasoned guides head up day hikes into various areas of the Wilderness. You hike up to Heart Lake (10,490 feet), the uppermost in a chain of four lakes; or to Seldon Pass (10,873 feet) with a sweeping view of 13,361-foot Mount Hilgard to the north and Mounts Henry and Goddard to the south. The trail up to Evolution Valley (9,200 feet), a meadow filled with wildflowers and tall grass along a meandering creek, gives grand views of the Sierras.

Guests can soak in two natural hot springs that Indians once used. Wildflowers surround the two chest-deep granite-lined tubs. One tub is hot (107 degrees), while the other is a cool 98 degrees.

Taking a hike to Donner Pass is another option. Donner Summit (8,019 feet) and Castle Peak (9,103 feet) can be easily reached from the Sierra Club's Clair Tappan Lodge, close to the Pacific Crest Trail. The beginning of spring is the best time to visit the meadows of the High Sierras.

Accommodations at the lodge are dormitory or family-sized rooms equipped with bunk beds and mattresses. You must bring your own sleeping bag. A professional chef prepares meals, but everyone is expected to help with brief daily housekeeping chores.

Unfortunately, logging in northern California's ancient forests is destroying the region's biological diversity and natural habitats. More than 90 percent of the ancient-forest ecosystem has been clearcut or developed. Environmental organizations propose curtailing unmilled log exports and other measures to protect what is left of the forests.

Tour operators:

Sierra Club Outings

COLORADO

Rocky Mountain National Park

Transportation: hiking
Accommodations: lodges/cabins
Price: $670-$765
Duration: 5 to 8 days
Seasons: summer

The mountains in the Rocky Mountain National Park look like giant woolly mammoths, albeit very pretty ones bedecked with garlands of pastel wildflowers and diamonds of glittering lakes. The peaks, however, are gray and foreboding. The valleys below clearly show the signs of being gouged out by glaciers during the Ice Age, when the woolly mammoths became extinct.

Estes Park, a small tourist town jammed with people during the summer season, is the gateway to the park. Western-style lodges in the vicinity serve as base camps for day hikes, which average 6 to 10 miles up steadily climbing trails. No special physical preparation is necessary, although you may tire easily at first due to the thin air. Estes Park lies at nearly ten thousand feet, and the hikes go up from there.

Some tours have two guides per trip in case your group (no more than sixteen people) splits into fast and slow tracks. Two guides also give the flexibility of long and short hikes to suit the different needs and capabilities of people on the tours.

Each day hike has a different character. One follows a trail along a stream to Dream, Bear, and Nymphy lakes. The peaks that form the Continental Divide loom directly over the lakes. Another trail to Mills Lake leaves the alpine pine forest and enters the very different world above the timberline.

Being above the trees (about twelve thousand feet) is a bit like setting to sea in a small ship. You experience a rush of freedom induced by the vast openness of sky. The high-altitude weather, which is unpredictable and volatile, gives the rush an extra edge.

A drive over the Continental Divide via Trail Ridge Road, the highest paved road in the United States, is also part of the tours.

Short hikes take you across the fragile tundra. The trails are limited and clearly marked; to prevent damaging the tundra, you are not allowed to stray from them. A summer trail over the divide used by Ute Indians over one hundred years ago is still plainly visible.

Tour operators:

New England Hiking Holidays   Roads Less Traveled

HAWAII

Transportation: motor vehicle/hiking/boat
Accommodations: hotels/lodges/bed & breakfasts
Land cost: $1,400-$2,000
Duration: 7 to 10 days
Seasons: year-round

There is much more to Hawaii than just golf courses and beaches. You can hike Waimea Canyon, monitor whales, explore tropical rain forests, or walk down into dormant volcanoes or along the burbling lava of an active one.

Hawaii, the largest of the seven islands, contains diverse ecosystems ranging from valleys, deserts, and tropical rain forests, to beaches, volcanoes, and snowcapped mountains. Tour operators try to give you a taste of each area of the 4,038-square-mile "Big Island."

At the Volcanoes National Park, you hike across the floor of the Kilauea Volcano, the world's most active volcano. According to local legend, Madame Pele, Fire Goddess of the island, resides there. The daughter of Haumea, the Earth Mother, and Wakea, the Sky Father, Pele melts rocks, creates mountains, and burns land—all the things expected of a volcano.

She also inflicts the "Curses of Pele" on those who take bits of lava as souvenirs—at least this is what many people believe. The legend does not mention a curse, but mailbags full of purloined lava arrive at the park's ranger station daily. Letters accompanying the returned lava beg that Pele release the offender from her curse.

Accommodations in the Volcanoes National Park are often at national park cabins or nearby inns.

Another hike in this volcanic region goes across the steaming crater of Kilauea Iki (Kilauea Volcano). On the 5-mile hike you feel the earth tremble and smell acid fumes. The molten magma beneath the Earth's thin crust bubbles upward sending signals in seismographic Morse code that read, "Tread lightly, puny human."

A volcano walk of a different sort traverses massive frozen lava flows on Mauna Loa (Long Mountain), which rises 32,000 feet from the ocean floor.

On Kauai, known as the "Garden Isle," you hike the Waimea Canyon, the "Grand Canyon of the Pacific." The steep, heavily eroded walls of the 15-mile-long, one-mile-wide, and 2,800-foot-deep canyon are colored in blues, purples, reds, and ochres.

The Kokee State Park is the best place to see elepaio, I'wi, apapane, and several other species of native Hawaiian birds. Other hikes on the island include a trail atop 2,500-foot-high cliffs in the Na Pali Coast Wilderness and in the native kao forest of the Kokee State Park. From the top of Nonou Mountain (1,259 feet) you get a panoramic 360-degree view of the island, the oldest in the Hawaiian chain, formed by volcanic action beginning over five million years ago.

A 7-mile hike (round-trip) along the Awaawapuhi Ridge through the ohia and koa climax forests is another feature of tours in Kauai. The forests contain unusual plant life and a rich variety of indigenous birds.

Maui is advertised as the least developed and least compromised of the islands. Besides the beaches, the main attraction is the dormant Haleakala Volcano in the Haleakala National Park. You hike the slopes of the 10,023-foot-high volcano, which is known as Maui's "House of the Sun" because legend has it the Polynesian god Maui made the sun move slowly across the sky by snaring it on the volcano's peak.

The National Park includes the Kipahula Valley, the Ohe'o Gulch, and a few miles of southeastern coast. The native Hawaiian goose, or nene, lives in the park. The goose's foot has adapted to walking on lava by reducing the webbing so it grips better. At one time, the bird nearly became extinct, in part because of the mongoose and other predators introduced to the island. A captive breeding and release program has increased the wild nene population to an estimated five hundred.

Another hike goes through the bamboo forests of the Waikomoi Forest Reserve, a native rain forest that shelters the endangered crested honeycreeper. In the forest you can find, and eat, ginger, guava, mountain apple, mango, and berries. Mountain pools along the trail make great swimming holes.

On some tours you can help monitor humpback whales. The whales calve in the Pailolo Channel between Maui and Lanai during the winter months. You count whales, record their movement, and help record their calls. You work with a marine biologist collecting base line data, photo-identifying individual humpback whales, and recording their mating songs.

Accommodations are lodges and bed and breakfasts with all the comforts of home. Minivans ferry you from site to site on the islands.

Hawaii is well on its way to becoming a zoo for its native wildlife. Bits and pieces of land are preserved for show, while the rest of the land is being converted for "productive" use. Golf courses are replacing entire ecosystems. The Islands have sixty-eight golf courses and another ninety-three are planned. A geothermal power plant on Hawaii threatens to destroy the last remaining lowland tropical forest in the United States. Half of Hawaii's rain forests have already been destroyed.

The "Big Island," Hawaii, contains many of the endangered plants and animals native to the islands. Of the once plentiful native monk seal only fifteen hundred remain. Half of the 140 original species of birds in Hawaii are extinct. Twenty percent of the endangered plant species in the United States are in Hawaii, and botanists predict that number may rise to 35 percent within two years. Feral pigs and goats do enormous damage in the tropical forest. The Hawaiian parks department has a program to eliminate the pigs and goats, but they remain a serious threat.

Tour operators:

Eye of the Whale

Journeys International

Nature Expeditions International

New England Hiking Holidays

Voyagers International

Wilderness Journeys

OREGON

Ancient Forests of Oregon

Transportation: hiking

Accommodations: resort lodges/hotels

Land cost: $525-$1,1990

Duration: 5 to 15 days

Seasons: April to December

The ancient forests of the Pacific Northwest are nearly extinct. By conservative estimates, only 5 percent of the forests that once covered the entire region remain, and stands of those patches are threatened by timbering.

The various hikes offered by tour operators into the ancient forests are informed recreation. The tour guides tell you a great deal about the life of the forest and why that life is important to your own.

The terrain is moderate with gradual elevation climbs. No special physical preparation is necessary. You carry only a light daypack and a camera. The tours go to the central Cascades, the high plateau of central Oregon, and to coastal regions. Vehicles take you from region to region.

Hikes in the central Cascades and the high plateau traverse Browder Ridge, Mill Creek Wilderness, and Breitenbush Gorge.

Browder Ridge is a designated Spotted Owl Habitat Area. The lumber companies' intent to cut down much of the owl's habitat sparked a bitter political debate that still rages in the halls of Congress and in the small communities whose economic life depends on the timber industry.

The Devil's Ridge trail goes into the Breitenbush River Drainage, once held sacred by the Indians because of the healing properties of the mineral hot springs found there. The hike is through a 750-year-old forest of Pacific yew.

The yew's bark and needles contain taxol, an important anti-cancer drug. The yew, considered a "trash tree" by loggers, is often left to rot on the ground once cut down. The yew is not endangered as a species, but its numbers are being greatly reduced by logging in the Cascade ancient forest. Plantations of yew trees are now being grown by companies that process taxol, which is also being produced artificially.

At day's end you return to a base camp at the Breitenbush Hot Springs Community near Detroit, Oregon. Breitenbush was a hot springs resort in the early 1900s but fell into disrepair. In 1977, it was restored and reopened as a self-reliant community. Members of the cooperative work to preserve the old growth forest around the springs. Nudity is allowed in the hot springs, so tours offer other base camps for those who do not wish to be so exposed.

One alternative, or addition, to the Breitenbush camp is Camp Sherman on the Metolius River in the central Cascades. From the camp an easy riverside trail rambles through forests of ponderosa pine, cedar, and giant Douglas fir, where white-headed woodpeckers can be seen and heard.

The Redwood Nature Trail follows the Chetco River through stands of three-hundred- to five-hundred-year-old redwoods and a grove of big Oregon myrtle. The hike goes to the steep rocky canyon of the Rogue River, one of the few protected wild rivers in the United States.

At the Oregon Caves National Monument you hike through a pristine forest of Port Orford cedar, one of the rarest and most valuable trees in the world. You pass through alpine meadows to a grandfather daddy of trees, one of Oregon's oldest Douglas firs. The trail leads into the Kalmiopsis Wilderness, an unusual area of the Siskiyou coastal range where several plants found nowhere else on earth grow.

In the Boulder Creek Wilderness you hike along the North Umpqua River to the Crater Lake National Park through a white-bark zone, the highest forest in the Cascades.

Another high hike goes to Waldo Lake, which is surrounded by high elevation forests of Engelmann spruce, Pacific silver fir, and mountain hemlock.

The Black Butte Trail takes you through an ancient ponderosa pine forest and a mixed conifer forest on the eastern side of the Cascades. These forests differ from forests on the western side. Your guide explains the difference and the ecosystems in the old growth forests.

On the coast, you hike the Drift Creek Wilderness on Cape Perpetua through the largest coastal Sitka spruce/western hemlock old growth ecosystem left in the Lower Forty-eight.

At day's end you stay in comfortable hotels or cabins with double rooms and private baths.

The Pacific Northwest forests are as ecologically important as tropical rain forests. They contain four to seven times more biomass than rain forests. The trees are critical in absorbing carbon dioxide and other man-made gases that contribute to the greenhouse effect.

The more expensive tours offered by Nature Expeditions International incorporate an eight-day or a fifteen-day field seminar program. As part of the seminar, a forest expert with an advanced degree in natural science explains the scientific facts of the earth's greatest conifer forest as you hike through it.

Tour operators:

Ancient Forest Adventures   Wilderness Journeys
Nature Expeditions
   International

WASHINGTON

Stehekin Valley, North Cascade Mountains

Transportation: hiking
Accommodations: cabins
Price: $825
Duration: 6 days
Seasons: September

The Stehekin Valley is also known as "The Enchanted Valley" or "The Shangri-la of the Northern Cascades," and it fits all of these descriptions. In the simple Stehekin Valley you find log cabins, horses, and wilderness. The alluring "Enchanted Valley" is removed from the everyday world, reachable only by boat, foot, or float plane. "The Shangri-la of the Northern Cascades" is home to majestic peaks, waterfalls, and wildflower meadows.

A tour of the valley starts with a ferry ride up 50-mile-long Lake Chelan, which is reminiscent of a Norwegian fjord with heavily forested mountains rising abruptly from the water's edge. The ferry leaves from the Lake Chelan National Recreation Area at the lower end of the valley and travels to the North Cascades National Park in the upper valley.

One 23-mile road leads from the lake into the park. It is only used by the park service to shuttle visitors and by the few permanent residents of the park. The Stehekin Valley Ranch, your base camp for day hikes into the valley, lies 8 miles up the road.

Accommodations are wood and canvas cabins with beds, showers, and flush toilets. Each cabin sleeps two to five people. Pillows are provided, but you must bring your own sleeping bag or rent one. You also must provide your own towels. Home-cooked meals are taken in the family style dining room. You do not have to cook, set the table, or otherwise trouble yourself.

Each day you are driven to a different trailhead for a day hike. In the lush North Cascades National Park you follow an old prospector's trail to 7,600-foot Sahale Arm. From the peak you can see range after range of serried mountains receding into the distance. Far in the distance is snowcapped Glacier Peak.

Another trail goes to Horseshoe Basin, where nineteen waterfalls tumble over steep granite rock faces. You hike to the 312-foot Rainbow Falls and to Agnes Gorge, an impressive chasm of waterfalls. Another hike goes up Park Creek Pass, one of the area's most scenic alpine passes.

The hikes range from eight to sixteen miles. Elevation climb varies from 2,000 to 6,500 feet. You will need a daypack to carry water and food. A pair of well-broken-in hiking boots are a must.

The weather can vary from sunshine to snow and back to sunshine. A wool hat and gloves, long underwear, rain gear, warm clothes, and extra socks are recommended.

More than 90 percent of the ancient forests in Washington have been clearcut or developed, destroying biological diversity and natural habitats. Various environmental organizations propose curtailing unmilled log exports and other measures to reduce pressure on the forests.

Tour operators:

Sierra Club Outings

MIDWEST

MINNESOTA/ONTARIO

Boundary Waters Canoe Area Wilderness

Transportation: canoe
Accommodations: inns/lodges
Land cost: $280-$600
Duration: 3 to 5 days
Seasons: July to September

The million-acre Boundary Waters Canoe Area Wilderness sprawls along 150 miles of the U.S.-Canadian border where Minnesota blends into Ontario. No roads cut through the boreal forests of birch, black spruce, tamarack red, and white pine, some as old as three hundred years. The Wilderness Area comprises one of the last intact natural areas in the Lower Forty-eight.

More than 1,200 miles of canoe trails wend from lake to lake. Sioux and Ojibwa Indians planting wild rice and hunting used many of the same routes you take. Land portages are easily made where the water connection is broken. On a portage, you help carry the canoe—otherwise it would not be an authentic canoe trip. Your gear is transported for you.

Black bear, moose, deer, foxes, beavers, loons, herons, and ducks live in the woods and on the lakes. The last twelve hundred timber wolves in the Lower Forty-eight also live in this area. You may hear a wolf, but you probably will not see one—or a black bear, either. But if you paddle quietly, you may spot a moose at dusk. The waterways are hunting grounds for ospreys, bald eagles, and the great grey owl, the largest owl in the United States. Unlike most other owls, it is a daytime hunter so chances of seeing one are good. The tours stress being quiet since noise scares off the wildlife.

Tours begin at different spots and take varied routes. You may start at Brule Lake for a northern lake trip, or paddle down the Little Indian Sioux River through a chain of lakes. Lac La Croix with its Indian rock paintings is also popular. Another route starts on the Granite River, a series of small interconnected lakes along the Minnesota-Canada border. The trip crosses into Canadian wilderness at Saganaga Lake, then loops back to the United States.

The trips are suitable for novices and experts alike. Overnight stops are spent at the few private lodges in the Wilderness Area. The U.S. Forest Service has bought and razed most of the private resorts and residences in the Wilderness Area.

The area is well-regulated. Customs officials staff checkpoints along the international border, such as in the middle Saganaga Lake, to check permits and identification papers. You are fore-warned of federal regulations, such as prohibition of cans and bot-tles, and are expected to obey. Substantial fines are levied without hesitation against violators.

Tour operators:

Canoe Country Escapes

Rainbow Adventures (women
  only)

Woodswomen Adventure
  Travel (women and children
  only)

NORTHEAST

MAINE

River Trips

Transportation: canoe
Accommodations: inns/lodges
Land cost: $300-$740
Duration: 3 to 5 days
Seasons: summer

Day-long canoe trips with overnight stops at inns are a delightful way to experience the Maine woods. These rivers, made for comfort rather than speed, demand no prior canoeing experience.

The Royal River courses slowly through pastureland and pockets of forest. The Back River cuts through pine forest and narrow, gray granite passages at Goose Rock and Open Mouth. When you are on the Little Androscoggin River, which is canopied by trees, you feel like you are in a world far removed from the nearby communities. The Ellis River, perhaps the prettiest river in Maine, flows through pastures and mixed forests of spruce, pine, and hardwoods. Moose live in these woods and drink from the river, so you may very well meet one on your trip.

The rivers flow to the ocean. On the Sasanoa, a tidal river, you follow the marshy shore of Hackemock Bay, where the marsh turns into pine woods and rock ledges. Seals visit the bay. Atlantic salmon swim up the reversing falls of the Sheepscat River, the banks of which are lined with march grass and rock ledges.

The tours include the two Abenaki Heritage rivers, Nezinscot and Cobbosseecontee Stream, where the Abenaki tribes of the Algonquin Nation once fished. The remote Nezinscot, an Abenaki word meaning "down the river by canoe," is fast-flowing but slows as it passes through overhanging forests of pine, oak, birch, and spruce.

The Cobbosseecontee Stream (Abenaki for "where the sturgeon occur") is a haven for ducks, herons, and loons. The slow-moving river winds through small ponds and marshes populated with muskrat and beaver.

Tour operators:

Canoe USA   New England Hiking Holidays

VERMONT

Transportation: canoe
Accommodations: inns/lodges
Price $300-$750
Duration: 3 to 7 days
Seasons: July to September

Starting in upper Vermont near the Canadian border, outfitters run the Upper Connecticut River and its tributaries, such as the Waits and Passumpsic rivers. The day-long or half-day trips are not taxing or difficult, even for novices.

Another favorite canoeing circuit runs through central and northern Vermont. The first two days are on the Winooski River as it cuts through the spine of the Green Mountains. The Winooski flows past the state capital of Montpelier, then cuts between Vermont's two highest peaks, Mount Mansfield and Camel's Hump. The fast-moving current carries you through rock-walled gorges and past wooded hills, pastures, and farmland. Along the way you can explore islands and rest on sandbars.

You then canoe the Lamoille River through rock gorges and open pastureland to the Passumpsic River, which joins the Connecticut River.

Another route starts on the White River near its confluence with the Connecticut. The White River offers 100 miles of canoeing, with stretches for various levels of abilities.

The Battenkill River, one of the loveliest rivers in Vermont, loops through valleys as it flows west to the Hudson River.

Portages from river to river when necessary are done by vehicle. The canoes are transported for you. Nights are spent in riverside inns with all the comforts of home.

Rivers are more than merely pretty places for cool fun. They created our landscape of valleys, canyons, and gorges. They are a determining factor of the riverine ecosystems so beneficial to wildlife and humans. Civilizations started in river valleys because the rivers deposited rich silt to nurture crops. Today, the bands of trees along rivers flowing through cultivated fields and pastureland are often the last refuges for wildlife in a highly developed area.

Tour operators:

Canoe USA

SOUTH

FLORIDA

Transportation: canoe

Accommodations: lodges/inns/tents

Land cost: $300-$800

Duration: 4 to 6 days

Seasons: February to March; September to November

The Ocala National Forest in central Florida sits atop a huge aquifer that supplies the state with most of its fresh water. Springs burble through the porous limestone creating "water trails," which are less-traveled than the hiking trails through the forest.

Within the national forest, Juniper Springs and Alexander Springs runs are on most tour itineraries. At Juniper Springs, a thirty-minute drive from the Fore Lake campground, you put in about fifty yards downstream from where the spring seeps from the ground.

The waterway is about six feet wide where you start and widens to nearly fifty feet by the end of the 6-mile trip. The creek winds through the Juniper Prairie Wilderness, a dense subtropical forest of cabbage palms and hardwood trees that overhang the banks. Bald eagles, herons, egrets, deer, and alligators are frequently seen along the way.

No canoeing experience is necessary and the trip is not physically demanding, since you paddle with the current downstream. The place is a refuge of solitude and quiet for humans and a sanctuary for the wildlife. Unfortunately, the solitude is occasionally scattered by low-flying Navy jets on practice bombing runs on the range belonging to the Ocala Air Base. You never hear the jets until they are nearly directly overhead.

Alexander Springs, a forty-minute drive from the Fore Lake campground, is very different from Juniper Springs. The water wells from an underground cave and forms a large, deep pool. You launch the canoes right into the pool. You can dive down twenty feet to the source of the spring surging from the rock crevice.

The waterway from the pool is perhaps a hundred feet wide and never narrows on the 6-mile trip downstream. The forest does not crowd the banks as on Juniper Springs Run. You do, however, find the same wildlife, including the limpkin, a three-foot waddling bird that daintily steps among the cattails to feed on large, round apple snails.

The clear-cutting of the forest is not apparent from the waterways, although it is clearly evident when you drive to the various put-in sites on the canoe trips. The U.S. Park Service leases forest tracts to logging companies. Conservationists are concerned that the forest is being over-cut, posing a threat to wildlife habitats. The park service maintains it is practicing sound land management and not endangering the wildlife.

The Ocala is "springs country." You can canoe the Rock Springs Run, which gushes from the base of a small limestone hill, down to Wikiva Springs. Local lore states that the Spanish explorer Ponce de Leon roamed the region looking for the elusive fountain of youth.

Accommodations on the canoe trips range from tents at the

Fore Lake campground, to rooms at the historic Ritz Inn in Ocala or the Lakeside Inn in Mount Dora, depending on the tour.

Tour operators:

Canoe USA   Wilderness Southeast

GEORGIA

Okefenokee National Wildlife Refuge

Transportation: canoe
Accommodations: cabin
Land cost: $320-$370
Duration: 3 to 4 days
Seasons: year-round

A "nothing-much-doing-in-this-wilderness" deceptiveness may fool the too-casual visitor to the Okefenokee Swamp. The wildlife is not obvious. But sighting a sandhill crane, a yellow-bellied slider turtle, or a river otter tells you there is more here than meets the eye. Many more creatures have private quarters deep in the swamp of Ogeechee lime trees, cypress forests, and peat bog prairies. You must have patience to find them.

The 438,000-acre Okefenokee Swamp, which straddles the eastern Georgia-Florida border, was once part of the ocean floor. Now it is mostly a peat bog 103 to 128 feet above sea level. Within the swamp lies the 358,981-acre National Wildlife Refuge.

A boardwalk built over the peat bog prairie on the east side of the park leads to a viewing tower, from which you can survey the grand sweep of the swamp low on the horizon under a broad sky.

Slow-moving Southern water flows through the Okefenokee. You have plenty of time on the canoe trails to look at, listen to, and smell the swamp life, although a swamp fart—a bubble of methane gas welling up from the swamp's bottom and bursting on the surface—is not to be lingered over. The gas is a product of vegetable matter decomposing on the swamp's bottom. The vegetable mat forms a liner that keeps the water from seeping out, creating the swamp in a never-ending process.

Aquatic trails divide stands of cypress and mangrove. Long beards of Spanish moss, hanging from cypress limbs, nearly touch the water. The air is thick with humidity, and the vegetation is dense. A pleasant "spookiness" permeates the swamp, as if you are in the palm of a gentle giant.

No special skills or previous canoeing experience are necessary before venturing into the swamp. Tour guides make sure novices are looked after. But be forewarned: the swamp is humid, muggy, and full of hungry mosquitoes.

You will paddle to the true headwaters of the Suwannee River, which flows into the Gulf of Mexico. The forest forms verdigris tunnels so you feel like a human hot dog rolled in a swamp bun. Deep in the forest you may, with luck, spot a rare wood stork or a very rare red-cockaded woodpecker with its magnificent crest. The red-cockaded woodpecker's existence is threatened by a diminishing habitat. The bird feeds and nests in diseased trees, which logging has stripped from the swamp's edge. Any remaining diseased trees have been marked in an effort to save the birds.

Okefenokee is an Indian word for "Land of the Trembling Earth," an accurate description of the peat bog prairies. The prairies, called "blow-ups" because they are literally blown up from the swamp's bottom by methane gas, are floating islands of various sizes. Grass and flowers, such as the jack-in-the-pulpit, colonize the bogs. The flowering plants are ground huggers with small blossoms. From a distance, the islands look lightly brushed with pastels.

Multiple species of local vegetation sprout on these floating prairies. The peat contains a detailed history of climatic changes as reflected in nature over hundreds of years. Scientists study peatlands to better understand how past periods of cooling and warming have affected plant and animal life—and to gain insight as to what we can expect in similar cycles in the future.

The swamp's quality of life is being degraded by development and timber operations on its edges and overuse by tourists and locals. Water pollution is seeping in; habitats are constricting. Animals go deeper into the swamp to avoid interlopers.

Most tour operators make base camp at the Stephen Foster Campground, the least populated of the park's three entrances. Accommodations are cabins with beds, private toilets, sinks, and showers.

Tour operators:

Mountain Travel/Sobek   Wilderness Southeast
  Expeditions

South America

ARGENTINA
Transportation: motor vehicle/walking/boat
Accommodations: hotels/lodges
Land cost: $1,500-$4,700
Duration: 17 to 21 days
Seasons: October to February

Argentina contains a variety of ecological regions, including tropical rain forests, steppes, montane forests, permanent glaciers, and seashore estuaries, and a variety of animal species, such as hummingbirds, pumas, guanacos (relatives of the Northern American camel), howler monkeys, fur seals, and penguins.

Tours to Argentina usually start with a visit to the Campos del Tuyu Wildlife Refuge, which is dedicated to the protection of "pampas" wildlife. Guides take you in search of the remaining population of pampas deer and birds such as the southern screamer and the southern lapwing. The pampas, a high country of treeless plains that resembles Montana, is an important nesting site for thousands of migratory birds from the Northern Hemisphere. At Punta Rosa, on the southern coast in the Peninsula Valdés area, scientists studying native birds welcome your help with banding, counting, and other tasks.

The Iguazu Falls National Park, a wild subtropical rain forest surrounding the horseshoe-shaped falls, offers a very different kind of experience. From the falls, footpaths lead deep into the jungle of giant ferns, vines, and reeds over sixty feet tall. A walk on the trestle bridge directly above the falls gives a bird's-eye view of the frothing water below.

At El Palmar National Park, another tropical jungle destination, trails go along the Los Loros stream and through open savannas dotted with Yatay palms. The capybara, the largest rodent on earth, lives in the park.

All tours go to Patagonia, a vast region in southern Argentina that encompasses extremes in weather and topography and a mix of polar and tropical animal species. Patagonia is bounded by the Andes to the west and the Atlantic Ocean to the east. To the north stands Cerro Aconcagua (22,330 feet), the highest peak in Argentina and the highest mountain in the world outside Asia. To the south is Tierra del Fuego, the end of the continent.

The barren, windswept Patagonian steppes come down the Andes like a giant stairway. Tinamou, falcon, and rhea, a tall flightless bird that resembles an ostrich, live on the steppe's grasslands. You find colonies of Southern elephant seal and Patagonia sea lion on the rocky beaches of the Atlantic coast. The largest colony of penguins outside the Antarctic gathers on the beach at Punta Tombo. Pods of Southern Wright whales cruise the waters.

National Parks on the tour circuit include the remote 7,000-acre Los Alerces National Park, where trails pass through forests of 1,000-year-old larches; Torres del Paine National Park; Los Glaciers National Park; and Fitzroy National Park.

The Torres del Paine National Park, known locally as "cuernos" (horns) for the rock spires that rise up to six thousand feet, is a region of pristine alpine lakes and mountains.

The Perito Moreno Glacier is the big attraction in Los Glaciares National Park, which is near Lago Argentino in southern Patagonia. The 200-foot-high, 3-mile-wide relic of the Ice Age is still growing. Blocks of ice weighing tons drop into a lake, shooting spray hundreds of feet into the air. Amazingly, the Chilean flamingos and black-necked swans that live on the lakeshore do not even look up at the booming CRACK!

The Fitzroy National Park, named for Captain Robert Fitzroy of the *HMS Beagle* on which Charles Darwin was a passenger, is a beech forest stretching across mountain slopes. The jagged peaks of Cerro Torre and Mount Fitzroy rise 11,073 feet in the background.

The last stop on the tours is usually Tierra del Fuego, "Land of Fire," so named by sailors on the *HMS Beagle* who explored the area in 1834. The sailors spotted columns of smoke on the land and reasoned where there is smoke, there is fire.

Tierra del Fuego is made up of a group of islands. Cruises leave for the Beagle Channel and the Strait of Magellan from Ushuaia (population 35,000), the southernmost city in the world, on Isle Grande, the largest of the islands. Darwin compared the channel to the Loch Ness glen in Scotland with its chain of lakes and firths.

A bus ride from Ushuaia takes you to Tierra del Fuego National Park. Huge Magellanic woodpeckers nest in the southern subarctic beech forests. Kelp geese, ashy-headed geese, and crested ducks live in the park's numerous bays and inlets.

Tour operators:

Explore Worldwide	Mountain Travel/Sobek
Innerasia Expeditions	Expeditions
International Expeditions	Safaricentre
Journeys International	Wildland Adventures

BRAZIL

Transportation: motor vehicle/boat/hiking

Accommodations: hotels/lodges/ranches

Land cost: $2,200-2,600

Duration: 16 to 20 days

Seasons: May to October

Brazil's Atlantic coastal rain forest is considered the number two "hot spot" for environmental conservation in the world. (Borneo being number one.) This region in Parana State was once one of the planet's richest and most extensive ecosystems. Now only 5 percent of the original forest remains, yet the region still contains some of the world's greatest ecological diversity. It also has the highest number of endangered species of any region in the world.

Tours to the Superagui National Park, located on the coast of Parana about one hundred miles south of Sao Paulo, give an up-close look at why the rain forest is humankind's best friend. On day hikes, naturalists explain the intricate interrelationship between life in Detroit, London, Sydney, Tokyo, and the fate of the rain forest. Hikes through dense jungle at Iguazu Falls make you intimate with the living, breathing life-form called "jungle."

Boat excursions around Paranagua Bay, guided by biologists and ecologists from the Guaraquecaba Ecological Station, scout some of the three hundred islands in the bay covered by rain forest and marshland. These islands are the last stand for some plant and animal species on the verge of extinction. The biologists and ecologists explain the delicate ecosystems and the efforts being taken to preserve them.

Brazil's southern Pantanal region is one of the biggest ecological reserves in the world and one of the most important wildlife habitats in South America. The lowland plain, overgrown with dense tropical vegetation, is nearly the size of former West Germany. The many rivers and lakes are magnets for rare species of birds. Jaguars, peccary, bobcats, and wild boar are among the many species of wildlife you may observe.

Trips into the area start in Manaus (population one million), which was a center of the rubber trade during the last century. Boats like the Pantanal Explorer II take you up the Cuiaba River into drowned forest and wetlands that are the last stronghold of the hyacinth macaw. On foot you explore the canyons of the Chapada dos Guimares, where jaguars roam. The boats are comfortable, expedition vessels with air-conditioned cabins, a library with literature about the region, and good food.

Many tours stay at Pantanal Camp on the Cuiaba River, the first ecological camp in the Pantanal. Resident ecologists and biologists lead walks into the jungle and explain the survival adaptations of the native flora and fauna. The camp has eight walk-in tents with twin beds, built-in ground sheets, mosquito netting, modern baths, and flush toilets. Gas or paraffin lamps provide light after sunset.

Other river cruises include a trip on the Amazon River in the Three Frontiers area, where Brazil, Peru, and Colombia meet. Boats, such as the *M/V Rio Amazonas,* a historic river vessel, make stops for nature walks and visits to Indian villages.

You also spend several nights ashore at lodges and camps, such as the Amazon Jungle Lodge, the Explorama Lodge, or the Explornapo Camp. The accommodations vary from beds and showers at the lodges to mattresses with mosquito netting and no running water at the camp.

The lodges in particular are comfortable base camps from which to explore the surrounding area on foot or by boat. The Amazon Jungle Lodge located on Lake Juma, 50 miles from Manaus, has a bar, a restaurant, and a sundeck. All excursions from the lodge are on foot or by canoe so as not to disturb the wildlife. Getting to the lodge is a bit of an adventure though.

Another lodge, the Ariau Jungle Tower, 20 miles from Manaus, can only be reached by canoe. Located between the Negro River and the Ariau Creek near the Anavilhanas Islands, the world's largest floating archipelago, the lodge is built on the branches of a 90-foot tree. A 150-foot high observation tower gives a view of the Negro River and the surrounding forest. All rooms have beds, a private shower and bath, and a veranda.

The Amazon village Tucano, 19 miles from Manaus, consists of sixteen wooden bungalows in the forest. Each bungalow has two rooms, twin beds, and a private bathroom. The village, on Puraquiquara Lake, is reached by a three-hour motorboat ride from Manaus. You explore the jungle on day hikes and canoe trips.

Deep in the jungle are two luxurious lodges, the Pousada Dos Guanavenas and the Floresta Amazonica.

The Pousada Dos Guanavenas, located 50 miles from Manaus on Canacari Lake's Silves Island, is a former refuge of the Guanavenas Indians. The lodge has thirty-two air-conditioned rooms with private balconies, a swimming pool, a sauna, telephones, electricity, and a restaurant. It won first prize at Brazil's Architectural Biennial for the use of regional materials. Daily trips by boat or on foot go into the surrounding jungle.

The Floresta Amazonica and the Cristalino Lodge share 54 acres of jungle in the highlands 30 miles from Alta Floresta. The lodges are located very far off the tourist track in the Mato Grosso Cristalino Forest Reserve. At the Floresta Amazonica the rooms are air-conditioned with private baths, televisions, and private verandas. There is a swimming pool and jungle paths that lead into the private reserve. The nearby Cristalino Lodge is a floating deck on the Cristalino River. The all-screened lodge has shared bathrooms and showers.

Manaus, the only urban center in a tract of tropical jungle three times the size of France, has become a hub for jungle excursions. Tourism is expected to become the region's chief source of foreign exchange within the next decade. Nature tourism is the top priority of Embratur, the Brazilian tourism authority. The growth of nature tourism—nearly 400,000 tourists per year are expected to visit the Amazon Basin during the next ten years—is an economic alternative to the clearing of the rain forest for farmland and pastures.

Unfortunately, at present, lumber companies continue to cut vast tracts of the rain forest. In addition, impoverished settlers continue to burn clearings in the forest to grow food. The soil is nutritionally poor and becomes cement-hard in a couple of years after the protective forest canopy has been removed. The farmers then burn out another clearing, thus continuing the cycle of wildlife habitat destruction.

However, farmers are not the chief ravagers of the rain forest. Large cattle and logging operations are more destructive. The

Brazilian government encourages the large-scale operations to create commodities for export. Cattle and timber products generate cash to pay down the country's crippling national debt. Pressure by the worldwide conservation community convinced some corporations not to purchase the products. McDonald's Corporation and Burger King, both large consumers of Brazilian beef, announced they would stop buying from ranches created from the rain forest.

Tour operators:

Exodus Adventure
Explore Worldwide
Forum
Journeys International
Lost World Adventures
Mountain Travel/Sobek
   Expeditions
New York Botanical Gardens

Questers Worldwide Nature
   Tours
Safaricentre
Sierra Club Outings
Voyagers International
Wilderness Southeast
Wildland Adventures

ECUADOR

Amazon/Andes

Transportation: motor vehicle/canoe/hiking
Accommodations: hotels/lodges
Land cost: $1,800-$2,700
Duration: 11 to 21 days
Seasons: year-round

Many Galapagos tours include trips into Ecuador's Andes and Amazon. Tours to these regions can also be taken independently of the Galapagos tours.

With their distinct ecosystems and cultures, the Andes mountains and the Amazon jungles are to South America what day and night are to twenty-four hours: two separate zones that comprise a whole. This is particularly true in Ecuador, where, within a single day, travelers can go from the Chimborazo Volcano's glacier to the Cuyabeno Amazone Rainforest Reserve deep in the jungle.

The journeys to either of these two worlds start in Quito, Ecuador's mile-high capital. A day trip by vehicle takes you to Otavalo's Indian market, famous for weavings. While in the highlands easy hikes are taken from village to village, into cloud forests, and on the slopes of 19,342-foot Cotopaxi, the world's highest active volcano.

During a day's descent from the highlands into the jungle you go from tramping across high mountains to paddling a dugout canoe along a river domed by trees and vines. Monkeys chatter and macaws crackle in the jungle canopy. Hikes through the jungle give a close look at the plant life and a sense of the world of the animals and the people who live there.

Indians often serve as guides on the tours' river trips and jungle hikes. They explain, through an interpreter, about medicinal plants and how to use them. If they come upon jaguar tracks, you may suddenly find yourself on a hunt. They point out monkeys high in the jungle canopy. Along the shore of Lago Grande, an oxbow lake hidden in the jungle, they identify various species of multicolored parrots, toucans, and macaws. The Indians help you see and hear the jungle as they do.

Individual tour operators have variations on the Andes/Amazon package, such as a visit to the hot springs at Banos, or a stay at the Cabanas Alihuani, or a comfortable rustic lodge on a bluff overlooking the River Napo.

Practically every tour goes to Las Selva Lodge, a cluster of palm-thatched cabanas deep in the rain forest. The cabanas are on stilts, and each has twin beds, a private toilet with a cold-water sink and shower, and kerosene lanterns. Meals are taken by candlelight.

A motorized dugout canoe takes you from Coca 60 miles down the River Napo to the Las Selva Lodge. If you are able to ignore the noise of the two-stroke outboard engine, you can pretend that you are exploring virgin territory.

Las Selva is on the shore of Garzacocha (Heron) Lake. Forty

species of birds live in the immediate vicinity, including hoatzin, boat-bill herons, red-bellied macaws, toucans, and screech owls. You get an eye-level look at monkeys and birds in the jungle canopy from a nearby 120-foot-high tower.

Naturalists conduct daily jungle excursions on foot or by canoe to introduce visitors to the wildlife of the Amazon Basin. A day-long canoe trip goes to Mandicocha Lake, where herons, king-fishers, horned screamers, striped bitteb, and harpy eagles abound.

The Cofanes, Secoyas, and Sinaos Indians have lived in the Ecuadoran Amazon for generations. The ethnic groups, each with distinct cultural traits, descended from the Tucano lineage. They share a common struggle to preserve their land and ways of life, which are being threatened by oil companies pushing drilling sites farther and farther into the jungle. The raw roads bulldozed through the jungle bring with them shantytowns, pollution, and service demands to an environment that is the antithesis of urbanization.

One site the oil companies want to lease is in the Yasuni National Park and the surrounding traditional tribal territory. Another is in the legal reserve of the Huaorani (Waorani) Indians, one of the world's most isolated peoples. The peril to the Hua-orani communities is immediate. In April 1992, a delegation rep-resenting 120 Amazonian tribes marched three days to Quito demanding legal title to their lands. The Ecuadoran government made sympathetic noises, but converting political promises into reality is more difficult. Indians and conservationists fear that the intrusion of commercial development will erode, if not destroy, the ecological systems on which the Indians and the wildlife are dependent. Due to pressure by the tribes, two oil companies, British Petroleum and Conoco, have already withdrawn from the area.

Coca, the jumping-off point for tours going down the River Napo, confirms the Indians' and conservationists' greatest fears of urbanization. The frontier honky-tonk town is a sprawl of bars and shanties. Tanker trucks belch exhaust into the air as they negotiate the mud streets. Spur roads leading to drilling sites have been slashed through the jungle. People in search of free land follow the roads and burn holes in the jungle to grow crops.

The Ecuadoran government, under pressure to pay its foreign debts and vitalize the country's economy, favors granting the leases for oil drilling. Oil is one of the country's few cash resources, yet reserves on the threatened land are estimated to hold only a twenty-year supply of oil.

The rain forests support a wildlife diversity that includes 4,000 species of flowering plants, 600 species of birds, and 120 species of mammals. Many species have already "disappeared," most of them unnamed plants, insects, or small creatures. But why should we worry about losing species of plants and animals anyway? Peter Raven and Ghillean Prance, writing in *Save the Earth* (McClelland and Stewart, 1991), explain, "Individual plants, animals, and fungi, as well as micro-organisms, will be the sources of products that transcend anything we can imagine now, used for purposes that have not yet even been conceived."

Experts are discovering that all the little bits and pieces of the Earth's life system are essential to the whole. A cause-and-effect relationship exists, for example, between what appears to be an insignificant insect and the food we eat. Brazil-nut trees cannot be grown on plantations because only the carpenter bee pollinates the trees, and the bee needs the mixed environment of a rain forest to thrive. Similarly, Raven and Prance note, the annual profits of the tomato industry have increased dramatically because of a gene for sweetness discovered in a wild tomato species from Peru.

Also writing in *Save the Earth*, Norman Meyers, an environmental consultant to several UN agencies, the World Bank, and other organizations, says, "We might be thankful for the wealth of the tropical forests next time we visit a pharmacist for medicine." There is a one-in-four chance that our purchase will derive from tropical forest plants. It may be an antibiotic, an analgesic, a diuretic, a laxative, a tranquilizer, or even just cough drops.

Tour operators:

Exodus Adventure Forum
Footloose Forays
Innerasia Expeditions
Journeys International
Learned Journeys
Mountain Travel/Sobek
    Expeditions

Questers Worldwide Nature
    Tours
Safaricentre
Voyagers International
Wanderlust Adventures
Wildland Adventures
World Expeditions

Galapagos Islands

Transportation: cruise ship/yacht/hiking
Accommodations: on-board
Land cost: $1,800-$4,900
Duration: 10 to 18 days
Seasons: year-round

Ecuador's best-known national park, the Galapagos Islands, lies six hundred miles off the country's west coast. The park straddles the equator atop a geological hot spot where the Cocos, Nazca, and Pacific plates collide. The archipelago, consisting of approximately eighty islands, rocks, and islets, was formed by hot lava oozing and exploding up from the ocean. Only eighteen of the islands are of significant size. The tours stop at the six main islands and some of twelve smaller ones.

Charles Darwin called the Galapagos a "living laboratory of evolution." His theory of evolution clicked into place after seeing the islands' remarkable wildlife. Biologists and naturalists who accompany many tours explain the ongoing research and conservation efforts.

Plaza Island supports the Galapagos Islands' largest population of land iguanas and a colony of bachelor sea lions. Blue-footed and masked boobies, red-billed tropic birds, and wallow-tailed gulls nest on the cliffs of the island's southern edge.

Espanola (Hood) Island (some islands have both Spanish and English names) is the world's only breeding ground of the waved albatross. From April to November the birds perform an elaborate, and loud, courtship ritual. Puenta Suarez, located on Espanola Island, is the only territory of the subspecies of marine iguanas, identified by bright red patches on their sides. A trail along the island's cliffs takes you close to nesting colonies of blue-footed and masked boobies, American oyster catchers, and Galapagos doves. You tread among three-hundred- to four-hundred-pound sea lions on your way to the water's edge to snorkel among bright tropical fish.

North Seymore Island is home to frigate birds, the robber barons of the sky. They specialize in harassing boobies taking fish and squid to their young. The frigates frighten the boobies with dive-bombing tactics so that the boobies cough up the food. The frigates then swoop down to catch their ill-gotten gains in midair.

Sea lions bask on the beaches of North Seymore Island. You can walk within touching distance of them, but do not stand between them and the sea. They may become aggressive if they feel their escape route is being cut off.

Isabela Island (Albemarle), the largest island of the archipelago, was formed by five volcanoes flowing together. On towering cliffs boobies, frigate birds, brown pelicans, Audubon shearwaters, and brown noddy terns nest. The birds feed in the richest fishing water in the Galapagos. The world's only equatorial species of penguin, the diminutive Galapagos penguin, lives on the cliffs at Tagus Cove.

At Puenta Morena you walk across the island's black lava to reach the habitats of flamingos, sea turtles, and penguins. A trail on the eastern side of the island leads up Volcan Alcedo (5,400 feet), where giant tortoises live.

Some tours offer an optional additional side trip up the volcano. The physically demanding 5-mile hike takes four to six hours. You carry up to forty pounds of gear in a backpack for a two- or four-night campout. The first 4 miles follow a steady, gradual ascent through a forest of leafless gray *palo santo* trees and scalesia, a member of the daisy family that grows up to 80 feet tall. Near the peak is a saltwater lake with an interesting ecological system. The final mile up to the crater's rim is steep, but the reward is worth it.

Huge tortoises live on the crater's rim and down in the caldera. They are the last of thousands that once lived on the island. In the days of sailing ships the tortoises were carted away to provide long-term on-board provisions. They were thrown into holds on their backs: months of fresh meat on demand.

The vegetarian tortoises laboriously climb the volcano for the food to be found on the mist-shrouded peak. Some of the creatures, which can live for 150 years, may have been born shortly after Darwin left the island. Hundreds of tortoises inhabit the volcano, slowly nibbling their way through the brush. If you get too close, one may hiss, but otherwise they ignore intruders—except for the wild donkeys, one of the feral animals introduced to the islands by man. The donkeys trample the tortoises' nests and compete with them for food. Wild pigs, goats, dogs, and rats also menace the tortoises.

Scientists at the Charles Darwin Research Station on Santa Cruz Island (Indefatigable) raise tortoise hatchlings to help preserve the species.

Fernandina Island (Narborough), across the Bolivar Channel from Isabela, is a perfectly sculpted, intact crater of a ruined volcano. It is the youngest of the Galapagos Islands and is still active. The last eruption occurred in 1984. Much of the island is rough lava that has not yet been broken down by plants.

At low tide, on a walk across the broad lava flow at the water's edge you find large marine iguanas grazing on algae. Cormorants also feed along the shore. Unlike other cormorants, these have evolved into flightless birds due to the lack of predators. Dolphins, porpoise, whales, sea lions, and sea turtles swim in the channel between Fernandina and Isabela Islands.

On Santiago (James) Island the tidal pools teem with octopus, starfish, and other sea life. Great blue herons, lava herons, oyster catchers, and yellow-crowned night herons feed in the pools. A walk along tidal pools takes you to a grotto where a colony of native Galapagos fur seals live. Being night feeders, the seals can be seen sleeping under ledges of grotto walls during the day. Wild goats and pigs roam the island.

Sea lions favor the red beaches of Rabida (Jervis) Island. Pelicans nest in the fringe of saltbushes behind the beaches, and pink flamingos strut their stuff in synchronized rituals behind the bushes that mask small lagoons. The broad-billed fly catcher, the Galapagos hawk, the Galapagos dove, and several kinds of Darwin finches also live on the island.

Santa Cruz Island is the social heart of the Galapagos. Puerto Ayora (population 8,000), the largest of four "urban centers" in the archipelago, is on Santa Cruz. The village is a cluster of houses, small shops, budget restaurants, boat repair yards, and the Hotel Galapagos.

The Charles Darwin Research Station and the Galapagos National Park Headquarters, where scientists conduct biological research and plan conservation projects, are located at nearby Academy Bay. In cooperation with the Galapagos National Park Services, the station's staff raises endangered iguanas and tortoises for return to the native islands on which they evolved. To further nurture native species, staffs of both organizations are developing programs to eradicate plants and animals introduced from the outside world.

International conservation organizations and private donors fund the Darwin station. Some tour operators, such as Inca Floats, Inc., also contribute to the station's budget. Operation funds for the Galapagos National Park comes from entrance fees and the Ecuadoran government.

In Santa Cruz's Tortoise Reserve, located in the highlands, giant tortoises live in their natural habitat. In Caleta Tortuga, a hidden mangrove lagoon on the island's coast, hundreds of sea turtles mate, mostly from November to March. Lava heron, great blue heron, golden spotted eagles, egrets, sharks, and manta rays also reside in the lagoon.

Most tours on the island stop at the rims of two enormous scalesia-forested sinkholes where vermilion flycatchers, Darwin finches, and short-eared owls live.

Floreana Island (Barrington) is another populated island. A walk down the green-tinted coral sand beach takes you to a lagoon where pink flamingos congregate. Devil's Crown, a shallow underwater crater, is great for snorkeling.

Nearby Santa Fe Island, part of the Barringtons, is the home of the Galapagos' largest land iguana. In addition, opuntia cactus, the "tree" of the Galapagos, can be found among the rugged landscape of the eroded lava formations.

Genovesa Island (Tower), the northernmost island in the archipelago, hosts a rich and varied bird life. Exquisitely colored red-footed boobies roost in the trees. Male frigate birds sit on desirable nesting sites in the dark green saltbushes and yodel rancorously to female frigate birds flying overhead. The amazingly loud call gets its force from air in the males' inflated red throat pouches.

The last stop on some tours is Daphne Islet, a small volcanic island with a large colony of blue-footed boobies in its crater. Due to the fragile ecosystem, only one boat per month is allowed to stop at the tiny island.

Although the islands are on the equator, the climate is surprisingly cool. The cold Humboldt and Peruvian currents, originating in the Antarctic, keep the temperature range in the sixties to nineties with December through March being the hottest season. In April the air and water temperatures begin to cool. Late September is the coldest time of the year.

Ironically, the greatest benefactors to the islands' upkeep and research facilities pose the most serious threats to the ecosystems. Tourists contribute thousands of dollars annually to the maintenance of the national park. However, the crowds of tourists stress the environment. To help mitigate this problem, off-season visits are encouraged as are efforts to limit the number of visitors allowed on any one island at a given time.

Tour operators:

Exodus Adventure	Geo Expeditions
Footloose Forays	Inca Floats
Forum	Innerasia Expeditions

International Expeditions

Journeys International

Learned Journeys

Lost World Adventures

Mountain Travel/Sobek
  Expeditions

Overseas Adventure Travel

Questers Worldwide Nature
  Tours

Safaricentre

Voyagers International

Wanderlust Adventures

Wildland Adventures

Woodswomen Adventure Travel
  (women and children only)

World Expeditions

World Wildlife Fund
  Explorations

PERU

Transportation: motor vehicle/boat/hiking

Accommodations: hotels/lodges/on-board

Land cost: $1,400-$2,800

Duration: 7 to 14 days

Seasons: year-round

The Amazon Basin is the world's largest wilderness area, covering 2.5 million square miles stretching over major portions of nine South American countries. The Amazon River and its 1,100 tributaries flowing through the basin contain 66 percent of all river water on Earth—40 percent of it in the Amazon River alone. The 25,000 species of plants found in the Amazon Basin rain forests contribute 20 percent of the oxygen found in the Earth's atmosphere. But the rain forests are not the "lungs of the Earth." They consume as much oxygen as they produce in the decay of organic matter. Rain forests do affect the atmosphere and climate, but not through supplying the world's oxygen, writes Catherine Caufield in her book *In the Rainforest* (University of Chicago Press, 1984).

A trip to the Peruvian Amazon usually involves a tour of the 13,000-square-mile Manu National Park, the largest protected tract of tropical rain forest in the world. Mountain grasslands, tropical rain forest and lowland jungles are all contained within the park's boundaries. Manu is an important link in the forest and river systems of the Madre de Dios region, located on the northern end of the rain forest that extends south to the Tambopata region, because it prevents fragmentation of ecosystems.

Manu is so essential to the Amazon Basin that the United Nations Educational, Scientific, and Cultural Organization (UNESCO) has declared it a biosphere reserve to be regulated by Peruvian scientists and international experts. Biosphere reserves are not recreation parks in the sense of a national park, but exist to protect natural resources and research how to manage the resources for sustainable use.

Biosphere proponents claim that biospheres are the emerging models for managing the entire global landscape. Core areas in biospheres are to be preserved in a pristine state, while the fringe areas are to be made productive without destroying the habitat. UNESCO has designated three hundred biosphere reserves in seventy-five countries.

Tours into Manu are confined to the "buffer zone," one of the biosphere reserve's three designated zones. The outer zone is for land use, mostly farming and logging. The second zone, the "buffer," contains research activities and controlled tourism. The core inner zone is strictly preserved in its natural state without outside interference. Only authorized researchers are allowed into the core area.

Tours stay at lodges, typified by the Manu Jungle Lodge Explorer's Inn, which offers beds, private toilets, and good food. Day—and night—hikes take you away from the last vestiges of the human world. A canoe trip up the Manu River to the Cocha Otorango area takes you even farther into the jungle wilderness.

Until you plunge into the Amazon jungle you cannot imagine how many varied life-forms share this planet. Scientists and naturalists who accompany many of the tours help sort out the tier upon tier of ecological systems, all of which are dependent on each other for survival.

"In the rain forest, no niche lies unused," writes Diana Ackerman in the *New Yorker* (June 24, 1991). "No emptiness goes unfilled, no gasp of sunlight untrapped. In a million vest pockets, a million life-forms quietly tick. No place on earth feels so lush. Sometimes we picture it as an echo of the original Garden—a realm ancient, serene, and fertile, where boas slither and jaguars lope. But it is mainly a world of cunning and savage trees. There is nothing mild-mannered or wimpy about rain forest plants. Truants will not survive; the meek inherit nothing. Light is a thick yellow vitamin they would kill for, and they do."

Tours also visit the Tambopata region, which is south of Manu and more accessible. The rain forest there, which contains over eleven hundred butterfly species, is the most biologically diverse forest outside the corridor of the east Andean slopes. Most tours include hikes and canoe trips into the Tambopata.

Several lodges, such as the Explorer's Inn, provide comfortable accommodations. The inn, a complex of seven separate thatched-roof bungalows, has thirty screened-in rooms with twin beds and private baths but no electricity. Biologists and ecologists on the inn's staff conduct specialized tours into the Tambopata reserve.

Rivers are another route tours take into the Amazon Basin. The cruises usually leave from Iquitos, the only major city on the Upper Amazon. No roads from the outside world penetrate the jungle to Iquitos; planes or boats are the only transportation in or out. The river excursions, aboard either a wooden, twin-decked riverboat or a modern, 75-foot cruise ship, go up the Amazon River into the Manu National Park, up the Rio Tigre and its small tributary, and up the Nahuapa River. Alternative trips are to the Madre Selva Reserve and up the Ampiyac River with stops at Bora and Huitoto Indian villages.

Naturalists and environmentalists give on-board lectures about the riverine and jungle ecosystems. They also lead hikes into the jungle for a firsthand look at the rain forest. The cruises give you a cursory and neatly packaged view of the Amazon, but they do at least introduce you to the rain forest and stress the importance of conserving the habitat.

The Amazonian rain forest environment is being destroyed in several ways. There are plans to build seventy-nine hydroelectric dams in Amazonia over the next twenty years, threatening to flood more than 56,000 square miles of pristine rain forest. In addition, the world's tropical rain forest is burned and bulldozed at the rate of 63,000 square miles each year.

One major negative effect of rain forest destruction is the build-up of carbon dioxide in the global atmosphere that may lead to global warming. Scientists have warned for years that increased levels of carbon dioxide in the atmosphere may result in drastic climate and ecological changes worldwide. Every year an additional four billion tons of carbon accumulates in the atmosphere. Roughly 30 percent of this surplus comes from the accelerated burning of tropical forests.

Tour operators:

Amazonia Expeditions
Amazon Tours & Cruises
Exodus Adventure
Forum
International Expeditions
Mountain Travel/Sobek
    Expeditions

Overseas Adventure Travel
Safaricentre
Wilderness Travel
Wildland Adventures

VENEZUELA

Transportation: motor vehicle/boat/hiking
Accommodations: hotels/lodges/ranches
Land cost: $1,800- $3,000
Duration: 4 to 15 days
Seasons: year-round

Venezuela has the usual offerings of an Amazonian tour—jungle wildlife, rain forest, a mighty river—plus that weird place, the Auyan-tepui. Life atop the 3,212-foot mesa is so strange Arthur Conan Doyle made it the setting for his 1912 novel *The Lost World.* In the novel an explorer discovers a world of prehistoric plants and dinosaurs. On the Auyan-tepui the prehistoric part is true, and you are the explorer.

The Auyan-tepui ("tepui" is the Pemon Indian word for mountain) is a fragment of a massive sandstone plateau that once covered the region. Flora and fauna isolated on the mesa for over a million years have retained primitive traits. A species of toad that lives on the mesa, the *Oreophrynella quelchi*, cannot hop or swim. The protective environment never forced the toad to evolve beyond the stage when it emerged from the ocean that covered the region 1.8 million years ago.

Tours include a one-day fly-in to the Canaima National Park, an area approximately the size of Belgium with a population of less than fifty thousand. You land at Kavak, a small town in the Kamarata Valley on the eastern face of Auyan-tepui. You visit a Pemon Indian village, where the style of the adobe and thatched dwellings has changed little over thousands of years.

The Indians serve as guides on a walk across the savanna and through rain forest to the Kavak Canyon, so narrow and deep that sunlight penetrates only briefly. The small river that spent millions of years sculpting the gorge still flows.

Tours next stop at Angel Falls, which spill off the Auyan-tepui. Discovered in 1935 by American bush pilot Jimmy Angel, the falls are the highest waterfall in the world, fifteen times higher than Niagara Falls (167 feet). Walking paths at the base provide easy access for a close-up look at this natural wonder.

The three-day stay in the 7.4-million-acre Canaima National Park is time well spent. The virgin wilderness contains exotic flora (much of it still unclassified), jaguar, tapir, and rare tropical birds, such as the golden cock-of-the-rock. The wildlife is surprisingly sparse, but the landscape is a showstopper. The sheer walls of the isolated fortress mesas shoot 4,600 to 6,900 feet out of the jungle. The Pemon Indians believe gods live on each mesa.

You take excursions by motorized dugout canoe on the Canaima Lagoon. A ride up the Carrao River, dotted with small tropical islands of pink- and white-sand beaches, takes you to Orchid Island.

The Gran Sabana, the world's third largest national park, lies south of Canaima. To reach the park you first fly to the mining town of Icabaru, then take a jeep up a rugged dirt road to Kawaik High Jungle Lodge, 3,000 feet above the surrounding rain forest. On a hike down into the jungle you spot some of the 250 indigenous species of birds and plants.

On the hike Pemon Indian guides give quick lessons in jungle survival, from finding food—Brazil nuts, palm hearts, and water-bearing vines—to weaving watertight containers from "babacu" palm leaves and making clothes from "matamata" bark. They teach you which jungle plants to use for an upset stomach and how to treat bruises with "Bengue" bark.

Northern Venezuela is Amazonas Territory, the country's wildest and least-populated area. The 1,340-mile-long Orinoco River, the eighth-largest river in the world, serves as the "highway" into the region. You travel from Ciudad Bolivar on a modern excursion boat up the mile-wide Orinoco, which means "father of our land." Gray "delfines" and the pinkish brown "toni-nos"—freshwater dolphins—leap out of the water as they chase schools of fish.

The Camturama Amazonas Resort on the bank of the Orinoco is a popular layover. From there you can take river excursions to the Atures Rapids and nearby islands. Inhabitants of the nearby Coromoto Indian village demonstrate how to use bows and arrows.

Tours go to several parks and wildlife refuges in the northern region of the country. The 250,000-acre cloud forest of the Henri Pittier National Park, 6,000-feet above the coastal tropical low-lands, is the most accessible in Venezuela. Thousands of birds migrating inland use Porstachuelo Pass, a V-notch in the mountains, as an aerial highway.

The park contains four hundred species of birds—nearly half the reported bird life in Venezuela. The rare white-tipped quetzal, the blood-eared parakeet, the blue-capped tanager, the ochre-breasted brush-finch, the buffy hummingbird, and the russet-throated puffbird are all part of Henri Pittier's flying rainbow.

Mount Avila National Park, a two-hour drive from Caracas, is another cloud forest rich with bird life. Bright-blue macaws and tiny hummingbirds flit among the orchids and bromeliads in the forest's upper canopy. You can explore the forest on guided hikes or horseback excursions.

Forty miles off Venezuela's Caribbean north coast lies the Los Roques National Park. The park's 556,345 acres encompass 360 islands, coral reefs, and sand cays. Only forty of the Los Roques Islands have names. Forty-five species of birds, including boobies, herons, and frigate birds, inhabit the islands. Giant sea turtles nest on the beaches in season. Snorkeling among tropical fish gives a look at the underwater wildlife.

The Matiyure Wildlife Sanctuary, home to over two hundred bird species, mammals, and reptiles also lies on Venezuela's Caribbean coast. American flamingos, scarlet ibis, frigate birds, and the rare American crocodile live in the sanctuary's unique ecosystem found only in Venezuela and Colombia. Accommodations are at the Le Cedral, a working ranch.

Accommodations on the jungle tours are usually in lodges or jungle camps with individual cabins. The cabins provide basic comfort: beds and private baths.

Tours also go to the *llanos*, 220,000 square miles of grasslands, marshes, and savannas where the interior great plains meet the Amazon jungle. Wildlife on this "Serengeti of South America" includes red howler monkeys, caimans, giant anteaters, ocelots, and capybara, the world's largest rodent. You visit Ye'wih Valley ("Hidden Valley of the Jaguar"), which was named after the Panare Indian word for jaguar.

The annual flood cycle creates an ever-changing ecosystem on the *llanos*. In the wet season, June to November, rains flood the vast plains, and wildlife are attracted by the plentiful food. During the dry season, December to May, most animals congregate around the remaining wetlands, making game viewing convenient.

You tour the *llanos* by jeep, horseback, or riverboat, depending on the season.

Base camps for the *llanos* tours are usually working ranches. The Dona Barbara Lodge, used by many tours, is located on a 95,000-acre working ranch/wildlife sanctuary near the Upper Apure River. The home-cooked food, including local jungle fruits, is served in a communal dining hall.

Prudence advises taking antimalarial tablets prior to visiting the lowlands. Otherwise, the only other health hazard is overexposure to the sun. Sunscreen, industrial-strength insect repellent, and clothing suitable for hot and rainy conditions are recommended. Temperatures range from daytime highs in the low 80s to nighttime lows in the 70s.

Tour operators:

Cheesemans' Ecology Safaris
International Expeditions
Journeys International
Lost World Adventures
New York Botanical Gardens

Questers Worldwide Nature
    Tours
Safaricentre
Wildland Adventures
World Expeditions

PART III

Family

Tours in this section are adapted especially for families with children ranging in age from three to twelve years, although teenagers would probably enjoy most of the trips, too. Many of the trips described in the Comfortable Wilderness section are suitable for families. However those tours do not place emphasis on the needs of young children as these tours do.

The definition of "family tours" varies considerably among tour operators. One program offered enables a child to stay abreast of schoolwork while on an extended trip. Other international tours have special in-country orientation sessions for children, and many tours have a person designated to give children special attention and instruction.

The family tours, however, do all have several things in common: The pace is adapted to children; accommodations are chosen with their comfort in mind; and, most importantly, the tours are designed so the children have fun while learning about new places, cultures, animals, and the environment. Some tour operators will even custom-design a trip for your family. In addition, great care is given to health matters; the trips do not go to areas where there may be health risks.

Many of the tour operators closely question the parents and children about why they want to go on the trip. Tour operators tell horror stories about children being forced to take a trip "for their own good."

International family tours range from trekking in Nepal or caribou-watching in Canada, to exploring rain forests in Central and South America. North American tours include hiking in New

York's Finger Lakes Forest or Utah's Arches Park, rafting in Alaska, and traveling the Bozeman Trail in Montana by covered wagon.

A happy and successful family trip depends on choosing a journey appropriate for the age level and interests of your children.

Africa

KENYA/TANZANIA

Transportation: motor vehicle
Accommodations: hotels/lodges/tents
Land cost: $3,000-$5,000
Duration: 14 to 20 days
Seasons: year-round

On a typical tour to Kenya and Tanzania, you and your children are eased into the world of African wildlife. After settling into your hotel in Nairobi, you are driven to the Nairobi National Park, located a few miles from the city center. The park, enclosed on three sides, is a bona fide wild game park with few concessions to the nearby urban area.

Animals migrate in and out of the park from the plains that stretch southward to Tanzania. In the park you will see the full spectrum of plains and forest animals found in East Africa. Lions, cheetahs, and rhino are common, as are wildebeest, giraffe, zebras, impala, and hartebeest. Abundant bird life includes turacos, mousebirds, vultures, ostriches, and secretary birds. A walk along the Athi River takes you to the hippo pool where you can observe these "underwater horses." (Hippos run submerged along the bottom of the river like horses run on land.)

Next, the tours usually spend several days in Amboseli National Park, a four-hour drive from Nairobi, and then return to the city for a day before heading out again for a week or more at various game parks: Masai Mara, Tsavo, Lake Naivasha, Samburu, Serengeti, and Ngorongoro. For more details on East African game parks, see COMFORTABLE WILDERNESS: Africa/Kenya/Tanzania.

Some tours include a visit to Malindi on the Indian Ocean coast. The city, a blend of African-Indian-Arabian influences, is interesting for parents and children. At the Watamu Marine National Reserve you can snorkel among brilliantly colored fish in the coral gardens. Miles of unspoiled, white-sand beaches are perfect for building sand castles and beachcombing. The city's restaurants offer a smorgasbord of international food.

Tour operators:

Africa Adventure Company   Voyagers International
Journeys International   Wildland Adventures
Overseas Adventure Travel

Asia

NEPAL

Transportation: motor vehicle/hiking

Accommodations: hotels/lodges/tents

Land cost: $1,200-$1,700

Duration: 16 to 20 days

Seasons: October to April is the prime time. Some tours are offered year-round.

The only way to experience the real Nepal is by hiking. Family trips are designed so that even a three-year-old, the minimum age accepted, can hike the Pokhara Valley or the Annapurna foothills. (However, tour operators prefer children at least five years old.) The children of the tours' Sherpa staff accompany their parents, so your children will meet new playmates and perhaps make a life-long friend. On some tours, a Sherpa guide is assigned to each child.

Life in Nepal revolves around the family. Loyalty to kin comes before loyalty to king or nation. The goals and needs of the individual are subjugated for the good of the family. These hospitable people, whose willingness to share and to give is legendary, outdo even themselves when opening their homes and lives to another family. Since not many families trek Nepal, you and your children will be welcomed and honored guests.

Tours start from Nepal's capital, Kathmandu. The city's Old Bazaar and labyrinth of narrow streets lined with small shops are a treasure trove for children and adults. The Hindu and Buddhist temples provide an introduction to Eastern religions. Day hikes from Kathmandu go into the Himalayan foothills and the Kathmandu Valley.

The tours next fly, or take a chartered bus, to Pokhara (2,950 feet), located 100 miles west of Kathmandu in a valley beneath the Annapurna Massif. For centuries the town has been a cultural crossroads where a rich variety of races and religions meet. Some people claim that the forest in J.R.R. Tolkien's *Hobbit* was inspired by the surrounding Ghorapani forest.

From Pokhara you can hike to Hyangja, a Tibetan refugee camp. There you mingle with the refugees, who fled their country when the Chinese invaded, bartering for curios and hearing their stories of political, cultural, and personal persecution. You stay overnight at a local hotel.

Tours take different routes from Pokhara, but they all follow a common direction before looping back on their final stage. One route follows a fairly steep trail through a forest that leads to a campsite above the Pokhara Basin. From the ridge you get a spectacular view of the 20,000-foot peaks of the Annapurnas, Dhaulagiri, Machapuchare, and Manaslu mountains to the north. The Pokhara Valley spreads below to the east, south, and west.

You carry only a light daypack on the treks. Pack horses and porters carry your personal gear and the food and camping equipment, including fuel for cooking. Responsible tour operators do not use wood for their fires. While a boon to the local economy, tourism poses an environmental threat in the mountains of Nepal, especially for the scarce forest. Providing services for tourists has increased the demand for wood for cooking fuel. As a result, most of the mountains and valleys have been denuded of their once dense forests.

Accommodations on the trekking trips are guesthouses and camping. When camping, the tours' staffs do all the work, including cooking and washing up. You and your children are encouraged to help set up tents and generally lend a hand, but these trips are not roughing it. In the mornings, hot tea is brought to you while you are still snuggled in your sleeping bag. Temperatures at night drop into the thirties and forties. Daytime temperatures range from 60 to 75 degrees.

Another typical trekking route goes to Suiket and over a ridge above the Yangri Khola Valley to a campsite at 6,000 feet. The trek continues over a 7,000-foot pass, then descends to the village of Landrung, where you visit a school. There is plenty of time to meet the villagers. If young children tire, porters will carry them in specially designed wicker baskets—if the child weighs under fifty pounds. Another route follows a ridge to Naudanda village and a campsite at Kare (5,700 feet). Both routes take you close to the sheer face of the Annapurna Massif without a long approach or ascending to high altitude (anything over 9,000 feet).

Both of the routes then make a steep descent on a long series of stone steps to the Modi Khola River. Crossing the river on a suspension bridge can be a bit breathtaking for young and old alike. The five-hour hike ends at a campsite on the outskirts of the village of Ghandrung or Tirkhedunga.

The tours then climb again through a dense rhododendron forest to Ghorapani Pass (9,350 feet), stopping at villages to meet local children. On some tours you spend a day on the ridgetop and have the option of either climbing Poon Hill (9,940 feet) or visiting villages. Other tours descend more quickly into the Modi Khola Valley.

A well-maintained trail follows the contours of the Modi Khola

Valley and leads down through fields and forests to the village of Birethanti, on the banks of a river.

The trail then climbs up to the village of Chandrakot, perched high above the convergence of two gorges, and joins a major foot route linking central and western Nepal. You meet a Chaucerian stream of people on the trail—religious pilgrims, traders with pony caravans, other trekkers, and villagers heading for market.

You camp at Yarsa after a five-hour hike in a high meadow near a temple away from villages. The Annapurna Range stretches across the horizon as far as you can see. An even more impressive view is from the Shiva Temple, a six-hour hike along the ridge.

The descent takes you to Phewa Lake, where you row across to a lakeside campsite near a grove of giant Boddhi trees, considered sacred by Buddhists.

Still another trekking route starts in Gorkha, the ancient capital of Nepal, a five-hour ride by minibus from Kathmandu. The trek is similar in nature to the ones described above: you climb 8,000-foot passes, visit villages, have fantastic views of Annapurna, and walk through forests. However, on this tour, you have the option of a two-day raft trip down the Trisuli River to the bazaar town of Narayanghat. A short jeep ride then takes you to the Royal Chitwan Wildlife Reserve on the Indian border.

The 360-square-mile Chitwan park is known for Bengal tigers and one-horned rhino. You ride on an elephant's back looking for these and other wild animals hiding in the 10-foot-tall grass and the dense forests. The park's forest, riverine, and aquatic habitats are home to wild boars, sloth bears, various species of deer and leopards, and more than three hundred species of birds. For children, and adults, riding an elephant on a wild game drive is like living a Rudyard Kipling story. On a raft or canoe trip down the Rapti River you may spot crocodiles.

While touring Chitwan, accommodations are at the Tiger Tops Jungle Lodge or the Tiger Tree Tops Tented Camp. Visits to Tharu villages show you a culture distinctly different than that of the hill people.

Family tours to Nepal involve more than just walking from one beautiful place to another for grand views of stunning mountains. Opportunities are created for your children to meet and interact with local children. Schools are visited when you stay in villages, and parents always find a common interest to discuss—children.

No special physical requirements are necessary for these treks, although being fit makes them much more enjoyable.

For more information on Nepal see NOT ORDINARY TRIPS: Asia/Nepal.

Tour operators:

Above the Clouds Trekking
Himalayan Travel
Journeys International

Overseas Adventure Travel
Wildland Adventures

Central America

COSTA RICA

Transportation: motor vehicle/train
Accommodations: hotels/lodges
Land cost: $1,700-$2,000
Duration: 10 to 12 days
Seasons: December to August

Volcanoes, rain forests, beaches, cloud forests, and exotic wildlife make Costa Rica an exciting destination for the whole family. Tours concentrate on national parks and reserves that are easily accessible from San Jose, the capital.

Costa Rica's wildlife parks and reserves shelter numerous species of wild birds, mammals, reptiles, amphibians, and insects, including 490 species of butterflies. The rain forest contains 8,000 species of trees and plants, including 1,200 species of orchids. The Poas Volcano National Park, an hour's drive from San Jose, is home to two 8,800-foot volcanic peaks—one active, one dormant—in a surrounding cloud forest. Steam curls from the active crater, which last erupted in 1989. The dormant crater, a half-mile higher, is surrounded by a cloud forest where wild hummingbirds, emerald toucans, tapir, and coati (similar to the raccoon) live.

The lush primary forest of the Carara Biological Reserve, a half-hour drive from San Jose, is home to monkeys, agouti (a rodent about the size of a rabbit), crocodiles, and boat-billed herons. One of the few remaining populations of the Meso-american scarlet macaw also lives in the 11,614-acre reserve. You explore the forest on an easy hike led by a naturalist.

The tours then continue for an hour or so past Carara on a narrow paved road through a tropical forest coastal range to the town of Quepos. From there a dirt road leads over a set of hills to the Manuel Antonio National Park on the Pacific Coast.

A limited trail system penetrates a small section of the park's tropical forest, where capuchin and squirrel monkeys live. White-crowned parrot, blue-crowned manakin, blackhooded antshrike, and rufous-backed antwren live in the forest's canopy. However, you may have difficulty pulling your family away from the beaches to explore the forest. Four beaches separate the park's 1,687 acres of tropical forest from the blue Pacific.

Tours also visit the Selve Verda lowland forest, in the northeast region near the Nicaraguan border. Jaguar, tapir, and toucans, which are usually only seen in pet stores, live in the forest. Most tours stay at the Selva Verde Lodge, which has its own private 500-acre nature reserve. On walks through the reserve, a resident naturalist explains how the plants and animals are dependent on one another to maintain the forest's ecological balance.

A trip to the northwest Guanacaste province gives you an opportunity to meet other families—turtle families. At night you watch as green sea turtles crawl out of the surf, dig a nest, and lay their eggs. The best turtle nesting time is from November to April. During the day you explore the Palo Verde Wildlife Reserve. You stay at the luxurious Ocotal Resort on the Pacific Coast.

No special health precautions are necessary when visiting Costa Rica. Some tours, such as Wildland Adventures, accept

children as young as two years old. The Costa Rican people absolutely adore children and may invite you and your children into
their homes.

For more details on Costa Rica see COMFORTABLE WIL-
DERNESS: Central America/Costa Rica.

Tour operators:

Journeys International   Wildland Adventures

North America

CANADA

Canadian Rockies
Transportation: hiking/raft/canoe
Accommodations: lodges/tents
Land cost: $510-$2,200
Duration: 5 to 7 days
Seasons: June to September

Tours to the Canadian Rockies offer a potpourri of experiences—
horseback riding, a float trip, heli-hiking, and even hiking with
goats. The trips are designed to give children hands-on access to a
variety of wilderness encounters.

A horseback/hiking/float trip, offered by Overseas Adventure
Travel, is based at the Goat Mountain Lodge in the Blaeberry
Valley, 150 miles west of Calgary, near the small town of Golden.
On the drive from the Calgary International Airport you pass
through stunning Banff National Park and Lake Louise.

The four-bedroom log lodge, located at the base of Goat
Mountain, in a meadow surrounded by a forest, accommodates a
maximum of twelve guests. A large sitting room with a fireplace
serves as a communal gathering place. Family style meals are prepared from locally grown ingredients.

Each child is given a logbook in which to record personal

accounts of daily trips to local sites. The Blaeberry River, fed by a glacier 18 miles away, flows through the valley. Thompson Falls tumbles down the mountain 4 miles from the lodge.

One hike follows a mountain stream through an old growth forest of British Columbia cedar and Douglas fir to Mummery Glacier. A guide explains the forest's ecosystem of decaying trees, fungi, mosses, and flowers. The trail comes out of the forest into an open glacial moraine. Thundering waterfalls, huge blocks of ice, and the massive glacier loom overhead. Your guide explains the geological formation of the glacier.

Children are also given instruction in how to use a compass and map and how to find their way in the mountains.

Another day hike on the tour begins with a helicopter ride. You land on the rugged Red Indian Ridge of the Van Horne Range above Goat Mountain and hike the seldom-traveled ridgetop (8,000 feet), following a mountain goat path. Alpine flowers, mosses, and lichens make good subjects for children to sketch in their logbooks, as are the views of the Purcells, the Selkirks, the Rockies, and the Columbia Valley.

The tour also includes a one-day float trip down the Blaeberry River in inflatable rafts. The trip poses no threats but is not without thrills, especially when running through a canyon. Along the way, the ecology of mountain rivers is explained.

The final day trip is a horseback ride on the David Thompson Trail, which was blazed by Indians and used by fur traders in the early 1800s. No previous riding experience is necessary; the mountain-bred horses are surefooted and dependable. The guide recounts historical tales of the area as you ride through the forest and across streams. At lunch around a campfire, children are taught how to bake bannock, a flat bread.

If you and your family are looking for a more unique wilderness experience, Outer Edge Expeditions offers a goat-hiking trip that explores the Rockies west of Calgary. You spend five days hiking and camping in Kananaskis country near the Banff National Park. The goats carry all the gear and food. You hike through several different kinds of forest, up limestone peaks with hanging glaciers, and through meadows of wildflowers. The pace is leisurely. The guide is a storehouse of information about the geology of the Rockies, the history of the area, the animals, and their habitat. The trip provides a good introduction to backcountry wilderness.

Tour operators:

Outer Edge Expeditions   Overseas Adventure Travel

Northern Canada Caribou Watching

Transportation: hiking/canoe
Accommodations: tents
Land cost: $2,000
Duration: 7 days
Seasons: late August

Who knows the way of the wind? The caribou do. For some reason children love that line. Perhaps it is more poignant once you have followed caribou herds around the tundra of Canada's Far North.

The trip, offered by Wilderness Inquiry, leaves from Yellowknife in the Northwest Territories, a small town on the northern shore of Great Bear Lake. Guides scout the great ice shield, pitted with lakes and scraped nearly down to ancient rock by retreating glaciers, for the Porcupine caribou herds. Once the herds are located, you fly to where they are and set up a portable base camp: sleeping tents, a kitchen and dining tent, and a communal tent. When the herd moves, you move. If the herd stays reasonably close, you make day trips to observe them.

This trip is for those who relish all aspects of a wilderness experience —including flocks of voracious mosquitoes and biting black flies, wet feet, and the exhilaration of being beyond the call of modern civilization.

The caribou move in the largest migratory herds in North America and now number approximately two hundred thousand. Historically the caribou have been as vital to the indigenous peoples of the Far North as the buffalo were to the Plains Indians. In the past, entire villages faced a cruel, often deadly, winter if the migration did not occur on schedule or if the route shifted. Your guides explain the connections between the caribou, the native people's culture, and the fragile tundra ecosystem.

Tour operator:

Wilderness Inquiry

Vancouver Island Orca Whale Watching

Transportation: boat/kayak
Accommodations: tents
Land cost: $999 for adults; $499 for children ages 3-12
Duration: 4 days
Seasons: June to September

On this trip you observe the orca in the wild either from a motorized boat or a sea kayak, both of which are suitable for young children. The two-person sea kayaks are stable, flat-bottomed boats with foot-operated rudders for easy control and maneuverability, and you and your family are given operation and safety instructions before you venture out in them.

You paddle the waters of Johnstone Strait off the northeastern tip of Vancouver Island. You do not even need to get into a boat to see the whales. The base camp is located on a promontory overlooking Blackfish (a local name for the orca) Sound, one of the two channels used by the orca as they come in from the open waters of Queen Charlotte Strait to feed on salmon and to visit Robson Bight and the rubbing beach. The rubbing beach area has been set aside as an ecological reserve from which all boats are banned when the whales are present, giving them some peace and privacy. The whales rub themselves on the pebble beaches for pleasure and to cleanse their skin.

Up to a hundred wild orcas have been seen during a single day in Johnstone Strait as they congregate to feed, play, rest, and socialize. You can see family pods interacting together and 30-

foot-long individuals breach, taillob, fin, and spyhop—a much better show than trained tricks.

There are two types of orca whales: the larger primary salmon feeders that you will see and small transient groups of a different gene pool that can, and do, devour sharks.

Orcas have a sophisticated social and communication system. Acoustic hydrophones (underwater microphones) and special receivers are used to listen to their shrills and clicks. The orca is one of the few species, including *Homo sapiens*, in which different family groups have distinct dialects. A trained naturalist helps interpret the signals and tells you about the whale. Your observing is done so as not to adversely affect the whales in their natural habitat.

The base camp consists of a central dining and lounging building with a front deck for whale watching. You sleep in double-occupancy, roomy mountain tents with cots and mattresses. Meals are prepared by a cook. A maximum of ten people can occupy the camp at one time.

The weather is variable. In midsummer, daytime temperatures range from 70 to 75 degrees, but cool breezes off the water make it seem chillier. In the evening, temperatures drop to around 55 degrees. The water temperature remains close to 48 degrees year-round.

Tour operator:

Ecosummer Expeditions

UNITED STATES—WEST

ALASKA

Alagnak River Rafting
Transportation: floatplane/raft
Accommodations: tents
Land cost: $1,350 for adults; $895 for children
Duration: 11 days
Seasons: July

According to the Sierra Club, this tour, which includes an eight-day float down the Alagnak River, is "designed for parent(s) who would like to provide a daughter or son (age twelve to sixteen) the opportunity to mark the significant transition from adolescence to adulthood with a major wilderness experience."

The trip begins with a flight from Anchorage 240 miles south-west to Illiamna. There you transfer to a floatplane for the hop to Nonvianuk Lake, from which the Alagnak River flows. The river extends nearly 80 miles west-southwest until it joins the Kvichak River, which eventually flows into Bristol Bay and on to the Bering Sea.

The Alagnak River, part of the Wild and Scenic Rivers System, is not dangerous, having only a few small rapids. You cover only a few river miles each day, allowing ample opportunity for fishing and hiking. No previous rafting experience is necessary, but you should be in good physical condition. Helping with loading and unloading the raft, collecting firewood, and preparing meals is part of the trip.

Wildlife along the river includes brown bear, wolf, red fox beaver, and otter. Bald eagles, osprey, ptarmigan, spruce grouse, swans, and a variety of ducks are also frequently seen.

After arriving at the lower reaches of the Alagnak, you fly by floatplane south to Naknek Lake for a day at Brooks Camp in Katmai National Park. While at the camp, you can take a bus to the Valley of Ten Thousand Smokes, which was cratered by the 1912 eruption of Novarupta Volcano.

For more information on Alaska, see SAFE THRILLS: North America/United States/Alaska.

Sea Kayaking in Glacier Bay

Transportation: kayak

Accommodations: lodges/tents

Land cost: $950 for adults; $807 for children under 20

Duration: 5 days

Seasons: June to August

A kayaking trip to the Beardslee Islands in the Glacier Bay National Park Wilderness Waters is designed specifically for families with children between the ages of nine and fifteen. The tour operator, Alaska Discovery, allows younger children to participate only if they have sufficient wilderness camping experience.

The trip starts and ends in Gustavus, which is located on a peninsula west of Juneau where the Icy Strait flows down from Glacier Bay. The water is not as cold as the names make it sound; it varies between 46 and 64 degrees. During the first day, kayaking instruction is given to novices. You then load up the kayaks and wait for the tide before pushing off into Bartlett Cove.

For three days you explore myriad islands in this forested area, which is very different from the rugged, austere landscape found farther north in the park. Paddling along the intertidal zone you see seals, bald eagles, a variety of songbirds and shore birds, and perhaps an occasional black bear. At night, you set up tents on the beach or on the edge of the forest. Around the campfire the guide explains forest succession and old growth ecosystems.

The time on the water is geared to the physical ability of the children. Each child is carefully schooled in water safety procedures. Guides take care to explain about the life of the whales and the other marine animals and why these animals come to Glacier Bay. The interrelationship between the bay and the surrounding forest is put into a comprehensive context. The information is presented in a manner suitable to the ages of the children.

Accommodations in Gustavus are at the Glacier Bay Lodge or the Gustavus Bed & Breakfast.

Tour operators:

Alaska Discovery   Sierra Club Outings
Alaska Wildland Adventures

CALIFORNIA

Transportation: hiking
Accommodations: tents

Land cost: $1,135

Duration: 7 days

Seasons: July to August

The Big Pine Lakes in the John Muir Wilderness in the California Sierras is a cluster of alpine lakes surrounded by forest and glacier bowls. A camp by one of the lakes serves as base for day hikes into this high country (average altitude of 10,800 feet) that is not heavily visited.

The trip is designed to introduce parents and children to safety techniques for enjoying the wilderness. The trip is suitable for people from the ages of six to sixty who are in good physical condition. Experienced campers also find this area, with its many beautiful peaks and lakes, rewarding.

The trip is planned to coincide with when the wildflowers bloom. You take gentle walks through aspen and pine forests, past pools, streams, and waterfalls. Or you can make steep climbs to the high peaks.

You carry only a daypack on the climb up to the base camp. Packers haul the heavier gear—food, tents, sleeping bags, and cooking equipment. Each person is limited to twenty pounds of gear, plus an additional ten pounds per family. Everyone shares cooking and camp maintenance responsibilities.

Tour operator:

Sierra Club Outings

COLORADO

Transportation: hiking

Accommodations: tents

Land cost: $225 for adults; $150 for child

Duration: 7 days

Seasons: July

The San Juan Mountains in southwestern Colorado, near New Mexico, is one of the least visited wilderness areas in the state renowned for the Rocky Mountains. In this vast, roadless, alpine and subalpine region of glacial valleys and high peaks live elk, deer, bighorn sheep, golden eagles, ptarmigan, and black bears.

This hike loops through the mountains covering 15 to 20 miles in seven days. You walk 2 to 5 miles a day on well-maintained trails with no steep altitude increases traversing. On the three lay-over days you can climb the higher peaks, visit nearby lakes, or just relax. At night you camp at mountain lakes or along rivers. The easy access and gently graded trails makes this an ideal introductory hiking trip for families and children.

The trip is suitable for children of all ages. Parents of younger children are expected to guide them and carry their gear, if necessary. Parents with toddlers or infants are expected to carry them and a proportionate share of the group's gear.

Children are quizzed on why they want to make this trip. They must respond, in writing, to questions like, "What do I want to learn about on this trip?" "What do I like about nature?" "What are things I am worried about on this trip?" The information is used by the trip leader to help customize the trip to the children.

The average daily elevation gain will be well under 1,000 feet; the greatest gain comes on the second day, 1,200 feet in 3.5 miles. The trailhead lies at 10,160 feet (the hike's high point is 12,000) 60 miles southwest of Alamosa, Colorado.

Expect warm and sunny days, although summer snowstorms can occur in the high country. Afternoon rain squalls are very possible. Nighttime temperatures may drop to freezing. You should bring clothes for all weather conditions and a warm sleeping bag. Food, stoves, cooking gear, and first-aid kits are provided. Each person should have a canteen and some means of purifying water.

Tour operator:

Sierra Club Outings

HAWAII

Transportation: hiking/motor vehicle
Accommodations: lodges

Land cost: $770 for adults; $515 for children

Duration: 7 days

Seasons: April

This family trip explores Kauai's Na Pali coast, the Alakai Swamp, the Hanalei Valley, and the Waimea Canyon, the "Grand Canyon of the Pacific." The hikes are short and easy, allowing ample time to observe the natural world. The guide explains the ecosystems of each area. There is also plenty of time for fun on the beach and snorkeling.

The guides take care to make the hikes a fun learning experience for children. While exploring Waimea Canyon they learn why the various rock stratums are different colors. How the canyon was formed is explained in a way children will comprehend. The canyon becomes a living classroom for geology, botany, and natural science lessons.

For more information on Hawaii, see COMFORTABLE WILDERNESS and NOT ORDINARY TRIPS: North America/ United States/ Hawaii.

Tour operator:

Sierra Club Outings

MONTANA

Bozeman Trail Wagon Train

Transportation: covered wagon

Accommodation: tents

Land cost: $480 for adults; $380 for children ages 8 to 14; no charge for children ages 3 to 7

Duration: 4 days

Seasons: May to September

This tour lets you and your family follow the Bozeman Trail used by pioneers over one hundred years ago. The 36-mile trip goes along the Work Creek drainage, which runs parallel to the Beartooth Mountains, and over plains that were once Crow and

Sioux Indian territory. You cross Jackson Divide and descend into Stillwater Valley and Bridger Creek Canyon. The tour also includes rafting on the Yellowstone River.

The trip gives a taste of what Indians and early settlers saw when the West was still wide open. The wagons are authentic reproductions and care is given to recreate an Old West atmosphere. You are taught how to drive the wagons; when not in the wagon, you ride a horse alongside.

Meals, prepared in the chuck wagon, are eaten around a campfire. In the evenings, tales of western history are told and the local ecology is explained.

Tour operator:

American Wilderness Experience

UTAH

Arches National Park Adventure
Transportation: hiking
Accommodations: tents
Land cost: $370 for adults; $250 for children
Duration: 6 days
Seasons: May

The delicate stone arch of Utah's Arches National Park appears so fragile that you half expect the next desert breeze will blow it away. The park, formerly Arches National Monument, contains over one hundred such natural marvels, including wind-sculpted caverns, giant boulders balanced on pinnacles, and rugged massifs of 150-million-year-old stone dabbed in delicate earth hues.

The park is a nature playground for children and their parents. Short day hikes suited for kids three to six years old highlight this trip. Around the campfire a U.S. Forest Ranger gives talks about desert ecology and the importance of protecting the desert habitat.

Two summers spent as a ranger at Arches National Park inspired Edward Abbey to write two books advocating an ardent defense of nature, *Desert Solitaire* and *The Monkey Wrench Gang*. For Abbey, the desert was an environment that nurtured his soul. On hikes through Arches and other deserts in New Mexico and California, Abbey came to realize that without respect for the natural world, the human world becomes soiled and distorted. The Arches uncompromising beauty may inspire in your children a similar lasting respect for nature.

The trip will also make you and your family aware of the environmental threats to American deserts, such as inappropriate recreational use, mining, cattle grazing, and urban development. In particular, the growing popularity of recreational off-road vehicles (ORVs) has taken its toll. According to a study by the U.S. Fish and Wildlife Service, moderate ORV use has already reduced animal life in some desert areas by nearly 60 percent. ORVs break up the crust of closely set rocks, called desert pavement, that helps protect the land from wind erosion. According to the California Desert Protection League, heavy ORV use has stripped and scarred more than a million acres of land in the California desert in little over twenty years.

Base camp for your walks through the Arches is near Devil's Garden. The campground has restrooms and running water, but no showers or kitchen facilities. You must provide your own waterproof tent, sleeping pads and bags, and eating utensils. The trip organizer, Sierra Club, provides the cooking gear.

Expect warm days and cool nights. Wind, rain, and cold weather are possible during the desert spring, so bring warm clothes and raingear.

Arches National Park is located five miles north of Moab, Utah. The nearest large towns are Grand Junction, Colorado, and Provo, Utah, both 110 miles away.

Tour operator:

Sierra Club Outings

WASHINGTON

Stehekin Valley, North Cascade Mountains

Transportation: hiking
Accommodations: cabins
Land cost: $825
Duration: 6 days
Seasons: May through September

Day hikes from the Stehekin Valley Ranch base camp take you and your family to waterfalls, meadows of wildflowers, and over mountain passes. With young children you can spend a day dawdling along a stream observing how the stream, the meadow, and the forest work together. With older children you can take a 16-mile hike to a high pass. You can also follow old prospectors' trails through the North Cascades National Park. The atmosphere is very relaxed giving you and your family ample time to explore the natural world.

Accommodations are wood/tent cabins with beds, showers, and flush toilets. Each cabin sleeps two to five people. You must bring your own sleeping bags and towels. Home-cooked meals are served in the family style dining room.

For more details, see COMFORTABLE WILDERNESS: North America/United States/Washington.

Tour operator:

Sierra Club Outings

MIDWEST

MINNESOTA

Canoeing the Boundary Waters

Transportation: canoe
Accommodations: lodges/tents
Land cost: $1995 for family up to four
Duration: 5 to 7 days
Seasons: July to September

One of the best voyages you will ever launch starts by slipping a canoe into the lake, whispering to your child to be silent, and paddling into the morning mist to search for a moose.

Days in the Boundary Waters Canoe Area Wilderness along the Minnesota-Ontario border begin with such journeys. They end at either a campsite or a lodge, depending on your preference.

Tours start at various put-in sites along the 150 miles of wilderness straddling the U.S.-Canada border. Gunflint Lake is one spot popular with families. Accommodations are at the Gunflint Lodge, located on the lakeshore across from the Canadian border. The cabins, with one to four bedrooms, have fireplaces, full bathrooms, private saunas, and daily maid service. All meals are provided. A staff naturalist conducts a nature program seven days a week, including hikes and canoe trips just for children.

From Gunflint Lake you can take a two-day canoe trip that loops through a chain of lakes. You camp on shore at night. Or you can paddle the Granite River, one of the prettiest waterways in the Boundary Waters. On this trip you camp one night and spend the second at the Chippewa Inn.

For more details on the Boundary Waters, see COMFORTABLE WILDERNESS: North America/United States/Minnesota.

Tour operator:

Canoe Country Escapes

NORTHEAST

NEW YORK

Finger Lakes Forest

Transportation: hiking

Accommodations: tents

Land cost: $325 for adults; $215 for children

Duration: 6 days

Seasons: July

Finger Lakes Forest is Family Camping 101. Sierra Club, the trip's sponsor, geared the pace and the format especially for families with young children. Day hikes, which range in length from 3 to 6 miles round-trip, take your family through the forests, meadows, farmlands, and rolling hills of central New York. You explore sculptured gorges, swim in waterfall pools, and visit a bird sanctuary, a farm, and a winery.

The isolated base camp, which has a capacity of twenty people, consists of tent sites scattered in a meadow surrounded by woods. You and your children have plenty of time to explore the woods and fields or to row on Cayuga and Seneca lakes.

At night around the campfire, U.S. Forest Rangers and members of local conservation organizations give presentations on local conservation and/or cultural issues. On one evening a storyteller entertains the children.

You are expected to help with camp chores, such as cooking, cleaning, wood gathering, water pumping, and other general duties. Recycling is *de rigueur*.

You must provide your own waterproof tent, eating utensils, and plates. A wash basin is available, but there are no sinks at the campground.

Sturdy, comfortable footgear is essential. Although the days are generally warm and dry, temperatures at night drop into the 40s so bring warm clothes. It would also be a good idea to bring rain gear, just in case.

The fate of the forests in both New York State and the Northeast region is uncertain today. More than half of the 6.2-million-acre Adirondack State Park is privately owned, primarily by timber companies. In the Northeast, 84 percent of the forestland is owned by forty-five different timber companies, paper mills, and local families. The unprotected forests can be clear-cut for profit at will. New York State does not have the money to buy the forest land. Environmental groups, such as Sierra Club, keep a watchful eye on potential clear-cutting. When they feel a forest is in imminent danger, they bring the issue to the public's attention.

Tour operator:

Sierra Club Outings

South America

ECUADOR

Andes to Amazon

Transportation: motor vehicle/hiking
Accommodations: hotels/lodges
Land cost: $1,350-$1,700
Duration: 11 to 15 days
Seasons: year-round

The Andes part of tours to Ecuador starts in the country's capital, Quito, a mile-high city of sixteenth-century Spanish architecture mingled with modern glass-and-steel buildings. A couple of hours' drive from Quito is the Indian market at Otavalo, in the beautiful northern Imbabura Andean region. The Otavalo Indians are famous for their weavings, pottery, and baskets. As part of the tour you take a short hike through the rural countryside, where the people tend their terrace crops and stroll the shores of Cuicocha Crater Lake. You spend the night at a colonial-style inn. Minimum age on the tours is usually four years.

You also visit other villages in the Otavalo region known for producing certain crafts: Peguche (weavings), Iluman (hats), Carabuela and Natabuela (embroidery and weaving). You meet the artisans and can purchase goods before they go to the Otavalo market.

The tour route crosses the lower slopes of Mount Imbabura volcano to Lake San Pablo. Another stop is made at the pre-Inca ruin Caranqui, which has well-preserved pyramids.

The highland tours always include a trip to the 19,342-foot Cotopaxi Volcano, the world's highest active volcano, located south of Quito. In good weather you can drive to the tundra zone just below glacial formations. The region around the volcano's base is intensely cultivated, as are most of the highlands, and pop-ulated with many villages. The tours stop at various villages where you get a chance to meet the genuinely friendly people, who open their homes at the sight of a child.

The Amazon part of the tours starts with a flight from Quito to Coca, a frontier oil "boomtown" on the Napo River. The town gives you a firsthand look at the consequences of development in the rain forest.

From Coca, a two-hour ride down the Napo in a motorized dugout canoe takes you to Las Selva Lodge. The muddy brown Napo, a tributary of the Amazon River, cuts through dense jungle. The image of pristine wilderness is spoiled only by the buzz of the two-stroke outboard motor. But the motorized canoe is considered progress for the Indians who use the waterways to transport their goods.

Las Selva Lodge, on the shore of Garzacocha (Heron) Lake, is a cluster of palm-thatched cabanas on stilts. Each cabana has twin beds, a private toilet, and a cold-water shower. Kerosene lanterns provide light. Short excursions from the lodge take you into the heart of virgin jungle. Forty species of birds live in the immediate vicinity, including macaws, flycatchers, toucans, and parrots. A 120-foot tower near the lodge lets you view monkeys and birds in the jungle canopy.

Day-long canoe trips go to Mandicocha Lake, where herons, kingfishers, horned screamers, and harpy eagles hunt. On jungle hikes, a naturalist points out the intricacies of the rain forest ecosystem.

For more details on Ecuador, see COMFORTABLE WILDER-NESS: South America/Ecuador. Variations on these tours can be combined with a trip to the Galapagos Islands.

Tour operators:

Journeys International	Voyagers International
Overseas Adventure Travel	Wildland Adventures

Galapagos Islands

Transportation: boat

Accommodations: on-board

Land cost: $1,800-$2,400

Duration: 8 to 14 days

Seasons: year-round

No school course or television documentary will show you and your children the wonders of natural history as will a visit to the Galapagos Islands.

You and your family get a chance to see sea lions, blue-footed boobies, and tortoises that live on top of a volcano. You will watch pink flamingos strut through their mating rituals and see sea turtles lay their eggs on the beach. Research scientists at the Charles Darwin Research Station explain the intricate, interlocking ecosystems of the islands.

The family tours are safe, comfortable, educational, and fun. For details on the Galapagos, see COMFORTABLE WILDERNESS: South America/Ecuador/Galapagos.

Tour operators:

Journeys International   Wildland Adventures
Overseas Adventure Travel

PART IV

Raw Adventure

Trips in this section require you to push yourself to the limit. They are physically very demanding. You are taken out of your normal cultural and personal context. These trips go to some of the most remote, isolated wilderness regions on Earth. They are more than a journey to a strange land: they are an opportunity to discover things about yourself.

The three trips in this section take you to the deep jungles of Irian Jaya, to a remote region of Nepal recently opened to foreigners, and to the Sanctuary of the Concordia high in the mountains of Pakistan.

IRIAN JAYA

Trekking to Asmat, Dani, and Yali Peoples

Transportation: small plane/dugout canoe/hiking
Accommodations: guesthouses/lodges/tents
Land cost: $1,525-$4,000
Duration: 8 to 15 days
Seasons: May to August

At what price fun. In the coastal swamps of Irian Jaya the heat, humidity, and bugs suck out your vitality. In the highlands of Irian Jaya the heat, humidity, and steep mountainsides try your patience. You plod forward because pride refuses to let you collapse on the spot. But the trip to the tribes of Irian Jaya is exciting, certainly satisfying, and, you grimly admit with a grin, even fun.

Irian Jaya is on the western half of an island roughly the size of California (Papua New Guinea is on the eastern half). It is touted as the remotest, wildest, most removed place on Earth—an accurate description. Irian Jaya is the least developed, least populated, and least visited of any part of Indonesia, which governs the territory.

The Asmat peoples live in the southern jungle coastal region that stretches to the interior mountain range. World-renowned wood-carvers and artists, their extraordinary work is considered by ethnologists to be among the world's most important primitive art. The Asmat view their work not as art but as an expression of their spiritual life.

Their relationship with the spirit world is very intense. The spirits are not benign. They must be constantly appeased. Living in the jungle is not paradisaical but a fierce competition for survival. The Asmat were once ferocious headhunters because they believed life comes from the death of another human being. They would eat their victims to get that person's strength, courage, and spirit.

Gradually they gave up headhunting and cannibalism after contact with Dutch missionaries in 1938. However, battles with other tribes over stealing a pig or other offenses still occur. The Asmat are skilled bow-and-arrow hunters and gatherers of the jungle's flora. The sago palm is a principle staple of their diet. They live in large family groups, each group isolated from the others. Their culture is extremely ritualistic involving gift-giving—including exchanging wives—honoring ancestral spirits, and paying homage to spirits of the natural world.

This tour reaches the Asmat either by coming down from the central highlands or going up the rivers from the coast.

The trip down from the highlands starts with a flight to the small highland village of Langda. The first three or four days of the hike are extremely rugged as you haul yourself up and over tightly packed, steep-sided ridges. Porters carry the heavy gear, but the physical effort is still extreme. You must be in excellent physical condition.

The trails, where they exist, do not follow the contour of streams or hillsides. They take the shortest line between two points—straight up and straight down. Only when you reach the lowland jungle with its network of rivers flowing to the coast does the relentless climbing stop. But in the lowlands the daily rain causes flooding, forcing you to wade through the jungle. The midday sun is intense and the humidity near saturation point.

Along the rivers live uncontacted upper Asmat tribes. You may or may not see them.

When you reach the lowlands, you climb aboard a large dugout canoe. For eight days you explore the river system, stopping at Asmat villages, often spending the night. In the swamps the people live in large tree houses, where you also sleep.

Starting from the coast, you take a motorized dugout on the main river, Asyewtz, to the village of Warse on the Yet River. You continue on the Siretz River to the village of Amborep and upstream to Kaimo. Here you share dinner with the Asmat and spend the night in a villager's home or in a two-person tent.

This is the routine for the next five days as you make your way deep into the jungle and loop back to Warse, using the rivers and streams like interconnecting highways.

The highland trips to the Yali and Dani tribes are suitable "only for the extremely fit outdoor enthusiast. For the unfit or those unaccustomed to rugged terrain at high elevations with the potential of extreme heat, the trips are impossible," warns Ecosummer Expeditions.

The trip starts in the Grand Valley of the Baliem River (5,000 feet). You fly by small plane to Wamena, a grassy airstrip on the valley floor that has grown into a small town with services and supplies for hiking expeditions. A small hotel serves as your base for a couple of days as you take day hikes to acclimatize.

In the town market you see your first Dani. The tribesmen, wearing only *koteka* (penis gourds) and bone amulets through their noses, strike deals with Indonesian businessmen dressed in suits. The Dani have a long tradition of intertribal warfare, headhunting, and cannibalism.

An afternoon introductory hike goes along the southern edge of the Baliem Valley. You cross the Wamena River on a hanging bridge and hike a trail at the base of the ridges. You meet Dani on the trail and as you pass fields where they work their sweet potato patches.

"Dani" is a generic term applied to all the tribes of the Baliem Valley, which has been inhabited for more than forty thousand years. The men wear only penis gourds and the women grass skirts. However, they elaborately decorate their bodies with feathers, shells, and paint. Each family lives in a separate roundhouse within a fortified compound. They keep a sweet potato patch and pigs within the compound so the group can survive a siege. The pigs are raised as members of the family; the Dani believe they possess a soul similar to humans.

The Dani have a complex social organization, a language with an astonishing degree of cultural and linguistic diversity, an agricultural system based on well-understood resource management, and show considerable engineering skills in constructing suspension bridges. Their tools are low-tech—stone axes, planting sticks, and wooden hoes—but appropriate for the culture the Dani choose not to abandon.

On a ten-day trek in the Baliem Valley highlands you walk a average of four hours a day over terrain ranging from moderately hilly to extremely steep. Some segments of the trails are demanding requiring agility and coordination. You should be in very, very good physical shape. You go from village to village, stop at salt pools where women strain salt through banana leaf fibers, and perhaps partake in a pig roast.

You fly by small aircraft over the Central Range into Yali territory, to a cluster of thatched huts known as Kosarek. The Yali tribes, called Yalimo by their neighbors, were not contacted until the 1960s and 1970s, when missionaries began penetrating these remote regions. From Kosarek you trek to more remote highland valleys. You hike over Jenggo Mountain to the tiny missionary village of Anggruk high above the Yaholi River, the hub of many routes to distant villages.

Yali women wear only rattan waist hoops and the men penis gourds, which they start donning at puberty. The gourds, usually bright orange calabashes, some up to 2 feet long, are a fashion statement as well as protection and a nod to modesty.

The Yali are small in stature: the men just over 5 feet and the women a couple of inches shorter. They have a reputation as fierce and dangerous fighters. The Indonesian government allows them neither guns nor alcohol. They hunt with 6-foot bows that shoot arrows nearly as long. The southern Yali men wear thick coils of vines around their stomachs and chests. The hoops, sometimes measuring over 100 feet end-to-end, are also effective armor.

Hiking in Yali territory was well-described by James Polster recounting his trek in the *San Francisco Examiner* (21 October 1990):

"Towering jungle, thin bridges of lashed logs swinging at nose-bleed heights, wild orchids, cassowaries and birds of paradise flitting about, and mountain after mountain packed so closely together that traveling across a valley to a point a few hundred yards as the crow flies may take hours of scrambling down, then up precipitous trails often narrower than the sole of your boot."

The Anggruk-to-Korupun trek over Star Mountain fits this description. You climb steeply up and over the spine of the country through high mountain passes covered with ancient and giant sago palms, primitive tropical plants with fernlike leaves growing in a top cluster. You descend, or mud ski if it has been raining, to the Seng River valley, home of the Wickbone tribes. These tribes were responsible for the attacks and cannibalistic acts on missionaries in 1968.

You follow a maze of trails over watershed after watershed to the Kim Yal territory. Here you may encounter tribes seldom, if ever, visited by Westerners. Less than twenty years ago these people were very warlike and known to eat Westerners. Such was the fate of Phil Masters in 1968, the missionary who established the Korupun mission. Korupun, a mountain village of the Kim Yal tribes above the Erok Gorge, is now a peaceful mission station. You fly from the station back to Wamena.

On the treks porters carry your heavy gear. You take a daypack with water, energy food, camera, and rain gear. A full-time cook and numerous camp assistants accompany you. The guide is experienced in the area and is known by the tribes. You will be in no danger from the people.

Tour operators:

Ecosummer Expeditions
Mountain Travel/Sobek
    Expeditions

Turtle Tours
Wilderness Travel

NEPAL

Trekking the Mustang

Transportation: hiking
Accommodations: lodges/tents
Land cost: $2,639-$$3,300
Duration: 22 to 24 days
Seasons: May to September

The Mustang region, lying north of Annapurna and Dhaulagiri and surrounded by Tibet on three sides, was closed to foreigners in 1964 by Chinese, who invaded Tibet in 1959. In the 1970s, Tibetan Kampas (freedom fighters), reputedly aided by the American CIA, used Mustang as a staging ground for guerilla raids against the Chinese.

In 1992, the Government of Nepal declared Mustang open to trekkers—but only two hundred permits were given for the first six months.

The trek to Mustang is not technically difficult. No rock climbing is required and the passes are all under 12,000 feet. However, the route is physically demanding, and there are no comforts along the way. Once you cross the high pass to Lo Manthang, the fabled wall "capital" of Mustang, there is no turning back, whatever the reason. No accommodations suited to Western tastes or comfort levels exist, as few foreigners have visited the region in thirty years. The adventure lies in the physical and cultural isolation.

The people reflect the land. They live a simplistic life as basic as the stripped-down mountains around them.

The tour starts in Kathmandu, although the actual trekking begins in either Jomosom or Pokhara, depending on the tour operator. If you leave from Pokhara, about one hundred miles west of Kathmandu, the walking time is longer, giving you more time to get "in tune" with the experience. For details on Kathmandu and treks in the Jomosom and Pokhara regions, see COMFORTABLE WILDERNESS and SAFE THRILLS: Asia/Nepal.

From Pokhara, you climb Ghorapani Pass (9,800 feet) with great views of Dhaulagiri and Annapurna. For three days you walk to Jomosom, descending through rhododendron and oak forests and past terraced fields, then start a gradual climb to Larjung (8,400 feet). This is an unusual town of narrow alleys and tunnels connecting houses as protection from the winds of the Kali Gandaki gorge. The area is delightful walking country with apple orchards and fields.

For this trip you must be a strong, experienced hiker in good physical condition to undergo the hardships of outdoor living and long days on the steep trails. Many days are spent at altitudes above 10,000 feet. Camp gear and supplies are carried by porters and pack animals, but at high altitudes hiking even with a light daypack is very strenuous.

After the small town of Jomosom you trek along the river and veer toward the medieval-looking village of Kagbeni. Previously, foreigners were not allowed to go farther north. You have left behind the forest and green fields. This is the threshold to the arid, treeless, windy high country of the Tibetan Plateau. The climate, the mud-walled houses, how people dress, and their language reflect Tibet more than Nepal.

The trail leads up and out of the Kali Ghandaki River drainage to Ghemi (11,480 feet), which you reach after crossing several passes over 12,000 feet. The weather is dry and sunny with daytime temperatures in the 60s, although cold snaps and a chilly wind makes it seem colder. At Ghar Gompa, an old temple rich in *thankas*, books, and statues, you stand poised to cross the high pass to Lo Manthang (12,400 feet), the "capital" of Mustang. If the high route is impassable because of snow, you descend to Charang and take a lower approach.

You walk a landscape of alluvial fans, sharp-edged sandstone ridges, broad sandy terraces, and glacial moraines for three days. On the sparsely vegetated slopes graze sheep, goats, and horses. You visit ancient monasteries and walled villages and abandoned fortresses, all made of mud in this treeless high desert. You hike to Chosyere, the northernmost village in Mustang and, if permission is granted by the local authorities, take a day hike toward the Tibetan border.

The region lies within the expected range of the snow leopard, wolf, blue sheep, great Tibetan sheep, wild dog, and the chiru, a unique Tibetan antelope. But an actual sighting of the larger mammals is rare. The local herdsmen consider them competitors with their livestock for the scarce food supply and do not encourage their presence.

You retrace your route out of this distinctly Tibetan high plateau back to the peaks of Nepal.

Tour operators:

Above the Clouds Trekking   Mountain Travel/Sobek
Ibex Expeditions   Expeditions
Journeys International

PAKISTAN

Baltoro Glacier/K2 Concordia Trek

Transportation: trekking

Accommodations: tents/yurts

Land cost: $2,890-$4,300

Duration: 22 to 32 days

Seasons: August to September

Journeys to lofty places tend to be arduous and this trek is no exception. You must be in extremely good physical condition and experienced in off-trail hiking. You spend hours boulder hopping and scrambling over talus and loose scree. You must also have the mental strength to push through the fatigue and the uncertainty of venturing into such a physically daunting place. You must be self-reliant, flexible, and have a good sense of humor at all times. That is what a raw adventure is all about.

The trek is to K2 (28,741 feet), the second highest mountain in the world after Mount Everest. The route follows the world's largest glacier, Baltoro. It is a difficult and steep climb into a true wilderness of rock, ice, glaciers, and mountains. The area is home to ten of the world's thirty highest peaks. The glacial system is the largest in the world outside the polar ice caps.

You enter the country at twin cities of Islambad and Rawal-pindi. You only stay a day then fly up to the little town of Skardu on the banks of the Indus River, weather permitting. Flights in and out of Skardu being cancelled is a daily possibility. The mountain strip is approached via a high pass adjacent to Nanga Parbat (22,660 feet), the world's ninth highest mountain. The airstrip gets socked in frequently. Flights have been delayed anywhere from a day to a week.

Tradition says Skardu is the legendary Iskandaria, founded by Alexander the Great. It is the capital of the Balistan region and was once part of Ladakh (Little Tibet). Lying at 7,000 feet, it is the starting point for some of the world's best mountaineering. In the town's hotels, you meet an international crowd who all have tales to tell of their climbs.

Two years ago the roadhead was pushed pass Skardu up the warm, arid valley to Askole. Most of the tours to the K2 Con-cordia start walking from this village. It is the last village on the route. Once you leave, you must be self-sufficient for the next two weeks. At the edge of the village you step into a wilderness of rock and ice as you trek eight hours up the Braldu River and across the terminus of the Biafo Glacier to Jhula (10,200 feet). The trail etched in the cliffs of the Dumordo River requires a sure and unhurried step. You wade across the river if the water level is low. A rope bridge is used to cross the roiling torrent when the water is high.

You arrive at the Paiju Camp (11,000 feet) at the foot of the Baltoro Glacier after an eight-hour trek.

You and the porters—who carry the camping gear, food, supplies, and your personal gear—rest at Paiju for a day. The trek is demanding even without carrying heavy packs. Imagine what shape the porters must be in. Almost half the trek is over rough rock glacial terrain. It is highly recommended you embark on a physical training program of running, bicycling, and aerobics three months before your trip, and stay with it up to the day of departure.

Continuing upward, you climb seven hours up the glacier toward the head of Yarmandu Glacier. You have splendid views of Paiju Group and Liligo Peak (20,500 feet) and Trango Tower Group (20,300 feet to 21,600 feet). You lay over at Urdukas, a patch of green land at 13,557 feet. From there you see the granite massif of the Grand Cathedral.

After a seven-hour climb you arrive at Goro (14,000 feet), one step away from the K2 Concordia. But it is a sizeable step that requires another four to five hours to go perhaps a thousand feet.

You spend three days in the Sanctuary of the Concordia Surrounding you is K2 (28,741), Broad Peak (26,400 feet), Gasherbrum (26,180 feet), Golden Throne (23,989 feet), Mitre Peak (19,718 feet), and a vast array of other peaks.

On day hikes you go up to the K2 base camp (ten hours roundtrip) or to the Pakistan Army camp at Hidden Peak base camp.

Tour operators:

Above the Clouds Trekking
Himalayan Travel
Ibex Expeditions

Mountain Travel/Sobek
Expeditions

PART V

Not Ordinary Trips

Trips in this section will appeal to travelers seeking a one-of-a-kind wilderness adventure. Universities, research institutes, and conservation organizations sponsor most of the trips. No special skills or knowledge is necessary to join the expeditions, which are open to everyone. Travel and accommodations vary from motor vehicles and comfortable lodging to backpacking and sleeping in tents.

The trips range from tracking elephants in Tanzania, wolves in Canada, or grizzly bears in Alaska; to swimming with dolphins; studying chimpanzees; or monitoring whales. Tropical rain forests in Central and South America, ecosystems in the Himalayas and Thailand, and the Colorado Plateau are a just few of the locations for these mostly research-oriented trips.

Africa

MALI

Tracking Hannibal's Elephants

Transportation: mobile field vehicle/hiking

Accommodations: tents

Land cost: $1,672

Duration: 14 days

Seasons: July to August

Tour sponsor: Foundation for Field Research

In the desert region of Gourma in Mali, 100 miles southeast of

Timbuktu, three hundred unusual elephants survive—but just barely: Encroaching farmland has reduced their habitat; cows, sheep, and goats have denuded the dunes of grass and scrubs on which they depend; and farmers compete with them for scarce water.

Scientists find it nothing short of a miracle that this herd has not been driven to extinction, as many other species in the region have been, including roan antelope, dama gazelle, korrigum, and ostriches.

These elephants remain enigmas to wildlife experts. They are the northernmost herd of elephants and the last viable one in the Sahel Desert. But exactly what type of elephant they are remains a puzzle. Some scientists postulate that they are a unique sub-species—the West African savanna elephant (*Loxodonta africana*). Others consider them a blend of the forest elephant and the savanna elephant. Another theory is that they are closely related to the now-extinct North African elephant, the kind that Hannibal took over the Alps on his unsuccessful raid on Rome.

On this tour, you get to participate in two aspects of a save-the-elephants project: botany and sociology.

You first help Malian botanist Assetou Kanoute document exactly what the elephants eat and do not eat as you follow the herds through the region between Mopti and Gao, where the Niger River makes a large loop. This information will be helpful in future herd management. Transportation is a sixteen-passenger truck that also carries camping equipment and research supplies.

You also help dig out silted water holes. Water availability is becoming a source of conflict between the elephants and the local population. Overuse by the thousands of goats, donkeys, sheep, cattle, and camels of the local herdsmen has diminished the water supply. Locals threaten that the conflict may be resolved by killing the elephants.

As part of the sociology team, you will help determine how the elephants and the local communities can share the water sources. The sociology team also investigates why the elephants are not hunted by the local people, even though their ivory tusks fetch a good price.

This project is funded in cooperation with Friends of Animals, the Malian government, and actress/conservationist Brigitte Bardot. The Foundation for Field Research is assisting in the botany and sociology studies.

Help Secure a Home for One of Man's Ancestors

Transportation: mobile field vehicle/hiking

Accommodations: tents

Land cost: $1,672

Duration: 14 days

Seasons: March to May

Tour sponsor: Foundation for Field Research

The other research project in Mali involves helping to create a protected home for the *Pan troglodyte verus*, a species of chimpanzee similar to Plio-Pleistocene man. The chimpanzees are the northernmost of their species and may provide clues to the evolution of mankind. How they have adapted to the arid conditions of Mali's Bafing region may indicate how the forest-dwelling Plio-Pleistocene man adapted to life on the savanna. It is theorized that *Homo sapiens* learned to walk upright in order to see over the savanna's tall grass.

The seven hundred remaining chimpanzees currently live in the Bafing-Makana Faunal Reserve, but neither they nor their habitat is under official protection. Poaching, the use of the chimpanzees' flesh in medicinal and religious practices, illegal exportation, and loss of habitat have reduced the chimpanzees' population.

The reserve may become a national park if a feasibility study now being conducted by Tufts University, the University of Maryland, and the Jane Goodall Institute is accepted by the Malian government. The chimpanzee, which has already disappeared in four African countries and is on the verge of extinction in five others, would be protected within the proposed park.

The study documents the seasonal range of the Bafing reserve, its types of habitats, and the numbers and grouping of chimpanzees within its boundaries. Joint use of the habitat by humans and the chimpanzees, interactions between villagers and the chimpanzees, and threats to the animals are also part of the study.

You assist the Tufts team by collecting plants and seeds used by the chimpanzees, recording their calls at various locations, and monitoring nesting materials. Other tasks include identifying foods the chimpanzees eat, observing a particular chimpanzee over time to help determine population fluctuations in the community, documenting the conditions of vegetation and water sources used by the animals, and interviewing the local people about the hunting of the animals.

Your home base is a mobile research unit—two heavy-duty trucks, one for cargo and one for passengers. The base camp consists of wall tents, camp beds, hot showers, a field kitchen with an experienced cook, tables, chairs, lanterns, research equipment, radios, generators, and computers. The mobile unit is also used to conduct eco-tourism workshops for Mali wildlife park personnel. The workshops provide information on how to keep the national parks and cultural diversity intact.

The research requires hiking through the bush and camping. In the bush camps you sleep in a tent on a sleeping pad. A field shower is provided. The field manager cooks all your meals. When the camp is moved to another research site, porters transport all the gear, and you ride to the next site in the truck.

TANZANIA

Backcountry Explorations

Transportation: motor vehicle/hiking

Accommodations: lodges/tents

Land cost: $5,500 (including airfare from New York)

Duration: 11 days

Seasons: January

Tour sponsor: Four Corners School of Outdoor Education

This trip goes to some of the better-known national parks and to places the average tourist never visits. But then, average tourists do not take this trip. The goal of the tour is to study wildlife and ecosystems unhindered by other visitors or by restrictions imposed in other game parks. The trip, led by African experts and natives, is intended to be an educational adventure. Local guides help you track animals and explain the properties of indigenous plants. They also take you to their homes for a family visit.

From Nairobi, Kenya, you take a bus south through the Amboseli National Park to Arusha, near Mount Kilimanjaro in Tanzania. Local guides join you there. The hands-on safari starts at the Lake Manyara National Park, a three-hour drive from Arusha. The saline lake, fed by springs coming from the base of the Great Rift Valley wall, covers two-thirds of the 123-square-mile park.

More than three hundred species of birds congregate at the lake, including African spoonbills, lesser flamingos, red-billed oxpeckers, sacred ibis, black-winged stilts, and white pelicans.

You track lions, buffalo, elephants, and other large animals along the edge of the lake. Search the branches of low-lying acacia trees when looking for lions. Manyara is well known for its tree-climbing lions, although actually seeing one in a tree is unusual. Waterbuck, Masai giraffe, zebras, impala, baboons, blue monkeys, and Syke's monkeys live in the forest of wild fig, tamarind, and mahogany. Hippos enjoy wallowing in the marshy glades, while elephants prefer the dense forest.

When you hike the 1,800 feet from the lake to the top of the rift escarpment, you climb through five vegetation zones, each a habitat for different species of animals.

Accommodations at Manyara are *bandas*, round huts made of brick with tin conical roofs thatched over for appearance's sake. *Bandas* are modeled after the housing found in most of the native bush settlements, although in the settlements the *bandas* are constructed of wattle and mud.

You next take a two-day walking safari based out of the Lake Eyasi Chemchem Camp. You hike around the lake observing the bird life and go into the bush in search of bigger animals. The Wahazabe, last of the East African bushmen, live in the region. Your guide, a member of the Wadtoga people, may arrange a meeting. The guide will take you to his home for a firsthand look at the lifestyle of the pastoral Wadtoga.

The camp consists of walk-in safari tents, hot showers (when the water supply allows), and a mess tent with tables and chairs where the tour staff prepares meals. A nice, cool spring serves as an alternative to a shower.

You then camp seven nights on the road. The tents are car-camping style with full-sized, zip doors and a ground sheet. Foam mattresses and pillows are provided. Safari beds are provided upon request, but none are as comfortable as the foam on the ground. The field toilet and shower are in separate tents for privacy. The mess tent sits twelve comfortably.

From Lake Eyasi you drive to Africa's "Garden of Eden," the Ngorongoro Crater. This 12-mile-wide extinct volcano caldera is a natural amphitheater that contains herds of nearly every species of East African plains animals, including leopards and black rhino. A Masai village is also in the crater.

You practice animal tracking techniques for two days within the crater. The group leaders discuss this volcano ecosystem and the threats to the wildlife posed by humans and climate changes.

Ngorongoro is a short drive from the Serengeti Plain, renowned as Africa's premier game park for observing large herds of wild game. On the way you stop at Olduvai Gorge, where anthropologists Mary and Louis Leakey discovered skull shards of the 1.75-million-year-old "Nutcracker Man." Two days are spent tracking on the Serengeti and simply being awed by the grandeur of the land, the sky, and the herds of animals. For more information on East African game parks, see COMFORTABLE WILDERNESS: Africa/Kenya/Tanzania.

The final day of the tour you stay at Gibbs Farm, a coffee/vegetable farm with four-star accommodations. You hike into the Ngorongoro Conservation unit to visit caves excavated by elephants searching for minerals.

The leaders of the trip are Dr. James Halfpenny, Wesley Krause, and Janet Ross. Dr. Halfpenny, who specializes in tracking, has researched animal tracking for the National Geographic Society. He also taught at the National Outdoor Leadership School in Kenya. Wesley Krause, who speaks fluent Swahili, also taught at the leadership school and has guided safaris for years. Janet Ross is a director of the Four Corners School of Outdoor Education.

ZIMBABWE

Black Rhino Watch

Transportation: hiking
Accommodations: house/tents
Land cost: $2,200
Duration: 11 days
Seasons: July to September
Tour sponsor: Earthwatch

The black rhino is facing a severe crisis. Over the past twenty years its population has declined dramatically from 65,000 to an estimated 4,000. About half of the surviving rhino live in Zimbabwe. To develop an effective management policy for the conservation of the black rhino, accurate population information is necessary. This Black Rhino Watch project involves collecting up-to-date information on population densities of black rhino in different parts of Zimbabwe and identifying individual animals.

In other words, you walk around in the bush tracking black rhino or signs of them, such as dung. When you see one, you take its picture, make notes on its behavior and movements, and detail the vegetation it eats and where. You walk about ten miles each day through scrub. You must be physically fit to easily do the daily hike and to run if charged by a wild animal.

One of the natural hazards of this project is the uncertain temperament of the black rhino. You are thoroughly briefed on how to avoid being charged and how to behave if you are charged by a rhino, an elephant, or any large predator. An armed ranger accompanies you into the bush as a precaution against wild animals and poachers who hunt in the research area.

You work in the Sengwa Wildlife Research Area on the southeast border of the Chirisa Safari Area, 150 miles east of Harare, Zimbabwe's capital. The Chirisa area adjoins the Chizarira National Park to the north. The Sengwa River meanders across the valley floor of the research area bounded by escarpments and sandstone cliffs.

A charter plane flies you from Harare to the research site. For the first two days and last two days you stay in a large modern house at the Sengwa Wildlife Research Institute. Otherwise you camp in the bush, sleeping in a tent on a bedroll. You must bring your own sleeping bag. The camp will move as necessary to find the rhino. You will be expected to help with camp maintenance and cooking. You will be in the field eight days.

By 7A.M. each morning you are in the field with a trained tracker searching for black rhino, who like to feed in the morning coolness. The tracker/scout directs the search and instructs you how and in which direction to follow the spoor. The scout also places you in a safe position to photograph the black rhino once one is sighted. By eleven o'clock it becomes too hot for field work. You spend midday in camp and return to the field for a couple hours around three-thirty.

No special skills or knowledge are required. The research staff gives you guidance and oversees the work.

For more information on Zimbabwe, see COMFORTABLE WILDERNESS and SAFE THRILLS: Africa/Zimbabwe.

Asia

NEPAL

Trekking the Himalayas
Transportation: hiking
Accommodations: tents/guest houses

Land cost: $2,400

Duration: 35 days

Seasons: April to May

Tour sponsor: Wildland Studies

This trip takes you from subtropical forests to high mountains and into mythical hidden valleys as you collect data to help establish a new national park. The Makalu-Barun Conservation Area, in the remote Barun Valley of eastern Nepal, is the country's largest undisturbed ecosystem. The area is under consideration to be included as part of a major international biosphere reserve that will encircle the Mount Everest region.

After an orientation in Kathmandu, you fly to Tumlingtar on the Arun River, accessible only by plane or foot. The twelve-day hike from Tumlingtar to the Makalu base camp goes into roadless country where few outsiders have visited. The trek begins in the lowland Sal forest near the Indian border and passes through the intensively cultivated Himalayan middle hills. On the way you investigate the unique agro-ecology of the area, including innovative and traditional agro-forestry systems. These systems hold great promise for integrating economic development with the urgent need for reforestation and soil conservation.

You climb through a cool and cloudy subalpine zone of rhododendron forests that support the most abundant wildlife in this part of Asia. Red panda, black-faced langur monkeys, the indigenous honey guide, and other birds live in the forests.

Finally you reach the Arun region, most of which lies above 14,000 feet. The alpine environment includes habitat for some of the highest elevation terrestrial plants and insects known. You cross Shipton Pass into the headwaters of the Barun River and establish a study site. Here you collect baseline data critical to management of the giant rhododendron forests, the alpine fell fields, and the stands of Himalayan alder.

Base camps are established for a few days, and then you hike to another study area. You carry a medium-weight backpack for five to eight hours a day when on the move. Porters help carry the month's supply of food, as this trip is totally self-sufficient. Local guides lead the way. This is basic backcountry trekking and camping.

You work closely with Nepali scientists and representatives of the Woodlands Mountain Institute. You help assess pressing environmental concerns, investigate ecological impacts, examine traditional cultural methods of farming, and survey plant and animal distribution. No previous field research experience is required. All necessary skills will be taught onsite. Those who successfully complete the program can earn college credits.

The data collected is crucial to preserve one of the last intact ecosystems of the Nepalese Himalayas in a manner that balances the needs of 35,000 indigenous people and the protection of the environment. The local residents—Sherpa, Rai, Lhomi, Tamang, Brahmans, and Chetris—are part of the study and a key element in the project. Isolated and poor, these people practice traditional trading, herding, and farming. They share a mutual dependence on natural mountain resources.

A growing human population threatens the fragile Himalayan ecosystems. Environmental degradation in the Himalayas, such as deforestation and subsequent soil erosion, affects the several hundred million people living on the plains of India. Disasters, such as the catastrophic floods in Bangladesh, are connected to the clearing of the Himalayan forests. How to maintain the integrity of the Himalayan ecosystem is the major focus of this study.

THAILAND

Hill Tribes, Jungle Forest, and Big City

Transportation: motor vehicle/hiking

Accommodations: hotels/tribal housing

Land cost: $2,500

Duration: 7 weeks

Seasons: January to March

Tour sponsor: Wildland Studies

What is going on behind the picture-postcard Thailand of golden Buddhas, resort beaches, and Bangkok's neon lights? You find out on this hiking trip, which takes you through roadless back-country to assess the plants and animals of the tropical ecosystems. You stay with hill tribes in their villages to learn about threats, mainly from the timber industry, to their territory and their culture. You experience big city environmental hazards of air pollution and clip joints.

The trip has three parts: backpacking in Khao Yai National Park, visiting the hill tribes, and exploring other national parks, protected landscapes, and wildlife reserves.

You begin in Bangkok, an environmentally distressed city. The traffic congestion, noise level, air pollution, and overcrowding are a city planner's nightmare. Nevertheless, you cannot fail to enjoy yourself in this extremely interesting city full of naturally friendly people. In preparation for your excursions into the countryside you interview national specialists in wildlife, forestry, park management, and agriculture. But you still have time to sample the food, sights, and people of the city.

The first backpack field trip goes to Thailand's largest national park, Khao Yai. Local experts acquaint you with the plants and animals of the subtropical ecosystem. The park harbors the country's greatest diversity of plants and animals, including an indigenous deer species.

The second trek goes into the hills bordering the Thai-Laos-Burma border, an area referred to as the "fourth world" and "The Golden Triangle," in reference to the opium trade. You stay with the Hmong, Lisu, Yao, Karen, and Akha, disenfranchised hill tribes from those three countries, which took over, not always peacefully, the tribes' traditional territories. In many respects the hill people are refugees on the land where they have lived for hundreds of years.

Daunting challenges face the tribes. Overpopulation due to births and immigration has increased dramatically in recent years. The food supply is stretched thin. The people are forced to farm marginal land and to drastically shorten the fallow periods essential for the fields' recovery. Competition for land causes conflicts within villages and between tribes.

Thai farmers, facing land shortages, push their way into the hills, burning off forest to create fields. Logging companies clear-cut acres of hardwoods, which the tribal people use to build houses. The Thai government declared a logging ban to conserve the rapidly disappearing teak forests, but outlaw loggers and tribal people continue to cut down the trees. For more details on the hill tribes see SAFE THRILLS: Asia/Thailand.

The destruction of the highland forests and watersheds and the declining populations of wild animals and plants are Thailand's most urgent environmental challenges. As in many countries experiencing rapid economic growth, Thailand faces trade-offs between development and conservation of natural resources. This trip gives you firsthand information about those difficult choices and their ramifications.

Base camp for the hill trips is Payap University, Thailand's oldest private university, on the outskirts of Chiang Mai. The university's staff and local experts provide background information and arrange contacts with the hill tribes.

On the trip's third segment, the group, with a maximum of fourteen participants and two instructors, splits into teams. Each team selects a wildlife reserve, a protected landscape, or a national park in which to conduct an ecological survey. Thailand's protected lands are sanctuaries for wild elephants, tigers, Malayan sun bears, gibbons, many species of deer, and other mammals. The bird life is also profuse.

Thailand is a poignant model for other countries attempting to balance economic and social needs with conservation of the world's last tropical forests. The project studies the challenges of conservation in the developing world and explores strategies by which economic development might proceed.

No special knowledge or skills are necessary for this trip. College credits are earned by those who successfully complete the work.

Central America

BELIZE

Research and Swim with Dolphins

Transportation: boat/swimming
Accommodations: cabanas
Land cost: $1,290-$1,490
Duration: 8 to 10 days
Seasons: July to December
Tour sponsor: Oceanic Society Expeditions

Dolphins seem to have an affinity for man. Ancient Greeks recorded how dolphins saved drowning sailors, and such stories are still heard today. Dolphins talk to us, play with us, and help us with technical and academic research projects, such as those of the U.S. Navy and John Lily.

Physically, dolphins have a larger brain than do humans. They are gregarious, problem solvers, and live in an organized society. But we do not know much about them. We do not understand their language or why they behave as they do. This project will assess and analyze communication and social behavior in pantropical spotted and bottlenose dolphins.

In order to organize their society, dolphins must share information concerning sex, location, and identity of individuals. You help naturalists make underwater video and acoustic records and take still photos. Virtually no underwater data has been collected on deep-water spotted dolphins. You may help discover links between dolphin behavior and acoustic communication.

The project's goal is to better understand wild dolphins in order to help protect them worldwide and preserve their habitats.

Information is collected from a 23-foot skiff and by underwater viewing to determine sex and age of individual dolphins. You assist in identifying individual dolphins, making field notes on observed behaviors, photographing, and using other data collection methods. No experience is necessary, but being comfortable with swimming and snorkeling is essential. You must bring your own mask, fins, and snorkel.

The project's headquarters are Blackbird Island on Turneffe Atoll. Accommodations are double occupancy cabanas with private facilities, each with an open porch to the sea.

Not all your time is spent working. Blackbird Island is adjacent to the barrier reef. Excellent snorkeling on the reef, second only to Australia's Great Barrier Reef, is literally at your doorstep. Nearby Soldier's Cay is a sanctuary for nesting roseate terns and crowned pigeons. You also take a full-day excursion to Lighthouse Reef Atoll, the Blue Hole, and Half-moon Cave, a seabird rookery with four thousand red-footed frigate birds.

Optional trips go to the Chan Chich Nature Reserve, inland rain forests, and Mountain Pine Ridge. For details on Belize, see COMFORTABLE WILDERNESS: Central America/Belize.

COSTA RICA

Help Save a Dry Tropical Forest

Transportation: hiking
Accommodations: share a house
Land cost: $1,275
Duration: 10 days
Seasons: late June to July
Tour sponsor: University Research Expeditions Program

When the Spanish arrived in Central America in the 1520s, most of the land was covered with dry tropical forests. Today, these unique forests, of which only 2 percent of the original remain, are in greater danger of extinction than rain forests. Understanding how the dry tropical forests' ecological systems work and their needs is essential to the forests' survival.

This trip takes you to Lomas Barbudal Reserve (literally "bearded hills"), a 6,000-acre national park in Costa Rica's northwest Guanacaste Province. The forest, home to over 450 species of flowering plants, 250 varieties of bees, and 200 species of birds, anteaters, armadillos, monkeys, and iguanas, is one of the few undisturbed dry forest environments in the New World tropics.

You walk hilly terrain to observe, track, and record the behavior of birds, bees, beetles, and ant colonies living in and around the reserve. The orchid bee species, which lives in only about six thousand acres, is of special interest. These bees are important because they pollinate many trees in the forest. Understanding the interdependence of the bees and the trees helps researchers gain a broader understanding of the interlocking ecological system.

You assist in discovering the preferred habitats and the biodiversity of the wildlife in the forest. The information will be used to determine the interdependence of the flora and fauna. Other work is to help develop educational material on the conservation project to be used by local school children in the city of Bagaces. No previous experience is necessary to participate.

Accommodations are at the New Center for the Conservation of Nature in Bagaces. You will share with other team members a house with electricity, good beds, and private baths with flush toilets and cold running water.

North America

CANADA

Wolves of Banff and Jasper National Parks

Transportation: cross-country skiing/hiking

Accommodations: resort/lodges

Land cost: $1,960

Duration: 6 days

Seasons: March

Tour sponsor: Four Corners School of Outdoor Education

As wolves are making a comeback in regions where humans once killed them off, understanding the ways of wolves is gaining new urgency. The wolf has been reintroduced into the eastern U.S.

wilderness parks, and an effort is afoot to bring them back into Yellowstone National Park. More than twelve hundred wolves already live in upper Minnesota. If humans and wolves are to coexist, much more needs to be known about the habitat require-ments, territorial range, feeding patterns, and societal structure of wolf packs.

Few chances exist to study wolves in remote areas relatively unaffected by humans. This trip takes you to places where this is still possible. Wolf biologists and naturalists lead you into Banff and Jasper national parks and the Kananaskis forest to track and observe wolves in conditions similar to those that existed in North America before the Europeans came over.

The research project involves noting wolf howls and discern-ing possible meanings of the communication. You record the population biology of the wolf/prey system—which means docu-menting deer, caribou, moose, bighorn sheep, and goats in the wolves' territory.

You visit kill sites, track wolves and their prey, and make plas-ter casts. Wolf experts present evening programs on wolf manage-ment and reintroduction programs in the United States. Data gathered on this trip becomes part of the base study.

You cross-country ski and hike over moderately rugged ter-rain, covering up to 5 miles round-trip daily. Nordic skiing skills are a prerequisite. No special knowledge of wolves is required, but you must be in good physical condition. Expect zero tempera-tures and windy conditions.

MEXICO

Search for the Rare Deer of Isla de Cedros

Transportation: hiking

Accommodations: tents

Land cost: $699

Duration: 7 days

Seasons: February to March

Tour sponsor: Foundation for Field Research

On the Isla de Cedros, located on the Pacific Coast midway down the Baja California peninsula, lives a rare type of deer. The Cedros Island deer, a subspecies of the mule deer, is so rare it was once considered extinct. However, a 1980 survey discovered three hundred of the skittish and shy deer living on the island. This project is a follow-up population count of the deer, which are illegally hunted for sport by islanders and mainlanders.

Isla de Cedros (Island of Cedars, so named by Spanish explorers who mistook the pines for cedars) is the largest of Mexico's Pacific-coast islands (21 miles long and 3 to 9 miles wide). Rare species of plants, reptiles, and mammals are also indigenous to the island. About six thousand people live in two villages on the island's southeast corner; most are employed at a fish cannery.

To enjoy this trip you must like working and camping in the wilderness. Isla de Cedros is mountainous, with slopes of loose rocks reaching nearly six thousand feet. You hike this landscape of desert shrub, chaparral, and juniper to two stands of pine on mountain crests. The deer live there and at other inland areas. You also make landings by inflatable boat along the island's east coast, and then search the shore area and nearby canyons for deer. The search requires backpacking into the interior where you camp.

When not backpacking, you stay at the base camp on the island's cobblestone beach. The camp consists of roomy two-person walk-in tents, a field kitchen with two cooks, tables, chairs lanterns, hot water showers, and a latrine.

Explore the Vanishing Rain Forest of Mexico

Transportation: hiking
Accommodations: house
Land cost: $1,495
Duration: 14 days
Seasons: year-round
Tour sponsor: Earthwatch

Mexico's rain forest, which once stretched from Veracruz to Chiapas along the Gulf of Mexico, now only exists in isolated fragments. The remaining sections of the rain forest are being cut down at the rate of up to one hundred hectares each day. This fragmentation causes extinction of wildlife and damages ecosystems.

According to biologists Robert MacArthur of Princeton University and E.O. Wilson of Harvard, the smaller a forest fragment the fewer flora and fauna species it supports. Their rule of thumb is that decreasing the area of a forest island tenfold halves the number of species it can maintain. The extinction rate goes up the longer a fragment has been isolated and the farther it is from a large habitat of the same kind.

The purpose of this project is to determine which bird and mammal species inhabit forest fragments in the vicinity of the Los Tuxtlas Biological Reserve, a region which has the northernmost tropical rain forest on the American continent. The study is important for understanding the impact of forest destruction on biological diversity and how different species cope with the reduction of their habitat. The information will be useful to determine which forest fragments should be preserved.

The research site is about two hours south of the city of Veracruz. You stay in a house on the beach of the Gulf of Mexico three miles from the research station. Meals are prepared by the staff.

You walk the forest setting up nets and traps to capture birds and animals for a census count. The nets are checked every half hour and the captured birds brought to the processing station. You also conduct a visual census of birds, animals, and vegetation. You go to various forest fragments and spend four days in each.

No special skills or knowledge are necessary. The professional team of biologists gives you field training in how to set the nets, handle the wildlife, and record data.

The walking conditions are not difficult, but the heat and humidity can be exhausting. The temperature averages 78 degrees, but the high humidity strengthens its effect. The hottest months are between March and May; the wettest months are September and October. December and January are the coldest months with temperatures around 50 degrees.

UNITED STATES—WEST

ALASKA

Tracking Grizzly and Black Bears

Transportation: motor vehicle/hiking

Accommodations: motels

Land cost: $1,895

Duration: 7 days

Seasons: September

Tour sponsor: Four Corners School of Outdoor Education

On this trip you get to watch grizzly and black bears eat breakfast. Their local cafe is Salmon Creek, near Hyder, Alaska, where they wade into the water and swipe fish onto the bank.

The trip starts with a drive up the Cassier Highway from Terrace, Canada, to Hyder through glacier-cut, waterfall-lined green valleys, passing under the toe of Bear Glacier. The country is some of the most primitive and spectacular in western Canada.

The goal of this research project is to develop a comparative natural history of the bears. You observe them from as close as a hundred feet. You learn how to track the bears and how to identify their signs and tracks, of which you make plaster casts. No attempt is made to stalk or approach the bears except under controlled and safe conditions. Professional naturalists, scientists, and guides oversee the trip.

You spend four days at Salmon Creek documenting the bears at dawn and dusk. During the day you track bears, make casts, and travel upstream to a glacier.

The final two days are spent in Terrace, British Columbia, tracking Kermode black bears. The Kermode is a white-phase (not albino) black bear found almost exclusively in this part of British Columbia. Fewer than one bear in ten is a white "ghost bear." You drive up the Kitsumkalum River to find the bears and take casts of their tracks. The Terrace town dump is the other bear observation site.

The program is limited to a maximum of sixteen participants.

Wrangell Mountains Wildlands

Transportation: hiking

Accommodations: tents

Land cost: $1,750

Duration: 41 days

Seasons: June to July

Tour sponsor: Wildland Studies

This is not a postcard tour. It is designed for an in-depth understanding of Alaska's alpine ecology, botany, geology, and human ecology. The Wrangell-Saint Elias National Park serves as the field study classroom.

Base camp is the town of McCarthy, located in the heart of the Wrangells and adjacent to the terminus of the Kennicott Glacier. A 64-mile road from the highway cuts through the national park to the town on the Kennicott River. Hand-operated carts hanging from a cable are the only way across the river. The town has weekly mail and passenger service by light plane; there are no televisions or telephones.

The mountains' main crest rims the area to the north, culminating in 16,390-foot Mount Blackburn, the core of an old volcano. The broad, forested Chitina Valley, cut by braided rivers and gravel floodplains, lies to the south. Humans share this country of spruce, poplar, and aspen forests beneath the continent's largest montane ice fields with bears, moose, and wolves.

Your headquarters are at the "Old Hardware Store," a remnant of the old mining days that looks like part of a Western movie set. The building, a National Historic Site, contains an extensive library and a large kitchen with a wood-burning stove. Sleeping accommodations are tents along nearby McCarthy Creek.

You take two extensive and sometimes rigorous backpack hikes into the wilderness. One goes up the 25-mile-long Kennicott Glacier to study the glacier's movements, features, and its impact on the climate and habitat of the area. Your investigation includes how the environment at the glacier's edge affects the movement of bears, Dall sheep, mountain goats, and moose.

Another hike goes into the mountain alpine region. You explore lush meadows and tundra, prime habitat for arctic ground squirrels, golden eagles, and grizzly bears.

Most hiking is bushwacking off-trail. You acquire map-reading and route-finding skills, just like a real explorer.

You earn college credits upon successful completion of the coursework. The information gathered will assist the National Park Service in formulating land-use plans for the area.

The alpine ecology focuses on two issues: the role of avalanches and grizzly bears in the diversity of subalpine and alpine plants, and the detrimental effect of mine tailings (residue) on plants in some areas around glaciers. You identify predominant alpine plants and study how they adapt to the extreme subarctic environment.

On wilderness hikes you note how the mountains continue to change. Ice Age geological forces that shaped the Wrangells are still at work—if you know where to look and what to look for. Three different fragments of the earth's crust collide beneath this southwestern section of Alaska, which borders the Yukon Territory. As a result, the Wrangell-Saint Elias National Park contains five of the fifteen highest peaks in North America. Recent uplifts have raised the mountains by more than forty feet in some areas.

Studying the issues involved in national park development— land ownership, access, level of development, and interpretation—is part of the experience. The research program seeks to unite the study of natural history with that of public policy. Your work involves inquiring how the special attributes of the Wrangell Mountains environment affect human habitation, development decisions, and land planning.

No special knowledge or skills are necessary, but you should be in good physical condition.

HAWAII

Ancient Cultures and Wild Environments

Transportation: motor vehicle/kayak/hiking
Accommodations: tents

Land cost: $1,200
Duration: 11 days
Seasons: June to August
Tour sponsor: Wildland Studies

This trip goes to the islands of Hawaii, Kauai, and Molokai to explore land and sea ecosystems and to study threats to the islands' integrity and the cultures they support. In addition to this serious stuff, you will have great fun snorkeling and hiking in the wilderness.

On Hawaii you travel with island environmental specialists on an extended backpacking trek along the Hilina Pali coast in the Hawaii Volcanoes National Park. You gather data to help assess the park's wildlands, wildlife habitats, ancient landscapes, and rapidly changing volcanic environments. Researching management options to protect these environments is part of the project.

On the island's Hamakua coast you hike the Waipio and Waimanu valleys investigating wildland management and the Hawaiian culture. You will get to compare and contrast how traditional and modern societies treat the land.

Development on the Kona coast is radically altering the land and the ecosystems. What is too much development? What is acceptable development? What should be absolutely and forever off-limits to development? You visit key sites important to Hawaiian culture—Kealekekua Bay, ancient sacred "heiaus," petroglyphs, and the birthplaces of kings while pondering these questions.

On Kauai you travel by foot and sea kayak to record habitat loss and the impact of development on the wildlife.

Traditional Molokai has the largest proportion of native Hawaiian citizens of all the major islands. The 38-mile-long island, which has few tourist destinations, is the "purest" in Hawaii. On Molokai you hike Halawa Valley and the Nature Conservancy of Hawaii Conservation Areas to assess alternatives for the island's long-term environmental and cultural sustainability.

For more information on Hawaii see COMFORTABLE WILDERNESS: North America/United States—West/Hawaii.

You can earn college credit for successfully completing the project's work.

MONTANA

Grizzlies and Wolves Wilderness

Transportation: hiking
Accommodations: Park Service housing
Land cost: $1,100
Duration: 3 weeks
Seasons: September to October
Tour sponsor: Wildland Studies

A confrontation brews in the Glacier/Bob Marshall Wilderness. Intense pressure due to logging and energy exploration threatens unprotected parts of the area that are crucial for the successful recovery of the endangered grey wolf. On this trip you help assess the status of the grey wolf populations and their habitats. The data will be used to develop options to preserve the ecosystem and its wildlife.

When you are done with the wolves, you go to the Glacier National Park and count grizzlies.

The Glacier/Bob Marshall Wilderness, an area larger than Rhode Island, stretches 100 miles south from the Canadian border and is flanked by the Northern Continental Divide. Glacier National Park lies on the northern side of this remote ecosystem.

When looking for grey wolves you hike the roadless Rocky Mountain Front Wilderness Area where they are recolonizing habitats. You help assess the area for potential winter habitat, denning sites, and dispersal corridors for the wolves. You take part in formulating innovative management strategies that serve the wolves, allow for some human recreation, and check development.

Having sufficient living space is crucial to wild animals. According to biologists, animals tightly confined in refuges of less than 125,000 acres may lose more than half their species in a few thousand years. In the United States, 30 percent of the national parks and 93 percent of the wildlife refuges are less than 125,000 acres.

In the Swan Valley, between the Bob Marshall and Mission Mountain Wilderness Areas, you investigate environmental impacts and assess the limits of acceptable change within the wilderness system.

No special skills are necessary. Experts teach you howling survey techniques, wolf sign identification, and how to assess wolf habitat. As you are traveling on foot cross-country, you learn map-reading and compass skills.

In Glacier National Park you may not actually see any grizzlies to count. They are hard to find. Rather, you record signs of the bears and assess their habitat. Wilderness managers need the information to make decisions and formulate management plans to protect the threatened bear.

College credits are earned for work successfully completed.

UTAH

Hiking the Colorado Plateau

Transportation: hiking
Accommodations: tents
Land cost: $825
Duration: 6 weeks
Seasons: April 7 to May 17
Tour sponsor: Wildland Studies

This tour takes you to the high desert wilderness of national parklands in southern Utah and northern Arizona, where you hike into the heart of red rock canyon country. Zion, Bryce, Glen, Capital Reef, Canyonlands, and Grand Canyon national parks are possible destinations. These parklands preserve some of the most pristine wilderness ecosystems in the United States.

You investigate critical challenges to the wilderness and explore potential management solutions. Proposals for massive development of energy resources and plans for expansion of recreation facilities threaten the character of the area. Coal and uranium mines, dams and reservoirs, abuse from overgrazing, and growing agricultural and recreational use all jeopardize the Colorado Plateau wildlands.

Plans exist to excavate up to forty uranium mines on public lands adjacent to Grand Canyon National Park. Dams and storage reservoirs are proposed upstream from Zion and Capital Reef national parks. Efforts are being made to develop oil, natural gas, and tar sands within Glen Canyon National Recreation Area.

You learn about the interwoven ecological, geological, and climatological factors that shape the plateau's environment. You help assess management alternatives to treating the parks as an ecosystem rather than as "islands" of wilderness. The research comes at a critical time. Congress, conservationists, and federal and management agencies are beginning to address the issues of the cumulative effects of external threats on an ecosystem-wide basis. Your team findings and recommendations could help shape the long-range plans to manage the Wilderness Areas.

A five- to seven-day trip in inflatable kayaks on the San Juan River exploring ancient Anasazi sites is also part of the trip.

No special skills or knowledge are required. College credits are earned by those who successfully complete the work.

WASHINGTON

Are Killer Whales Safe in Puget Sound?

Transportation: boat
Accommodations: house/on-board
Land cost: $1,695
Duration: 10 days
Seasons: June to September
Tour Sponsor: Zoetic Research/Sea Quest Expeditions

You cruise the Greater Puget Sound around the San Juan Islands photographing orca whales and recording their underwater vocals. The orcas, also known as "killer whales," are the top predator in the inland marine ecosystem. If numerous whales are found in Puget Sound that means plenty of food exists, indicating that the ecosystem is healthy.

This long-term project involves photo-identifying the whales and is useful in determining the life history of individual whales, the pod's social structure, and birth and death rates. The study helps identify the habitat needs of the orcas and what activities— too many boats, or pollution—adversely affects them.

Your task depends on the activities planned for the day. You may go out on the research vessel to photograph whales and note their movements. Onshore duties include identifying individual whales from photographs, entering data into computers, and visual and acoustic watches at the research facility.

Everyone, including the staff, participates in meal preparation, dishwashing, and routine cleaning of the research facility and living accommodations.

You stay in a three-bedroom waterfront house with all the conveniences of a home near Friday Harbor on San Juan Island.

The weather is generally quite nice with daytime temperatures ranging from 70 to 90 degrees. Nighttime temperatures range from 50 to 70 degrees. You should expect periods of cold, drizzly rain.

Minke Whale Search

Transportation: boat
Accommodations: base camp
Land cost: $559
Duration: 5 days
Seasons: September to October
Tour Sponsor: Zoetic Research/Sea Quest Expeditions

On this trip you kayak the Pacific Northwest's San Juan archipelago, often referred to as the "banana belt" because it lies within the rain shadow of the Olympic Mountains. Lots of rain falls. Four hundred islands, rocks, and reefs located just north of Puget Sound straddle the Washington-British Columbia border, whose shoreline is an ecozone between marine and land habitats.

Because of the abundant marine wildlife the area has been nominated for status as a National Marine Sanctuary. Thousands of harbor seals, hundreds of bald eagles, millions of migrating salmon and zillions of other aquatic things use the straits between the islands. The orca whale uses the San Juans as their core range. While studying the minke whales, you visit some of the orcas' favorite feeding, traveling, and play areas.

As part of a team of five you take observation notes and identification photos and make hydrophone recordings of minke whales. The ongoing study by nonprofit Zoetic Research helps to fill gaps in understanding the species' natural history. No one has ever reported seeing minke whales mate or calve, and their winter range is still unknown.

When not chasing the whales you explore San Juan Island, a popular tourist destination that has two National Parks.

MIDWEST

MINNESOTA

Tracking Timber Wolves

Transportation: motor vehicle/hiking

Accommodations: lodge

Land cost: $750

Duration: 12 to 14 days

Seasons: July to October

Tour sponsor: Earthwatch

Your task on this trip is to eavesdrop on wolves. You ride around the north woods of Minnesota in a van listening to wolves travel about and talk to one another. The object is to trace their daily movement patterns, their home range, and their travel routes and escape cover. You will also help gather data on how wolves interact with humans: Do they retreat from human habitation areas during the day? How do they cohabit with humans? Do they den near houses? Do they travel our roads at night?

You track the free-ranging timber wolves by monitoring previously attached Wildlink radio-collars. Testing this newly developed system is part of the project.

You work around the clock in six- to eight-hour shifts. Occasionally you may hike over rough terrain, streams, and swamps to investigate suspected kill sites.

The information gathered will be useful in protecting wolves and their habitat in the Great Lakes region. The wolf is classified as a threatened species in Minnesota and as endangered in other of the contiguous forty-eight states. Efforts are under way to reintroduce the timber wolf to its historical ranges. The success of such efforts depends on knowledge of its behavior and habitat needs in areas where humans are a significant presence.

Results of the study will aid state and federal agencies in developing a management plan that will assist existing timber wolf populations to survive and will allow them to expand to new, suitable ranges in Wisconsin and upper Michigan.

One wolf typically roams over 85 square miles. The largest population of timber wolves in the lower forty-eight states, about twelve hundred, lives in Minnesota. There are a few packs in Wisconsin and scattered individuals in Michigan and Montana. Each wolf pack is a family group. Wolves are very social animals whose survival depends on cooperation.

Accommodations on the trip are cabins with modern toilets, shower facilities, and running water. The research area is near the Boundary Waters Canoe Area Wilderness. In your free time you can canoe the many lakes or hike the forest. Temperatures range from 40 degrees to 90 degrees and humidity becomes high. Insect repellent against black flies, deer flies, and mosquitoes is essential.

SOUTH

FLORIDA

Wild Dolphin Societies

Transportation: boat
Accommodations: house/duplex
Land cost: $2,495
Duration: 14 days
Seasons: June to October; December and January
Tour sponsor: Earthwatch

Recent large-scale deaths of bottlenose dolphins along the Atlantic seaboard and the northern Gulf of Mexico have given new urgency to discovering the effects of human-caused pollution on the species. That is one aspect of this project. Another goal is to refine our understanding of the structure and dynamics of dolphin populations. How large an area is needed to support how many dolphins and what habitat needs are essential to maintain a dolphin population?

You will help capture, sample, mark, and release dolphins in the Sarasota area, Tampa Bay, and Charlotte Harbor. You will also photograph individual dolphins and note behavioral patterns, in particular, their whistling communication.

The dolphins are captured by encircling schools of them with a 1,500-foot-long net dropped in water less than five feet deep from a commercial fishing netboat. One or two outboard chase boats move rapidly through the area creating an acoustic barrier to help contain the dolphins. The chase boat crews check to ensure the dolphins are not being entangled in the net or otherwise injured.

Each dolphin is maneuvered into a sling and brought aboard the research vessel for measuring, weighing, and marking. Biological samples are also taken. Then the dolphin is released into the water.

The data is used to relate concentrations of contaminants in the dolphins to the possible influence of environmental pollution on the dolphins' immune systems. Understanding how bottlenose dolphins relate to each other and to the environment is essential for conservation management as well as for understanding the evolution of their social system. An important element of the study is to measure the energy expenditures of individual dolphins to help determine if the environment is supporting their food requirements.

The project is part of a twenty-one-year study of the Sarasota dolphin community.

No special knowledge is necessary, but you should be a strong swimmer.

South America

CHILE

Catching Guanacos/Watching Pumas

Transportation: hiking
Accommodations: hotels/tents
Land cost: $2,150
Duration: 17 days
Seasons: November
Tour sponsor: Patagonia Research Expedition

The Torres del Paine National Park, located in Chile's southern Patagonia, is a composite of the Rockies, the Alps and the Himalayas, with parts of the Tetons, Glacier National Park, Yosemite, and Glacier Bay added for highlights. Over 95 percent of the park, which is an International Biosphere Reserve, is a wilderness of steppes, towering peaks, massive glaciers, moraine valleys, waterfalls, blue lakes, and lagoons.

This is your office on the trip.

Your work is to hand-capture newly born chulengoes (baby guanacos), ear-tag them, and put on a telemetry radio collar—all without falling in love, if you can, with the cute creatures with enormous, liquid-brown eyes who will follow you home if given a chance.

Guanacos, the progenitor of the llama, is one of four species of South American camels. The camel first originated and evolved on the plains of North America, flourishing as recently as 10,000 to 12,000 years ago, according to Dr. William Franklin, who leads the trip.

The base camp is near glacier-fed lakes and cool lagoons. You hike an average of 2 to 7 miles daily across shrub foothills ranging in elevation from 200 to 1,000 feet. Beech forest, Patagonia grassland, Andean alpine, and glaciers of the Torres del Paine park surround you. "Torres del Paine" is a combination of Indian and Spanish words meaning blue towers—which describes the granite spires seen everywhere. Twelve million years ago granite blocks pushed through the plain's sedimentary rocks to form the sheer vertical walls of the impressive mountains. They form the backdrop to your camp.

Over two hundred species of birds live in the park, including the Andean condor with a 14-foot wingspan, Chilean flamingos, peregrine falcon, austral parrots, Darwin's rhea, and black-necked swans. Patagonia puma, Andean fox, and austral viscacha are also present, but rarely seen.

An object of the research is to track the mortality rate of the chulengoes, a favorite prey of the puma. You observe mother-infant relationships and guanaco behavior. How behavior relates to environment is important to the study.

The legal harvest of chulengoes for their fine silky wool, and male guanaco for wool and meat, is a multimillion-dollar business. An important aspect of the research is to determine at what rate guanaco can be harvested without interfering with their normal reproduction and social organization. Information you gather will be an important contribution to wildlife conservation and management programs.

No special skills or knowledge are necessary. You are taught how to approach, catch, and mark the chulengoes without causing harm. The weather varies from sunny to cool with rain, but it is always windy. You must be psychologically prepared to deal with constant strong winds.

ECUADOR

Study a Rain Forest

Transportation: hiking
Accommodations: field station
Land cost: $1,395
Duration: 13 days
Seasons: July
Tour sponsor: University Research Expeditions Program

If you want to know the details of a rain forest's life, this is your trip. You will record the intimate habits of the rain forest plants and their personalities. You will photograph them and take samples to study at the nearest laboratory. This could be the start of a lasting love affair with plant life.

The trysting place is the 10-square-mile Maquipucuna Tropical Reserve on the Andes' western slope, north of Quito, Ecuador's capital. Hardwoods, tree ferns, and orchids once completely covered these mountains, which are now nearly denuded. But the forest within the reserve has never been cut.

The project is to inventory the reserve's plant species, collect and prepare samples, and record details about the habitat. You also attach identification tags to trees along the trail system. The information will be used for future land management and ecological plans.

A fledgling trail system is under development in the steep terrain. Field work is moderately strenuous, especially when the afternoon rains turn the trails into mud. The days are hot and the evenings cool. Stinging ants and poisonous snakes, no more dangerous than rattlesnakes, live in the forest. It is recommended that you start taking an antimalarial drug one week prior to departure. Be sure to bring an insect repellent containing DEET.

Accommodations are the reserve's field station, a wooden building with bunk beds, kitchen, indoor plumbing, and flush toilets.

You work with Ecuadoran students and scientists under the direction of Dr. Grady Webster of the University of California-

Davis Botany Department. Wilderness experience or a background in field botany, biology, or plant ecology would be useful but are not prerequisites. Expertise in photography and Spanish would also be useful.

PERU

Amazon River Dolphins and Rain Forest

Transportation: boat/hiking

Accommodations: riverboat

Land cost: $1,890-$2,850

Duration: 8 to 15 days

Seasons: March to July

Tour sponsor: Oceanic Society Expeditions

Amazon River Basin dolphins, like other dolphins of the world, are at high risk from human abuse of the environment. River dolphins face special challenges of habitat degradation caused by pollution, irrigation, and urban development.

On this project you collect data to assess the effects of human activities on the Amazon dolphins' environment. You help gather information on the dolphins' environmental requirements so effective conservation measures can be implemented. Solid scientific data is necessary to protect the dolphins and to establish marine sanctuaries.

At Iquitos you board the *Delfin*, a 76-foot traditional three-deck wooden riverboat with double occupancy compact cabins, shared shower/bath, a dining room, and a sun deck. The ship is your living quarters during the trip. You cruise one day up the Tahuayo River, a narrow tributary of the Amazon, to the Pacaya-Samiria National Reserve, where the Maranon and Ucayali rivers join to form the Amazon. Along the rivers you see great and snowy egrets, yellow-billed terns, and yellow-headed caracara.

Nine days are spent in the reserve, the largest in Peru, which has enormous stretches of untouched tropical rain forest. This pristine habitat of the pink dolphin, the manatee, and other aquatic species was once slated for oil drilling. Pressure from environmental groups has temporarily stalled the plan, but the possibility exists that drilling could still happen.

You assist researchers in studying individual dolphins, estimating their age and sex. You document their patterns of association with others in the group. Data gathering is done from motorized skiffs, by onshore observation, and by swimming with the dolphins. The Amazon dolphins are the largest species of freshwater dolphins in the world. Some grow to nine feet in length.

You will also have ample time for nature hikes in the reserve. Jabiru, horned screamers, ringed kingfishers, anhinga, slate-collared hawks, toucans, yellow-crowned parrots, and other jungle birds live in the marshy swamplands.

Heat, humidity, and insects are facts of jungle life. What you cannot escape be prepared to deal with by bringing industrial-strength insect repellent and a sense of humor. Daytime temperatures average between 81 and 90 degrees, but the humidity intensifies the heat. Nighttime temperatures average between 65 and 70 degrees.

No experience or special skills are required, although knowing how to swim is a plus.

PART VI

PART VI

Special Needs

The trips in this section are designed for people with special needs caused by physical or other disabilities. For example, tour operators are experienced in handling wheelchairs and other support equipment. On trips suitable for those in wheelchairs, a vehicle with a lift is used when needed, and the tour operators know how to aid people when transferring from a chair to a kayak. Visually impaired individuals are assigned a personal guide, and a signing guide accompanies the hearing-impaired. Some tours, such as those organized by Search Beyond Adventure, have nurse escorts for people who require medical assistance.

On the tours for individuals with behavioral disorders, the staff-to-tour participant ratio is one-to-one. So, if a person needs assistance getting dressed or eating, that aid is available. In addition, the tours are relaxed and flexible to help reduce stress, which can trigger some behavioral disorders. The tour groups are divided into smaller groups according to capability and interests.

The trips described here are not watered down versions of the other eco-journeys in the book. The tours include kayaking in Canada, dogsledding in the Boundary Waters Canoe Area Wilderness, canoeing the Florida Everglades, and exploring rain forests in Belize and Costa Rica.

Central America

BELIZE

Transportation: charter bus

Accommodations: hotels/lodges

Land cost: $925-$1,000

Duration: 8 days

Seasons: January to May; September to December

Forest covers 70 percent of Belize, a wild garden with national boundaries. Ninety percent of the country, which is roughly the size of New Hampshire, has not been developed or planted or in any way exploited. The second largest barrier reef in the world, after Australia's Great Barrier Reef, lies just offshore. You sample the jungles and beaches for a firsthand look at how various ecosystems comprise a country.

You travel to the Cockscomb Basin Wildlife Sanctuary, the world's only jaguar reserve. Ocelot, margay, the reclusive tapir, peccary, monkey, and jaguarundi, which resembles a very large brown cat, also live in the reserve. Naturalists explain in detail the inner workings of the tropical rain forest.

The Crooked Tree Bird Sanctuary, which consists of eight interconnected lagoons, is accessible only by boat and is your next destination. The endangered jabiru stork nests in the sanctuary. An estimated one hundred nesting sites remain in all of Central America for the jabiru, an impressive bird 5 feet tall with white plumage, a black head, black beak, red collar, and a 12-foot wingspan. Howler monkeys, including the rare black howler, also live in the sanctuary.

The tour includes the options of going to Mexico's Yucatan region or to Tikal, a Mayan ruin located in the disappearing jungles of eastern Guatemala.

For more details on Belize, see COMFORTABLE WILDERNESS: Central America/Belize.

Tour operator:

Search Beyond Adventure

COSTA RICA

Transportation: van

Accommodations: hotels/lodges

Land cost: $1,895-$1,985

Duration: 9 days

Seasons: March to May; mid-September to December

Costa Rica's cloud forest and rain forest, active volcanoes, marsh-lands, rivers, and sea water estuaries are home to numerous species of birds, mammals, reptiles, amphibians, insects, and plants.

On this tour you sample diverse parts of this environmental potluck. You visit Poas Volcano National Park, a big—and active —volcano capped by a cloud forest, and stop at Manuel Antonio National Park on the Pacific Coast, where capuchin and squirrel monkeys live in the jungle fronting the park's four beaches.

In the northeastern Guanacaste Province you visit one of Central America's few remaining primary dry tropical forests in the Santa Rosa National Park. A trip to the coral reefs of the Cahuita National Park is optional.

For more information, see COMFORTABLE WILDERNESS and NOT ORDINARY TRIPS: Central America/Costa Rica.

Tour operator:

Search Beyond Adventure

PANAMA

Transportation: bus

Accommodations: hotels/lodges

Land cost: $1,895-$1,985

Duration: 10 days

Seasons: March to May; September to mid-December

Jungle wildlife in the Soberania National Park and in the Darien Jungle, a roadless track that stretches south to Colombia, are the main offerings of this tour. You take the Pan-American Highway to Yaviza, where the road ends at the edge of the Darien Gap, home territory of the Choco Indians.

The newly created 1.5-million-acre Darien National Park lies 15 miles beyond the end of the road. The park, the second-largest protected area in Central America, is one of the world's most biologically diverse ecosystems. However, as an established entity, the park exists more on paper than in reality. The huge area is patrolled by only fourteen rangers at three stations. Between them they have only one vehicle and a couple of radios. Such limited means is not enough to contain the threats to the park.

The chief threat is the influx of ranchers and their cattle invading from central Panama. They cut and burn the jungle to clear land for grazing and raising crops. Lumber companies surreptitiously pay farmers to clear forested plots and then buy the valuable mahogany and cedar. Aid to maintain the park's integrity has come from environmental groups and the U.S. government. Asociacion Nacional para la Conservacion de la Naturaliza (ANCON), Panama's most influential conservation organization, works hard to establish the park. ANCON's partner in the U.S., the Nature Conservancy, provides funding and technical assistance through its Latin American "Parks in Peril" program. The U.S. Agency for International Development has also put money into the Darien project.

On an excursion to the San Blas Islands, 90 miles off the Atlantic Coast, you visit Cuna Indian villages. The Cuna are perhaps the most environmentally conscious and politically aware of the indigenous Central American tribes. Before the Spanish arrived five hundred years ago, the Cuna occupied the entire southern isthmus and part of coastal Colombia. They guided Balboa to his "discovery" of the Pacific Ocean, which they had known about for generations. When the Spanish attempted to enslave them, the tribe fled into the mountains of eastern Panama and on to the San Blas Islands, where most of the 30,000 Cuna now live in a 100-by-30-mile autonomous reserve. Some Cuna still live in the mainland jungle.

The Cunas are perhaps best known for *molas*, intricately sewn panels of reverse applique the women use to decorate their blouses. They invented the *mola* when missionaries discouraged their custom of body painting in favor of clothes. *Molas* are valued art objects and are now exported worldwide.

The tour also includes a visit to the Panama Canal and a drive up Baru Volcano.

Tour operator:

Search Beyond Adventure

North America

CANADA

Big Salmon River

Transportation: canoe/van
Accommodations: tents
Land cost: $2,000
Duration: 24 days
Seasons: August

The Big Salmon River, a tributary of the Yukon River, is a premier canoe route in the Yukon Territory. The trip starts on Quiet Lake, located 125 miles north of British Columbia and spawning ground of the red Chinook salmon, after which the Big Salmon is named. On the trip you see the big fish fighting up rapids to get to their home lake.

The Big Salmon meanders out of Quiet Lake and through Sandy and Big Salmon lakes before dropping over the edge of an ice shield plateau for a 220-mile-plus run to the Yukon River.

During the first days of the trip you paddle the length of Sandy and Big Salmon lakes practicing your paddling techniques on these tranquil lakes ringed by forests and mountains. In the evenings, from the lakeshore camp, you may see moose coming for a drink.

Leaving Big Salmon Lake you start down the swift-flowing

river, being careful to avoid logjams and "sweepers"—trees that hang out over the water. The Big Salmon Range rises to the west and Mount Saint Cyr and Tower Peak to the east. For three days you run the twisting river surrounded by hundreds of miles of untouched wilderness. The river is fast but not technically demanding—until you hit a two-mile series of rapids below Moose Creek. The rapids are more fun than dangerous as you run an obstacle course of boulders and scattered rocks.

You travel 10 to 50 miles per day on the river. Past the rapids the river flattens through a wide, low valley. You sit back and cruise, admiring the Big Salmon Range on the right and the Semenof Hills on the left. But do not relax too much. A mile and a half above Headless Creek the river makes a sharp left, then a right "U" turn. This combination is the fastest and roughest section of the river.

After you successfully pass this test you can once again admire the scenery—purple hills far downriver marking the Yukon River. The next day you pass an abandoned village at the mouth of the Big Salmon before joining the mighty Yukon.

What an ugly brute of a river! The Yukon looks like mud coffee left on boil too long. The silt-laden river churns and swirls and leaps down the narrow channel hemmed in by high, steep banks. For five days you take a thrilling ride past "hoodoos" (sand pillar and arches sculpted by the wind) and abandoned gold mining villages. You run the famous Five Fingers Rapids, where many "Klondikers'" rafts and boats were smashed to pieces.

And then, suddenly, it's over. You coast into Dawson, where Jack London and Robert Service found scenes and characters for their fiction and poems. Dawson still nurtures its Gold Rush image with honky-tonk saloons, such as Diamond Tooth Gertie's, and false storefronts. But today it also has modern conveniences, such as hot showers in the comfortable hotel where you stay.

This trip caters to people with and without disabilities, giving all a chance to explore aspects of human nature as well as wilderness nature. The group consists of ten to twelve participants and two tour staff members.

Severe weather conditions are more the norm than the exception. Days can alternate from hot and sultry to cold, made more so by rain and driving wind. Wilderness experience is not necessary, but previous canoeing experience is extremely helpful. The trip is not without danger. Cold water, sweepers, and logjams pose threats. It takes two to five days to evacuate an injured person out of this remote area. Safety is stressed again and again on the trip.

The journey actually begins in Minneapolis for a 3,000-mile van ride through some of the most scenic country in North America. Driving time is three-and-a-half days, each way, to Johnson's Crossing, Yukon Territory. Or you can fly to Whitehorse and join the trip at Johnson's Crossing, a four-and-a-half-hour bus ride from Whitehorse.

Tour operator:

Wilderness Inquiry

Queen Charlotte Islands

Transportation: kayak

Accommodations: tents

Land cost: $1,195

Duration: 12 days

Seasons: August to September

The Queen Charlotte Islands, 480 miles northwest of Vancouver on the southern end of the Alaskan archipelago, are called the "Galapagos of the North Pacific." Haida Indians, who lived there centuries ago, called the islands Haida Gwaii. Both names mean essentially the same thing: a beautiful and bountiful place.

The plentiful land allowed the Haida to develop a sophisticated society. Ample salmon runs and an abundance of wild game guaranteed the survival of "the People of the Raven." The tribe had leisure time to contemplate the source of their good fortune. They carved totem poles from red cedar as homage to the generous nature gods. You see these still-standing prayers on your trip around the islands.

An overnight ferry ride from Prince Rupert takes you to Graham Island, where you catch an early morning ferry for a short ride to Moresby Island, launching point for the kayak trip. You are given kayaking instructions and time to practice before you paddle to the first overnight campsite. No previous kayaking or camping experience is necessary.

For the next eight days you paddle along the islands' shores forested with Sitka spruce, Douglas fir, and hemlock up to one thousand years old. You see bald eagles, seals, salmon, orange and purple starfish, and perhaps orca whales. The stable, 21-foot touring kayaks hold two or three people plus your gear.

The group consists of a maximum of twelve people plus two members from Wilderness Inquiry. The trip is open to everyone. You paddle about 8 miles per day, although this can vary from 5 to 15 miles, depending on the weather conditions. Rain and wind could slow you down. The average daily temperature range is from 45 to 75 degrees. The greatest danger is the cold water, so everyone is required to wear a wet suit and a life jacket.

On Tanu Island you stop at the ruins of an old Haida village, where totem poles guard the sacred sites. After a day's layover on the south side of the island, you push off again to explore Kunga Island and Darwin Sound, reputedly where the highest concentration of bald eagles nest. On Bischof Island, at the end of Darwin Sound, you soak in hot springs.

Then comes some more excitement. You venture back out to the open sea in the kayak, where you sit mere inches above the waterline. Bobbing on the waves, you eventually regain your confidence and start to feel a sense of control tempered by prudence. You have cut the security ties to your normal environment, and you are doing just fine.

You explore the sea caves of the Limestone Islands on the way to Skedans, another ancient Haida village. You go among several totems and the moss-covered remains of a longhouse, a building where the community held "potlaches." A day is spent exploring the island on foot and by kayak. You paddle around the kelp beds of Fairborn Shoals, where sea otters and seals hang out. At Cumshewa Inset you explore another Haida site.

A day later you return to Moresby Island and turn homeward.

Tour operators:

Search Beyond Adventure   Wilderness Inquiry

MEXICO

Copper Canyon

Transportation: charter bus/train/motor vehicle/hiking

Accommodations: hotels/hostels

Land cost: $935-$985

Duration: 8 days

Seasons: January to March

Copper Canyon, located in northern Mexico, is one of the most extensive, isolated, and unexplored canyon systems in the world. The Tarahumara Indians live within the 23 square miles of this largely undeveloped national park.

A train ride takes you through the forest and gorges of this region, which is four times larger than the Grand Canyon, via a series of bridges and tunnels. Jeep and truck rides give you a closer look at the canyonland's ecosystems, wildlife, and rare varieties of birds. You also visit isolated Tarahumara villages deep in the canyons.

Logging in the canyonlands threatens the Tarahumara way of life. Tree cutting destroys wildlife habitat, causes erosion, and prevents the area from developing into a world-class wilderness park.

For more details, see SAFE THRILLS: Mexico/Copper Canyon.

Tour operator:

Search Beyond Adventure

UNITED STATES—WEST

HAWAII

Transportation: rental vehicles

Accommodations: cabins

Land cost: $1,395-$1,455

Duration: 8 days

Seasons: January to March

Cabins at the Kokee State Park are your base camp for a tour of Kauai. The elepaio, the I'wi, the apapane and other indigenous birds live in the park's native koa forest. Highlights of the tour include Waimea Canyon, the 15-mile-long, one-mile-wide, and 2,000-foot-deep "Grand Canyon of the Pacific"; the rugged Na Pali coast with 2,500-foot-high cliffs; the Kalalau Valley; and, of course, the beaches.

For more details on Hawaii, see COMFORTABLE WILDER-NESS and NOT ORDINARY TRIPS: United States/Hawaii.

Tour operator:

Search Beyond Adventure

MIDWEST

MINNESOTA

Boundary Waters Canoe Area Wilderness

Transportation: canoe

Accommodations: lodge/tents

Land cost: $585-$765

Duration: 6 to 8 days

Seasons: April to November

More than twelve hundred miles of canoe trails wind from lake to lake through the million-acre Boundary Waters wilderness that sprawls 150 miles along the Minnesota-Ontario border. Tour operators have their favorite routes starting at different put-in points. The routes also vary with the seasons. A spring trip may start from Snowbank Lake (Fernberg Trail); an August trip takes a circle route; an autumn trip may make trips from a base camp, returning to the lodge daily.

For details on the Boundary Waters, see COMFORTABLE WILDERNESS: United States/Minnesota.

Tour operators:

Nantahala Outdoor Center   Wilderness Inquiry

Search Beyond Adventure

Boundary Waters by Dogsled

Transportation: dogsled/pulk sleds/nordic skis

Accommodations: lodge/snow shelter

Land cost: $425

Duration: 5 days

Seasons: December to March

The Boundary Waters wilderness in the winter is beautiful. And traveling during this time of year allows you to avoid the mosquitoes and the biting black flies.

You travel on cross-country skis or snowshoes. Mobility-impaired people travel in a pulk, a small sled pulled by one or two trained dogs. Everyone takes turns riding in or driving the one large dogsled.

The trip begins with a one-mile hike across Bearskin Lake to the YMCA's Camp Menogyn lodge, located a few miles from the Canadian border. The base camp has indoor bathroom facilities, a sauna, and a kitchen. Everyone is expected to help with cooking, washing dishes, and general clean-up.

You spend a day practicing mushing the dogs on the lake and polishing your skiing technique. No previous experience is necessary in dogsled driving, cross-country skiing, or winter camping. Weather permitting, the group builds a snow shelter and spends the night. Snow shelters are surprisingly comfortable. Body heat and candles keeps the temperature reasonable enough to cook without gloves, but you do sleep fully clothed, including a hat, snuggled into a sleeping bag.

You next travel to Rose Lake on the U.S.-Canadian border to see palisades three hundred feet high. Another day trip goes to Daniels Lake. The frozen lakes are great for running the dogsleds. Portage trails through the forests are good for cross-country skiing. You travel 3 to 8 miles a day on the trails. The group is limited to fifteen persons accompanied by five Wilderness Inquiry staff members.

A variation of this trip is an eight-day trip for eight people that loops to remote lakes off the Gunflint Trail and back to the base camp lodge. You camp out in snow shelters for two nights.

Tour operator:

Wilderness Inquiry

NORTHEAST

MAINE

Chiputneticook Lake

Transportation: canoe

Accommodations: tents

Land cost: $395

Duration: 3 days

Seasons: July and September

Chiputneticook Lake, a chain of wilderness lakes along the Maine-New Brunswick border, forms a maze of interconnected bays and islands. Calm and picturesque, the lakes provide a perfect introduction to wilderness canoeing.

The trip begins and ends at Spednik Lake Park, across from the Canadian border. On the first day you paddle into Palfrey Lake, where you camp on a peninsula sticking out into Palfrey Cove. Although only a four hours' drive from Bangor, Maine, you feel eons removed from civilization.

The next day's goal is Birch Island on the upper reaches of Palfrey Lake. You paddle an average of 10 miles each day, but that distance varies from 2 miles to 30 miles, depending on the conditions, such as strong headwinds or rain. You should expect at least one day of rain. On two to four short portages from lake to lake you carry your gear in backpacks.

The group is limited to ten to twelve people with two Wilderness Inquiry staff members. The group may be a mix of able-bodied and impaired people. No previous canoeing or camping experience is required.

The lakes lie near the northern Appalachian Mountains where, as recently as ten thousand years ago, glaciers ground the mountains down to their underlying granite substratum. The granite makes for some smooth and accessible campsites and trails, however, rocks, mud, logs, and other obstacles can cause difficulties for wheelchair-users.

Tour operator:

Wilderness Inquiry

Allagash Wilderness River

Transportation: canoe
Accommodations: tents
Land cost: $725
Duration: 5 days
Seasons: September

Big lakes and a swift river make this trip a northern Maine combo platter. After a three-hour drive from Bangor, you camp on the shore of Long Lake. You spend the first day learning, or brushing up on, canoeing and camping skills. No previous experience is necessary.

You paddle the length of Long Lake, make a short portage over the dam at the lake's end, and set up camp at Sweeny Brook. The trip continues on streams through the woods, pass Round Pond, and down Five Fingers Brook, where it enters the Allagash River.

Now you are ready for fun. On the fast-flowing, but not danger-ous, river, you dodge islands and rocks as you head farther north up the Allagash Wilderness Waterway. The river eventually joins the St. John River, where you pull out and are met by a vehicle for a six-hour ride back to Bangor.

You paddle an average of 10 miles per day and make two to four portages carrying your gear in backpacks.

Like Chiputneticook Lake, the waterway lies near the northern Appalachian Mountains, where the granite makes for some smooth and accessible campsites and trails, but rocks, mud, logs, and other obstacles can cause difficulties for wheelchair-users.

For more information on Maine see COMFORTABLE WIL-DERNESS: North America/United States—Northeast/Maine.

Tour operator:

Wilderness Inquiry

SOUTH

FLORIDA

Paddling the Everglades and the Florida Keys

Transportation: kayak
Accommodations: tents
Land cost: $695
Duration: 8 days
Seasons: mid-January to February

The Seminole Indians called the Everglades "Pay-Hay-okee," which means grassy waters. This swamp-like subtropical area is actually a river, up to 60 miles wide at points, flowing south from Lake Okeechobee to the tip of Florida. You paddle through the maze of mangrove islands, bays, and channels of Florida Bay and into the interior of the Everglades National Park. You also spend a couple of days in the Florida Keys.

To protect nesting birds, landing is forbidden on the islands in Florida Bay.

For five days you explore the winding canals, creeks, and lagoons of the 1.5-million-acre Everglades National Park, although only the lower one-fourth of the river is in the park. You cover from 5 to 15 miles each day, frequently spotting pelicans, spoonbills, flamingos, and other varieties of the some three hundred bird species in the park. Unfortunately, increasing degradation of the environment is sharply reducing bird populations in the Everglades.

You next venture into Pearl Bay, a remote habitat of the endangered indigenous wood stork. Do not be surprised if a dolphin or manatee rolls up alongside your kayak.

You camp minimum-impact style on beaches or, in the Everglades, on chickees, elevated tent platforms. The group is limited to twelve to fifteen people, plus two Wilderness Inquiry staff members. No previous canoeing or camping experience is required.

After emerging from the Everglades, you make a two-day trip to the Florida Keys. The paddling experience is much different here. Instead of still, tea-colored water, the blue sea gives you a roller coaster ride on gentle swells. You kayak to Indian Key, site of an Indian massacre, and explore the native vegetation of Lignam Vitae Key. At the John Pennekamp State Park you snorkel on a coral reef. Marked water trails wind through the park.

Coastal wetlands like the Everglades can be up to twenty times richer in wildlife than the open oceans. The mixing of freshwater and seawater in such estuaries fosters one of the most productive habitats on Earth. What estuaries lack in wildlife diversity is made up for in sheer numbers. Thousands upon thousands of crabs, shrimps, worms, snails, oysters, mussels, and cockles, which attract the flocks of birds, live in the mud flats of the Everglades.

Unfortunately, the Everglades, the United States' greatest wetland ecosystem, is "in a state of collapse," according to National Audubon Society president Peter Berle.

In the 1930s, two hundred thousand wood storks, white ibis, tricolored herons, and other birds nested in the Everglades. Today, only two thousand to four thousand birds nest there.

"This ecological havoc was wrought through the expenditure of millions of public dollars and the construction of one of the world's largest plumbing systems," writes Berle in *Audubon Magazine* (March/April 1992). "The Central and Southern Florida Flood Control Project was designed to interrupt the natural flow of water as it seeped southward from Lake Okeechobee, through the Everglades National Park. The plumbers of the U.S. Army Corps of Engineers provided flood control and drainage, enabling the conversion of thousands of acres to agriculture."

As a result, the native wildlife suffered greatly. So far, the following animal species indigenous to the Everglades have been placed on the Endangered Species List: Florida panther, the wood stork, the snail kite, the American crocodile, the Cape Sable seaside sparrow, and the manatee.

Berle called on Congress to stop farm subsidies that encourage environmental destruction. Public dollars must be spent instead for the restoration of the Everglades, he argues.

Congress has taken limited action by instructing the Corps of Engineers to restore the Kissimmee River, north of the Everglades, back to its original meandering state. The engineers had remade the river into a straight ditch for better flood control.

The Everglades National Park is a World Heritage Site. Signatories of the World Heritage Convention (the United States is one) adopted by the UNESCO (United Nations Educational, Scientific, and Cultural Organization) General Conference in 1972, promised to preserve "the sites and monuments within its borders that are recognized to be of exceptional universal value."

Tour operators:

Search Beyond Adventure   Wilderness Inquiry

GEORGIA

Okefenokee Swamp Exploration

Transportation: canoe
Accommodations: cabins
Land cost $350-$400
Duration: 4 to 6 days
Seasons: year-round

Aquatic trails wind through cypress and mangroves and pass float-ing prairies of peat bogs in the Okefenokee, which literally means the "Land of the Trembling Earth." Day trips paddling through the swamp require no previous canoeing experience.

Accommodations are cabins, usually at the Stephen Foster State Park.

For more details on the Okefenokee, see COMFORTABLE WILDERNESS: United States—South/Georgia.

Tour operator:

Search Beyond Adventure

RIVER TRIPS

Three organizations have notable river-running programs for peo-ple with disabilities: Environmental Traveling Companions, Nan-tahala Outdoor Center, and Dvoraks Expeditions. The programs, designed to build trust, self-confidence, team-building techniques, and expand personal skills, give you hands-on wilderness experi-ence. The guides tell about the ecosystems, geology, and environ-mental issues of the rivers.

The canoe and kayak trips run rivers in California, Oregon, Colorado, Utah, Texas, New Mexico, and Alaska. International trips go to Costa Rica, Mexico, and Nepal. You camp along the rivers, which range from easy to challenging. The trips are from three to twelve days long. No previous experience is necessary for the majority of the trips. The tour operators school you in paddling techniques, camping skills, and safety precautions.

Tour operators:

Dvoraks Kayak and Rafting
  Expeditions
Environmental Traveling
  Companions

Nantahala Outdoor Center

LISTING OF TOUR OPERATORS

ABEC
1304 Westwick Drive
Fairbanks, AK 99712
(907) 457-8907

Abercrombie & Kent International
1520 Kensington Road
Oak Brook, IL 60521
(708) 954-2944
(800) 323-7308

Above the Clouds Trekking
P.O. Box 398
Worcester, MA 01602-0398
(508) 799-4499
(800) 233-4499
Fax (508) 797-4779

Adventure Associates
P.O. Box 16304
Seattle, WA 98116
(206) 932-8352

Adventure Network International
200-1676 Duranleau Street
Vancouver, BC V6H 3S5
Canada
(604) 683-8033
Fax (604) 683-6892

Adventure Tours of Asia
826 South Sierra Bonita Avenue
Los Angeles, CA 90036
(213) 935-3156

Africa Adventure Company
1620 South Federal Highway
Suite 900

Pompano Beach, FL 33062
(305) 781-3933
(800) 882-9453
Fax (305) 781-0984

Africatours
210 Post Street, #911
San Francisco, CA 94108
(415) 391-5788

Alaska Discovery
234 Gold Street
Juneau, AK 99801
(907) 586-1911

Alaska Wildland Adventures
P.O. Box 389
Girdwood, AK 99587
(907) 783-2928
summer only:
HC64 Box 26
Cooper Landing, AK 99572
(907) 595-1279
(800) 334-8730

Amazonia Expeditions
1824 NW 102nd Way
Gainesville, FL 32606
(904) 332-4051

Amazon Tours & Cruises
8700 West Flagler Street
Suite 190
Miami, FL 33174
(305) 227-2266
(800) 423-2791
Fax (305) 227-1880

American Museum of Natural
   History/Discovery Tours
Central Park West at 79th Street
New York, NY 10024-5192
(212) 769-5700
(800) 462-8687

American Wilderness Experience
P.O. Box 1486
Boulder, CO 80306
(303) 444-2622
(800) 444-0099
Fax (303) 444-3999

Ancient Forest Adventures
16 NW Kansas Avenue
Bend, OR 97701-1202
(503) 385-8633
(800) 551-1043

Arctic Edge
Box 4850
Whitehorse, Yukon Territory Y1A
   4N6
Canada
(403) 633-5470
Fax (404) 633-3820

Arctic Treks
Box 73452
Fairbanks, AK 99705
(907) 455-6502

Avant Garde Travel
P.O. Box 4621
North Hollywood, CA 91617
(818) 990-3439

Black Feather
1341 Wellington Street West
Ottawa, Ontario K1Y 3B8
Canada
(613) 722-9717
Fax (613) 722-0245
or
40 Wellington Street East
Toronto, Ontario M5E 1C7
Canada
(416) 861-1555
Fax (416) 862-2314

Boulder Adventures
P.O. Box 1279
Boulder, CO 80306
(303) 443-6789
(800) 642-2742

Canada Canoe Adventures
1029 Hyde Park Road
Suite 5
Hyde Park, Ontario N0M 1Z0
Canada
(519) 473-2109
Fax (519) 473-2109

Canadian Recreational Canoeing
   Association
Association Canadienne De Canotage
   Recreatif
1029 Hyde Park Road
Suite 5
Hyde Park, Ontario N0M 1Z0
Canada
(519) 473-2109
Fax (519) 473-2109

Canadian River Expeditions
3524 West 16th Avenue
Vancouver, BC V6R 3C1
Canada
(604) 738-4449
Fax (604) 736-5526

Canoe Country Escapes
194 South Franklin Street
Denver, CO 80209
(303) 722-6482

Canoe USA
N.E.H.H.
P.O. Box 1648
North Conway, NH 03850
(800) 233-2128
Fax (800) 728-4911

Cheesemans' Ecology Safaris
20800 Kittredge Road
Saratoga, CA 95070-6322
(408) 867-1371
(408) 741-5330

(800) 527-5330
Fax (408) 741-0358

Dvoraks Kayak and Rafting
    Expeditions
17921-B U.S. Highway 285
Nathrop, CO 81236
(719) 539-6851
(800) 824-3795

Earthwatch
680 Mount Auburn Street
Box 403
Watertown, MA 02172
(617) 926-8200
Fax (617) 926-8532

Ecosummer Expeditions
P.O. Box 8014-240
936 Peace Portal Drive
Blaine, WA 98230
(206) 332-1000
(800) 688-8605
Fax (604) 669-3244
or
1516 Duranleau Street
Granville Island
Vancouver, B.C. V6H 3S4
Canada
(604) 669-7741
Fax (604) 669-3244

Environmental Traveling
    Companions
Fort Mason Center
Landmark Building C
San Francisco, CA 94123
(415) 474-7662

Exodus Adventure
9 Weir Road
London SW 12 OLT
England
081-673-0859
    Australia:
    Exodus Expeditions
    81a Glebe Point Road
    Glebe NSW 2037
    (02) 552-6317
    Fax (02) 552-6318

Canada:
Market Square Tours
54 Donald Street
Winnipeg, Manitoba R3C 1L6
(204) 949-4279
(800) 661-3830
Fax (204) 949-0188

Denmark:
Topas Globetrotters
Skaersbrovej 11
8680 Ry
(86) 89 36 22
Fax (86) 89 36 88

Germany:
Deutshand Explorer
Huttenstrasse 17
4000 Dusseldorf 1
(0211) 379-064
Fax (0211) 370-630

The Netherlands:
Terra Travel
Haarlemmerstraat 24-26
1013ER Amsterdamn
(020) 62 751 29
Fax (020) 62 454 01

United States:
Safaricentre
3201 North Sepulveda Boulevard
Manhattan Beach, CA
(310) 546-4411
(800) 223-6040 (U.S.)
(800) 624- 5342 (California)
(800) 233-6046 (Canada)
Fax (310) 546-3188

Explore Worldwide
1 Frederick Street
Aldershot
Hants GU11 1LQ
England
0252 34 41 61
Fax 0252 34 31 70
    Australia:
    Adventure World
    73 Walker Street
    North Sydney NSW 2060

956-7766
Fax 956-7707

Belgium:
Divantoura
St Jacobsmarkt 5
2000 Antwerpen
03/233 19 16
Fax 03/233 21 39

Canada:
Trek Holidays
(800) 661-7265

Denmark:
Inter-travel
Frederiksholms Kanal 2
DK-1200 Copenhagen K
(33) 150 077
Fax (33) 156 018

New Zealand:
Adventure World
101 Great South Road
Remuera, P.O. Box 74008
Auckland DX69501
524 5118
Fax 520 6629

Switzerland:
Suntrek Tours
Birmensdorferstr 187
P.O. Box 8371,8036
Zurich
01/462 61 61
Fax 01/462 65 45

United States:
Adventure Center
1311 63rd Street
Suite 200
Emeryville, CA 94608
(510) 654-1879
(800) 227-8747
Fax (510) 654-4200

Eye of the Whale
P.O. Box 1269
Kapa'au, HI 96755
(808) 889-0227

Footloose Forays
Michael Ellis
P.O. Box 1179
Pt. Reyes, CA 94956
(415) 663-9206

Forum
91 Gregory Lane
Suite 21
Pleasant Hill, CA 94523
(510) 671-2900
Fax (510) 671-2993
(510) 946-1500

Foundation for Field Research
P.O. Box 2010
Alpine, CA 91903
(619) 445-9264
Fax (619) 445-1893

Caribbean Research Station:
P.O. Box 771
The Carenage
St. George's, Grenada (WI)
(809) 440-2330

Mexico Research Station:
Apartado Postal #1000
Tuxtla Gutierrez
29000 Chiapas, Mexico
Fax 52-961-2431

Four Corners School of Outdoor
Education
East Route
Monticello, UT 84535
(801) 587-2156

Foxglove Safaris
15 West 26th Street
New York, NY 10010
(212) 545-8252

Geo Expeditions
P.O. Box 3656
Sonora, CA 95370
(209) 532-0152
Fax (209) 532-1979

Great Expeditions
5915 West Boulevard

Vancouver, B.C. V6M 3X1
Canada
(604) 263-1476
(800) 663-8422
Fax (604) 8422

Guerba Tours and Safaris
Adventure Center
1311 63rd Street
Suite 200
Emeryville, CA 94608
(510) 654-1879
(800) 227-8747
Fax (510) 654-4200

Hemingway Safaris
1050 Second Avenue
New York, NY 10022
(212) 838-3650

High Adventure Travel
166 Geary Street
10th Floor
San Francisco, CA 94108
(415) 986-6445
(800) 428-8735
Fax (415) 616-2161

Himalayan Travel
P.O. Box 481
Greenwich, CT 06836
(203) 622-0084
(800) 225-2380
Fax (203) 622-0084

Ibex Expeditions
2657 West 28th Avenue
Eugene, OR 97405
(505) 345-1289
Fax (505) 343-9002

Inca Floats
1311 63rd Street
Emeryville, CA 94608
(510) 420-1550
Fax (510) 420-0947

Innerasia Expeditions
2627 Lombard Street
San Francisco, CA 94122

(415) 922-0448
(800) 777-8183
Fax (415) 346-5535

International Expeditions
One Evirons Park
Helena, AL 35080
(205) 428-1700

International Zoological Expeditions
210 Washington Street
Sherborn, MA 01770
(508) 655-1461

Joseph Van Os Nature Tours
P.O. Box 655
Vashon Island, WA 98070
(206) 463-5362
Fax (206) 463-5484

Journeys International
4011 Jackson Road
Ann Arbor, MI 48103
(313) 665-4407
(808) 255-8735
Fax (313) 665-2945

Ker & Downey Safaris
13201 Northwest Freeway
Suite 50
Houston, TX 77040
(713) 895-8753
(800) 423-4236

Kimbla
Adventure Center
1311 63rd Street
Suite 200
Emerville, CA 94608
(510) 654-1879
(800) 227-8747
Fax (510) 654-4200

Learned Journeys
Trans-Pacific Special Interest Tours
P.O. Box 30636
Santa Barbara, CA 93130-0626
(805) 682-6191
(800) 682-6191

Lost World Adventures
1189 Autumn Ridge Drive
Marietta, GA 30066
(404) 971-8586

Luxury Adventure Safari
30 West Mission Street
Suite 4
Santa Barbara, CA 93101-2498
(800) 733-1789

Mariah Wilderness Expeditions
P.O. Box 248
Point Richmond, CA 94807
(510) 233-2303
(800) 4-MARIAH

Montana Nature Conservancy
Big Sky Field Office
Power Block West
3rd Floor
P.O. Box 258
Helena, MT 59624
(406) 443-0303
Fax (406) 442-8311

Mountain Travel/Sobek Expeditions
6420 Fairmount Avenue
El Cerrito, CA 94530-3606
(510) 527-8100
(800) 227-2384
Fax (510) 525-7710

Nantahala Outdoor Center
U.S. 19W
Box 41
Bryson City, NC 28713
(704) 488-2175

National Audubon Society
950 Third Avenue
New York, NY 10022
(212) 546-9146

Nature Expeditions International
474 Willamette Street
P.O. Box 11496
Eugene, OR 97440
(503) 484-6529
Fax (503) 484-6531

New England Hiking Holidays
P.O. Box 1648
North Conway, NH 03860
(603) 356-9696
(800) 869-0949

New York Botanical Gardens
Bronx, NY 10458-5126
(212) 220-8647

Ocean Cruise Lines
Paquet French Cruises
Pearl Cruises
1510 SE 17th Street
Fort Lauderdale, FL 33316
(305) 764-3500
Fax (305) 764-2888

Oceanic Society Expeditions
Fort Mason Center
Building E
San Francisco, CA 94123
(415) 441-4106
(800) 326-7491

Outer Edge Expeditions
45500 Pontiac Trail
Walled Lake, MI 48390
(800) 322-5235
Fax (313) 624-5140

Overseas Adventure Travel
349 Broadway
Cambridge, MA 02139
(617) 876-0533
(800) 221-0841
Fax (617) 876-0455

Patagonia Research Expedition
124 Science II
Iowa State University
Ames, IA 50011
(515) 294-1240

Pioneer Tours
P.O. Box 22063
Carmel, CA 93922
(408) 626-1815
Fax (408) 626-9013
(800) 288-2107

Costa Rica:
Pioneer Tours
Aparado: 3070
Sebanilla, Costa Rica
(506) 25-8117
Fax (506) 53-4687

Quark Expeditions
980 Post Road
Darien, CT 06820
(203) 656-0499
(800) 356-5699

Questers Worldwide Nature Tours
257 Park Avenue South
New York, NY 10010
(212) 673-3120
(800) 468-8668
Fax (212) 473-0178

Rainbow Adventures (women only)
Susan Eckert & Associates
1308 Sherman Avenue
Evanston, IL 60201
(708) 864-4570

REI Adventures
P.O. Box 88126
Seattle, WA 98138-2126
(206) 395-7760
(800) 622-2236

Roads Less Traveled
P.O. Box 18742
Boulder, CO 80308
(303) 530-7350

Safaricentre
3201 North Sepulveda Boulevard
Manhattan Beach, CA 90266
(310) 546-4411
(800) 223-6046 (U.S.)
(800) 624- 5342 (California)
(800) 233-6046 (Canada)
Fax (310) 546-3188

Salen Lindblad Cruises
Frontier Cruise Lines
333 Ludlow Street

Stamford, CT 06912
(203) 967-2900
Fax (203) 325-3670

Sea to Sky Trails
11715 81 Avenue
Delta, BC V4C 7H7
Canada
(604) 594-7701
Fax (604) 597-3315

Search Beyond Adventure
400 South Cedar Lake Road
Minneapolis, MN 55405
(612) 374-4845

Sierra Club Outings
Dept. #05618
730 Polk Street
San Francisco, CA 94139
(415) 776-2211

Siria Tented Safaris
P.O. Box 7361
Davis, CA 95617
(916) 756-6214
Fax (916) 470-8062
(916) 835-1531

Society Expeditions
3131 Elliott Avenue
Suite 700
Seattle, WA 98121
(206) 285-9400
Fax (206) 285-7917

Special Interest Tours & Travel
134 West 26th Street
Suite 903A
New York, NY 10001
(212) 645-6260
(800) 525-6772
Fax (212) 627-1807

Sue's Safaris
P.O. Box 2171
Rancho Palos Verdes, CA 90274
(310) 541-2011
Fax (800) 541-2011

Sunrise County Canoe Expeditions
Cathance Lake
Grove Post Office, ME 14638
(207) 454-7708

Tamu Safaris
Box 247
West Chesterfield, NH 03466
(800) 766-9199

Third Eye Travel
33220 Sandpiper Place
Fremont, CA 94555
(510) 487-9010
Fax (510) 487-9010

Transiberian Tours
P.O. Box 5358
Whitehorse, Yukon Territory, Y1A
    4Z2
Canada
(403) 633-5470
Fax (403) 633-3820

Travel Dynamics
132 East 70th Street
New York, NY 10021
(212) 517-7775
Fax (212) 517-0077

Trek Africa
760 Market Street
Suite 524
San Francisco, CA 94102
(415) 399-0104
Fax (415) 399-0121

Turtle Tours
Box 1147
Carefree, AZ 85377
(602) 224-5844
Fax (602) 488-3406

Tusker Trail & Safari
P.O. Box 5444
Santa Monica, CA 90409-5444
(213) 399-1683
Fax (213) 399-3682

University Research Expeditions
    Program
University of California at Berkeley
Berkeley, CA 94720
(510) 642-6586

Victor Emanuel Nature Tours
P.O. Box 33008
Austin, TX 78764
(512) 328-5221
(800) 328-8368
FAX (512) 328-2919

Voyagers International
P.O. Box 915
Ithaca, NY 14851
(607) 257-3091
Fax (607) 257-3699

Wanderlust Adventures
65 Clarkson
Suite 207
Denver, CO 80218
(303) 777-5846
Fax (303) 777-5846

Whitewolf Adventure Expeditions
2565 West 2nd Avenue
Vancouver, B.C. V6K 1J7
Canada
(604) 736-0664
Fax (604) 736-2810

Wild Horizons Expeditions
West Fork Road
Darby, MT 59829
(406) 821-3747

Wilderness: Alaska/Mexico
1231 Sundance Loop
Fairbanks, AK 98709
(907) 452-1821

Wilderness Inquiry
1313 Fifth Street, SE
Box 84
Minneapolis, MN 55414-1546
(612) 379-3858

Wilderness Journeys
P.O. Box 807
Bolinas, CA 94924
(415) 868-1836
(800) 786-1830

Wilderness Safaris
4N 211 Locust Avenue
West Chicago, IL 60185
(708) 293-9288
(800) 762-4027
Fax (708) 293-9607

Wilderness Southeast
711 Sandtown Rd
Savannah, GA 31410-1019
(912) 897-5108

Wilderness Travel
801 Allston Way
Berkeley, CA 94710
(415) 546-0420
(800) 247-6700

Wildland Adventures
3516 NE 155th Steet
Seattle, WA 98155
(206) 365-0686
(800) 345-4453
Fax (206) 363-6615

Wildland Studies
San Francisco State University
3 Mosswood Circle
Cazadero, CA 95421
(707) 632-5665

WomanTrek (women only)
1411 East Olive Way
P.O. Box 20643
Seattle, WA 98102
(206) 325-4772
(800) 477-8735

Woodswomen Adventure Travel
   (women and children only)
25 West Diamond Lake Road
Minneapolis, MN 55419-1926
(612) 822-3809
(800) 279-0555
Fax (612) 822-3814

World Expeditions
Suite 747
Yonge Street
M4W-3C7
Toronto, Ontario
Canada
(416) 963-9163
(800) 387-1483
Fax (416) 963-5730

   Europe:
   World Expeditions
   Laederstraede 11B St.
   1201 Copenhagen K
   Denmark
   (01) 93 4660
   Fax (01) 93 4760

   Australia:
   World Expeditions
      3rd Floor
   377 Sussex Street
   Sydney NSW 2000
   (02) 264 3366
   Fax (02) 261 1974

   New Zealand:
   Venturetreks
   P.O. Box 37610
   164 Parnell Road
   Parnell, Auckland
   (09) 79 98 55
   Fax (09) 77 03 20

World Wildlife Fund Explorations
1250 24th Street NW
Washington, DC 20037
(202) 778-9683

Zegrahm Expeditions
1414 Dexter Avenue North
Suite 327
Seattle, WA 98109
(206) 285-4000
Fax (206) 285-5037

Zoetic Research/Sea Quest
   Expeditions
P.O. Box 2424
Friday Harbor, WA 98250
(206) 578-5767

GENERAL INDEX

Abbey, Edward, 249–250
Aberdares Mountains, 8, 14–16
Admiralty Island, 97–98, 186
African Wildlife Foundation, 27
Aleutian Islands, 185
Allagash Wilderness River, 319–320
Amazon Basin, 3, 129, 131–132, 134, 138, 139, 144, 210–215, 221–227, 254–255, 303–304
Amazon River, 141–142, 143, 144, 210, 221, 223, 303–304
Amazonas, 226
Amboseli National Park, 155, 156, 160, 232, 275
Andes (mts.), 140, 212–213, 254
Angel Falls, 142, 143, 144, 225
Annapurna Massif, 48–49, 171, 234–235
Annapurnas (mts.), 48–49, 51, 233–237
Antarctica, 3, 29–36
Antarctica Environmental Protection Agency, 36
Antarctica Project, 36
Appalachian Mountains, 124–126, 319
Appalachian Trail, 124–125
Arawale National Reserve, 8
Arches National Park, 249–250
Arctic National Wildlife Refuge, 89–93
Arenal Volcano, 70
Auyan-tepui, 224–225

Baja Peninsula, 82–85, 287
Banff National Park, 239, 240
Bering Land Bridge National Preserve, 102

Bering Strait, 61, 101
Beringia, 101–103
Bob Marshall Wilderness Area, 109–111, 293–294
Borneo, 36–42
Boundary Waters Canoe Area Wilderness, 198–199, 252, 298, 316–318
Boynton, Graham, 160
Breitenbush Hot Springs Community, 195
Brooks Range, 90–94

Californian Desert Protection League, 250
Canadian Rockies, 239–241
Canyon de Chelly, 105
Canyonlands National Park, 114, 117, 294–295
Carara Biological Reserve, 179, 238
Cascade Mountains, 194–195, 197–198, 251
Caufield, Catherine, 131, 221
Central Kalahari Game Reserve, 150, 153, 154
Cerro Aconcagua, 207
Cerro Torre, 128, 208
Charles Darwin Research Station, 218, 219
Chimborazo Volcano, 135
Chiputneticook Lake, 318–319
Chizarira National Park, 26–27, 170, 278
Chobe National Park, 5, 150, 153–154
Chukotka Peninsula, 102–103
Cockscomb Basin Wildlife Sanctuary, 174–175, 308

Commonwealth of Independent States, 101–103
Confederation of Indian Nations of the Ecuadorean Amazon, 136
Continental Divide, 106, 110, 190, 293
Convention on International Trade in Endangered Species (CITES), 28
Cordillera Occidental, 133
Cordillera Real, 134
Copper Canyon, 86–87, 315
Cotopaxi (volcano), 133, 213, 254
Cotopaxi National Park, 133
Crooked Tree Bird Sanctuary, 175–176, 308

Darien National Park, 310
Dark Canyon Wilderness, 115–116
Denali National Park, 187
Devon Island, 78–79
Dirty Devil Wilderness, 114–115
dolphins, 299–300, 303–304

Ellesmere Island, 78–81
Embratur, 211
Endangered Wildlife Trust, 165
Escalante Canyons Wilderness, 113–114
Etosha National Park, 20, 162–163
Etosha Pan, 20, 162–163
Ewaso N'giro River, 9
Exxon Valdez, 185

Falkland Islands, 30, 32–33
Finger Lakes Forest, 252–253
Florida Everglades, 320–322
Florida Keys, 320–321
Fossey, Dian, 23

Galapagos Islands, 216–220, 255–256
Gates of the Arctic, 93–94
Gila Wilderness, 111–112
Glacier Bay, 95–96, 245
Glacier Bay National Park, 99, 100, 186, 245
Glacier National Park, 109, 119, 294
Glen Canyon National Recreation Area, 113, 115, 117, 295
gorillas, 22–23
Graham Island, 74, 76–77, 314

Gran Sabana, 142–145, 226
Grand Canyon, 104–105, 295, 315
Great Smoky Mountains National Park, 125–126
Greater Yellowstone Coalition, 123
Greater Yellowstone Ecosystem, 119–120
Greenpeace, 184
grizzly bears, 186, 187, 289, 293–294
Guaraquecaba Ecological Station, 129, 130, 209

Hawaiian Islands, 107–109, 191–194, 248, 292–293, 316
High Arctic, 78–81
Himalayas (mts.), 49–50, 279–280
Honaker Trail Foundation, 115
Hulahula River, 90–91
Hwange National Park, 169

Icy Bay, 97
Iguazu Falls, 130, 209
In the Rainforest, 131, 221
Inside Passage, 186
Irian Jaya, 259–266

Jane Goodall Institute, 273
John Muir Wilderness, 188–189, 246

Kakamega Forest, 7
Kalahari Desert, 4–5, 150, 162
Kamchatka Peninsula, 60–62
Kanoute, Assetou, 272
Kenai National Park, 185, 187
Kenai National Wildlife Refuge, 185
Kenyatta, Jomo, 8
Kilauea Volcano, 107, 191
Kitich Game Reserve, 9
Kluane National Park, 77–78
Kodiak Island National Wildlife Refuge, 185
K2 (mt.), 267–268

Labyrinth Canyon Wilderness, 117–118
Ladakh, 43–47, 267
Lake Arenal, 70
Lake Louise, 239
Lake Manyara National Park, 12, 13, 159–160, 275

Lake Naivasha, 6, 232
Lake Nakuru, 7
Lake Nakuru National Park, 159
Lake Turkana, 8, 10–11
La Selva Biological Station, 179
Los Glaciares National Park, 128, 207–208

Makalu-Barun Conservation Area, 279
Manu National Park, 139–140, 221–223
Manu River, 140, 222
Manuel Antonio National Park, 71, 181–182, 238, 309
Marshall, Robert, 93, 110
Masai Mara National Reserve, 155, 157, 158, 232
Mathews Range, 9–10
Mauna Loa, 192
Misty Fjords National Monument, 97
Monteverede Cloud Forest Reserve, 72, 178–179
Moremi Wildlife Reserve, 4–5, 150, 151–152
Moresby Island, 74–76, 314
Mount Cayambe, 133–134
Mount Elgon, 7
Mount Elgon National Park, 7
Mount Everest, 48, 49, 53–54, 171, 267, 279
Mount Kenya, 6, 9, 14–16
Mount Kilimanjaro, 3, 6, 12, 17–19, 156, 275
Mount McKinley, 187
Mount Roraima, 143
Mount Saint Elias, 97
Mustang region, 264–266

Namib Desert, 20, 162, 164
Namib-Naukluft National Park, 20, 163–164
Na Pali Coast Trail, 107
Na Pali Coast Wilderness, 99, 192
National Academy of Science, 129
Nile (river), 10
Ngorongoro Crater, 13, 155, 158, 233, 276
North Cascades National Park, 197, 251

Ocala National Forest, 202–204
off-road vehicles (ORVs), 250
Okavango Delta, 3–5, 21, 150, 151, 152–153
Okavango River, 4–5, 150
Okefenokee National Wildlife Refuge, 204–206
Okefenokee Swamp, 204–206, 323
Oregon Caves National Monument, 195–196
Organization for Tropical Studies Center, 180
Orinoco River, 143, 144, 226
Owen-Smith, Garth, 165

Palo Verde National Park, 69
Pan troglodyte verus, 273
Pantanal region, 129, 209–210
Papua New Guinea, 55–60, 259
Patagonia, 127–128, 207–208, 301
Pokhara Valley, 171, 233–234, 265
Pribilof Islands, 184
Prince William Sound, 185
Puget Sound, 296–297

Queen Charlotte Islands, 74–77, 313–315

Rainforest Action Network, 131
Ranthambhore National Park and Tiger Reserve, 171
Redwood Nature Trail, 195
Rio Negro, 144
Rio Usumacinta, 87–88
Rocky Mountain National Park, 190–191
Royal Chitwan Wildlife Reserve, 171, 173, 236

Sapodilla Cays, 67–68
Samburu Game Reserve, 8, 9, 155, 158–159, 233
San Andreas Fault, 100
San Cristoval Mountains, 75
San Juan-Anasazi Wilderness, 118–119, 295
San Juan Mountains, 246–247
Sangay National Park, 133, 136

Sariska Tiger Reserve and Wildlife Sanctuary, 171
Save the African Endgangered Wildlife Fund, 165
Save the Earth, 215
Schaller, George, 23
Serengeti National Park, 155, 157–158, 233
Serengeti Plain, 27, 157–158, 166
Seward Peninsula, 187
Shaba Game Reserve, 9
Sibiloi National Park, 6
Sierra Madre, 86
Sierra National Forest, 188–189
Singh, Arjan, 171
South African Centre for Ivory Marketing, 154
South Luangwa National Park, 24, 166–167
Stehekin Valley, 197–198, 251
Strait of Magellan, 127, 208
Superagui National Park, 129, 130, 209

Tana River Primate Reserve, 8
Tatshenshini River, 98–100
Tibet, 43, 265
Tierra del Fuego, 207, 208
Torres del Paine National Park, 127–128, 207, 300–301
Tortuguero National Park, 182
Tsavo National Park, 11–12, 155, 156–157

Uhuru Peak, 17, 19

Utah Wilderness Coalition, 114
UNESCO, 139, 222, 322

Vancouver Island, 73–74, 242
Victoria Falls, 5, 25, 27, 167, 168
Virunga Volcano, 22–24
Volcanoes National Park, 107, 191–192, 292
Waimea Canyon, 108, 191, 192, 248, 316
Waimoku Falls, 109
Weminuche Wilderness, 106
Western Canada Wilderness Committee, 100
Western, David, 160
whales, 296–297
Wild and Scenic Rivers System, 244
wolves, 293–294, 297–298
World Bank, 215
World Wildlife Fund, 176
Wrangell-Saint Elias Mountains, 97, 290–291
Wrangell-Saint Elias National Park, 99, 290–291

Yellowstone National Park, 119, 121–123, 286
Yellowstone Park Preservation Council, 122
Yukon, 77–78, 311–313

Zambezi River, 5, 25–26, 28, 167, 168–169
Zanskar, 43–47
Zoetic Research, 297

GEOGRAPHICAL INDEX

AFRICA
Botswana, 3–5, 149–155
Kenya, 5–20, 155–162, 232–233
    Mount Kenya/Aberdares, 14–17
    Mount Kilimanjaro, 17–20
Mali, 271–274
Namibia, 20–21, 162–165
Rwanda, 21–24
Tanzania, 5–15, 17–20, 155–162,
    232–233, 274–277
Zaire, 21–24
Zambia, 24–26, 166–168
Zimbabwe, 26–29, 168–170, 277–278

ANTARCTICA, 29–36

ASIA
Borneo, 36–42
India, 43–47, 170–173
    Ladakh/Zanskar, 43–47
Irian Jaya, 259–264
Nepal, 47–55, 170–173, 233–237,
    264–266, 278–280
Pakistan, 266–268
Papua New Guinea, 55–60
Russia, 60–62, 101–103
Thailand, 62–66, 280–282

CENTRAL AMERICA
Belize, 67–69, 174–177, 283–284,
    308
Costa Rica, 69–72, 177–183,
    237–239, 284–285, 309
Panama, 309–311

NORTH AMERICA
Canada, 72–82, 239–243, 285–286,
    311–315

    Canadian Rockies, 239–241
    Big Salmon River, 311–313
    High Arctic, 78–82
    Queen Charlotte Islands, 74–77,
        313–315
    Vancouver Island, 73–74, 242–243
    Yukon, 77–78
Mexico, 82–89, 286–288, 315
    Baja, 82–85
    Copper Canyon, 86–87, 315
    Rio Usumacinta, 87–89
United States:
    Alaska, 89–93, 184–188, 243–245,
        289–291
        Admiralty Island, 95–98
        Alagnak River, 243–244
        Aleutian Islands, 185
        Beringia, 101–103
        Brooks Range/Arctic National
            Wildlife Refuge, 89–94
        Gates of the Arctic, 93–95
        Glacier Bay, 95–98, 244–245
        Icy Bay, 95, 97, 98
        Inside Passage, 186
        Misty Fjords, 95–98
        Pribilof Islands, 184–186
        Tatshenshini River, 98–101
    Arizona, 104–106
        Canyon de Chelly, 105–106
        Grand Canyon North Rim,
            104–105
    California, 188–189, 245–246
    Colorado, 106–107, 190–191,
        246–247
    Florida, 202–204, 299–300,
        320–322
    Georgia, 204–206, 323

Hawaii, 107–109, 191–194, 247–248, 291–293, 316
Maine, 124–125, 200–201, 318–320
    Allagash Wilderness River, 319–320
    Chiputneticook Lake, 318–319
Minnesota, 198–200, 251–252, 297–298, 316–318
    Boundary Waters Canoe Area Wilderness, 198–200, 251–252, 316–318
Montana, 109–111, 248–249, 293–294
New Mexico, 111–112
New York, 252–253
North Carolina, 125–126
Oregon, 194–196
Tennessee, 125–126
Utah, 112–119, 249–250, 294–295
    Escalante Canyons Wilderness, 112–114
    Dark Canyon Wilderness, 115–116
    Dirty Devil Wilderness, 114–115
    Labyrinth Canyon Wilderness, 116–118
    San Juan-Anasazi Wilderness, 118–119
Vermont, 201–202
Washington, 197–198, 251, 295–297
Wyoming, 119–123

SOUTH AMERICA
Argentina, 127–129, 206–208
Brazil, 129–132, 208–212
Chile, 127–129, 300–301
Ecuador, 133–139, 212–221, 254–256, 302–303
    Andes Mountains, 212–216, 254–255
    Galapagos Islands, 216–221, 255–256
Peru, 139–142, 221–224, 303–304
Venezuela, 142–145, 224–228

Author's Note

I began traveling as a young boy in Carthage, Illinois, by drawing Amazonian river systems in the dust and voyaging down the imaginary waterways through lush jungles. I next traveled in ninth grade study hall while furtively reading the books of Richard Haliburton instead of studying Latin.

Those early journeys fired my lust to try the real thing. A year studying in Europe only increased the heat of my desire. Peace Corps service in an isolated Ethiopian village led to a four-year circumvention of the world.

In those years of travel I was awed and thrilled by the diversity of the lands and the cultures. I was equally struck by the commonality linking all peoples together and binding them to nature. I discovered "Mama" was the one word children spoke no matter the country.

Mark Twain got it right when he wrote, "Travel is fatal to prejudice, bigotry and narrow-mindedness."

My consciousness of commonality has deepened and matured over the past twenty years of traveling the world. It has also taken on a political cant.

Environmentalism is destined to supersede bottom-line economics as the defining political force. Author Jeremy Rifkin gave the moment a name: biosphere politics. French philosopher René Dubois gave it a rallying cry: "Think globally, act locally."

In his book, *Biosphere Politics,* Rifkin articulated the premises of the new politics and its political, economic, and social ramifications.

"Because biosphere politics is based on sustainable economic development, rather than ever-accelerating production, the ecosystem rather than the market dictates the spatial limits of political rule," he writes. "The task of the new organismic politics, then, is to ensure ecosystem sustainability on the local level and biospheric security on the global level.

"...Biospheric consciousness and politics mean far more than a sensitivity to cleaning up the enviornment. In a biosphere culture, life-style itself becomes a political issue, as citizens in each community begin to draw the connections between personal consumption choices and the effects those choices have on the environmental health of the planet and the economic well-being of people in other lands."

It is time we evolve beyond the economic morality that rewards individual gain at the expense of societal and the natural world's well-being. The great crime is that we have accepted as normal the dismemberment of the basic interconnecting unity of the human world and the natural world.

A shift of consciousness toward a more nurturing world will occur if animals, the Earth, and humans are honored as partners dependent on one another for common well-being. The destruction of wildlife habitat is the equivalent of burning down our own house. The continued elimination of species equals the killing of cells in the global brain, a source of wisdom needed for our own survival.

Rudyard Kipling synthesized the essence of the travel experience: "Travel makes one modest —you see what a tiny place you occupy in the world."

Stephen Foehr is an award-winning travel writer with credits in numerous magazines and newspapers. He lives in Boulder, Colorado, with his four-year-old son, Lucian.

Other Noble Press Books

GOING OFF THE BEATEN PATH
An Untraditional Travel Guide to the U.S.

Mary Dymond Davis

"A stimulating journey down the back roads and byways of the nation's active environmental movement." *Los Angeles Times*

"An exhaustive descriptive catalog...for all those cynical moments when one doubts that anything ever changes." *Utne Reader*

This year-round weekend and vacation guide provides travelers with over a thousand exciting and unusual places to visit. Places described range from the birthplace of George Washington Carver to Biosphere II. Its geographical index allows readers to find interesting places within hours of their home. Places described include:

- Wildlife refuges
- Cliff Dwellings
- Biking Trails
- National Forests
- Solar Energy Projects
- Hiking Trails
- Unique Museums
- Vegetarian Restaurants

$15.95, paperback, 466 pages

HANDLE WITH CARE
A Guide to Responsible Travel in Developing Countries

Scott Graham

"Graham's bottom-line message is that today's tourist must travel responsibly, especially in the developing and fragile areas of the world whose ecosystems–including their land, culture and local economies–depend on careful handling." *Vegetarian Times*

This guide shows how responsible travelers can get the most out of their travels in developing countries and help to preserve fragile ecosystems. Topics covered include dealing with poverty, supporting local economies, enjoying local cuisine, and booking local tours and volunteer vacations. The book is packed with anecdotes illustrating the problems of traveling to underdeveloped countries and how to overcome them.

$8.95, paperback, 168 pages

WHITE MEN DON'T HAVE JUJU
An American Couple's Adventure Through Africa

Pam Ascanio

"By the end of this lively tale, there's respect for a huge and magnificent continent, and a slightly different view of the world." *Travel Books Worldwide*

"The author's travel tips...make this a worthy supplement for would-be adventurers." *Publishers Weekly*

Pam Ascanio and her husband, Robb, a white middle-class couple from Florida, did what many people only dream of do-ing —they quit their jobs, sold their home, and took off on the journey of a lifetime.

This book is the story of their year of adventures in Africa, dur-ing which they got far more than they bargained for. Read this riveting memoir and discover Africa's power and grandeur for yourself; you may even be inspired to embark on your own African adventure.

$12.95, paperback, 346 pages

FREE THE ANIMALS!
The Untold Story of the U.S. Animal Liberation Front & Its Founder, Valerie

Ingrid Newkirk

"A moving story about extreme cruelty and extreme courage, and an inspirational and practical guide for anyone bent on challenging the system." – Oliver Stone

"...[the] dramatic and intriguing story of...the Animal Liberation Front. These are the people who, often at risk of life and limb as well as jail, break into laboratories and rescue animals from experimenters and vivisectionists." – from the Introduction, by Cleveland Amory

Written by bestselling author Ingrid Newkirk, executive director of People for the Ethical Treatment of Animals (PETA), **Free the Animals!** is the fascinating story of the pseudonymous "Valerie" and her transformation from law-abiding police officer to underground activist. A shattering account of one woman's struggle against the forces supporting the abuse of animals, **Free the Animals!** is an action-packed story of underground adventure, as well as an eloquent plea for the rights of animals.

$13.95, paperback, 372 pages

ECO-WARRIORS:
Understanding the Radical Environmental Movement

Rik Scarce

"...intriguing, if sometimes disturbing reading...a fine account for anyone looking for insight into the environmental movement." *New York Times Book Review*

"**Eco-Warriors** will help explain what it's all about." *The Progressive*

An in-depth and movingly eloquent look at the people, the actions, the history, and the philosophies behind such groups as

Earth First!, The Sea Shepherds, Greenpeace, and the Animal Liberation Front.

$12.95, paperback, 320 pages

EMBRACING THE EARTH
Choices for Environmentally Sound Living

D. Mark Harris

"This book is not only a call to action, it is the guide you need to act." *East West*

"**Embracing the Earth** encourages us to live an environmentally sound lifestyle 365 days a year [and] Harris makes you want to." *South Carolina Wildlife*

A practical guide on how to turn every day into an Earth Day. Contains over 200 do-able projects to begin living more lightly on the Earth. Charmingly illustrated and gently persuasive. Includes directories.

$9.95, paperback, 164 pages

TOWARD A SUSTAINABLE SOCIETY
An Economic, Social and Environmental Agenda for Our Children's Future

James Garbarino

"Garbarino's ideas for making the transition to social welfare systems based on innovative economics and environmental concerns are creative and interesting." *Library Journal*

Award-winning author James Garbarino takes the proponents of "unlimited capitalistic growth" head-on. In his fascinating account of what constitutes a sustainable society, Garbarino's convincing arguments illustrate the disastrous effects our current unrestrained consumer-oriented economic system will have on the environment and our children's future.

Picking up where *Small is Beautiful* leaves off, Garbarino

shows that the world's natural resources cannot keep pace with consumer demand. He also illustrates how our current economic priorities drain much-needed resources from our social welfare system, imperiling the future of America's children.

$19.95, cloth, 260 pages

DEFENDING THE LEFT
An Individual's Guide to Fighting for Social Justice, Individual Rights, and the Environment

David E. Driver

It is time to bring the "Reagan Revolution" to an end. **Defending the Left** will show you what you can do to see the "Progressive Renaissance" of the Nineties become reality.

This is an inspiring guidebook for Americans ready to end the conservative assault on human rights, equal opportunity, and the environment. It goes beyond single-issue advocacy books to demonstrate the common bond among different political concerns of the Left. And it offers many means–consumerism, use of the media, politics, and grass-roots organizing–that concerned individuals can use to make a difference.

$11.95, paperback, 288 pages